# Solidarity Between Species

For Sylvia,
art historian
and anthropologist of the future

# Solidarity Between Species

## Living with Animals Exposed to Pandemic Viruses

### Frédéric Keck

polity

Copyright © Frédéric Keck 2025

The right of Frédéric Keck to be identified as Author of this Work has been
asserted in accordance with the UK Copyright, Designs and Patents Act 1988.

First published in 2025 by Polity Press

Polity Press
65 Bridge Street
Cambridge CB2 1UR, UK

Polity Press
111 River Street
Hoboken, NJ 07030, USA

All rights reserved. Except for the quotation of short passages for the purpose
of criticism and review, no part of this publication may be reproduced, stored
in a retrieval system or transmitted, in any form or by any means, electronic,
mechanical, photocopying, recording or otherwise, without the prior permission
of the publisher.

ISBN-13: 978-1-5095-6687-7 (hardback)
ISBN-13: 978-1-5095-6688-4 (paperback)

A catalogue record for this book is available from the British Library.

Library of Congress Control Number: 2024941809

Typeset in 10.5 on 14pt Fournier Std by
Cheshire Typesetting Ltd, Cuddington, Cheshire
Printed and bound in Great Britain by CPI Group (UK) Ltd, Croydon

The publisher has used its best endeavors to ensure that the URLs for external
websites referred to in this book are correct and active at the time of going to
press. However, the publisher has no responsibility for the websites and can
make no guarantee that a site will remain live or that the content is or will
remain appropriate.

Every effort has been made to trace all copyright holders, but if any have been
overlooked the publisher will be pleased to include any necessary credits in any
subsequent reprint or edition.

For further information on Polity, visit our website:
politybooks.com

# Contents

| | |
|---|---|
| *Acknowledgments* | vii |
| *Opening: Covid-19 displayed as pandemic and zoonosis* | ix |

**Introduction: Wild thought about biopolitics**      1

| | | |
|---|---|---|
| **1** | **Biopower: Disciplining individuals, regulating populations** | 9 |
| 1.a | Public hygiene and mental health | 11 |
| 1.b | Biotechnology, biosafety, and biolegitimacy | 15 |
| | | |
| **2** | **Pastoral power: Watching over humans like sheep** | 21 |
| 2.a | A benevolent and sacrificial power | 21 |
| 2.b | Veterinary medicine and breeders' knowledge | 23 |
| | | |
| **3** | **Cynegetic power: Catching the prey's perspectives** | 33 |
| 3.a | Colonial slavery and hunting societies | 33 |
| 3.b | Virus hunters and disease reservoirs | 46 |
| | | |
| **4** | **Cryopolitics: Conserving collections in nature reserves** | 59 |
| 4.a | The mutations of influenza viruses | 59 |
| 4.b | The cold chain in markets and laboratories | 72 |
| 4.c | Storing living beings in reserves and museums | 78 |

vi                                   *Contents*

**5      Planetary health: Anticipating disasters with
        animals**                                                    95
5.a     Responsibility: From pandemics to global warming     96
5.b     Participation: The ideal of justice through war        108

**6      Sentinels: Building a new form of solidarity**         121
6.a     The frontiers of the immune system                      121
6.b     Remembering the signs of the past to prepare for
        future disasters                                                127

**Conclusion: Environmental pathologies, animal
        studies, and the critique of capitalism**        140

*Notes*                                                                146
*Index of Names*                                                   220

# Acknowledgments

This book, begun at the start of the Covid-19 pandemic, after a series of media interventions and online conferences that led me to repeat the positions defended in my previous book *Avian Reservoirs*, sometimes at the risk of caricaturing them, has benefited from discussions with long-standing interlocutors and encounters with new ones in very real seminars, which in my view must continue to nourish intellectual life, despite the new possibilities offered by digital work.

I would like to thank Mathias Delori, Katia Genel, Jakob Vogel, Maiween Roudault, and Denis Thouard for hosting me at the Centre Marc Bloch in Berlin in the spring of 2022, as part of the Marc Bloch Chair at EHESS, followed by a summer school in September 2022, at a time when Germany was an excellent vantage point for observing political transformations in Eastern Europe and for rethinking emancipation at the intersection of philosophy and the human sciences.

For the past five years, the Master's degree in Environmental Studies at the École des hautes études en sciences sociales has been a venue for the invention of interdisciplinary teaching practices and knowledge contents, from which this book is partly derived. Thanks to Christophe Bonneuil, Marc Elie, Thomas Leroux, and Geneviève Pruvost for allowing me to take part in this intellectual adventure.

I would like to thank Philippe Descola, Pascal Lamy, and Frédéric Worms for their invitation to teach at the European Anthropology Chair at the École normale supérieure de Paris between 2021 and 2023, as well as my PhD students, who took part in the seminar on human–animal relations: Keltoum Boumejdane, Rongtai Chen, Philippe Drugeon, Anna Dupuy, Mathilde Gallay-Keller, and Nan Nan. Thanks also to Emmanuel Didier for the seminar we ran together on "One Health" in 2022 as part of the "Humanités médicales" Master's program, and to Marc Fleurbaey for hosting me at the ENS's Centre de formation sur l'environnement et la société.

I was able to present the book's most daring hypotheses at the Cercle Lucien Herr's seminar on socialism. I would like to thank Milo, Sacha, and Ulysse Lévy-Bruhl for their discussion of these proposals, which owe them a lot.

This book has benefited from discussions I was fortunate to have for several years with Andrew Lakoff and Christos Lynteris. I am grateful to them for inviting me to present my research to colleagues at the Universities of Southern California in Los Angeles and St. Andrews in Scotland, as well as to Claire Sagan for inviting me to Vassar College, and to Domenico Perrotta for inviting me to the University of Bergamo and to the Congress of Ethnography and Qualitative Research in Italy.

Laurent Jeanpierre initiated this book on biopolitics and accompanied it with Bruno Auerbach and Stéphanie Chevrier through its wanderings to completion at La Découverte. I thank John Thompson for his early interest in the translation of this book at Polity.

The book benefited from the precise, helpful, and kind comments of Romain Graziani, Violette Pouillard, and Mélanie Roustan.

Joëlle Soler has built a strong link in her quest for "holy places" between the socialism of her homeland Tarn and the ecology of the Seine-et-Marne, where we now live. She knows how much I owe her, and for which I can never thank her enough.

# Opening:
# Covid-19 displayed as pandemic and zoonosis

If an anthropologist of the future were to curate an exhibition displaying how humanity has experienced Covid-19, in the way that anthropologists of the past have presented distant societies to European audiences in museums, she might choose four objects and four animal species, which would represent the "material culture" and "ethno-zoology" of humanity today. These objects and animals have indeed populated the imagination of contemporary societies during this pandemic, in ways that remain to be analyzed and understood. The Covid-19 pandemic led humans to globally disseminate objects that had appeared in different places over the past two centuries, standardizing them according to international norms and hybridizing them with more traditional techniques of epidemic control. But Covid-19 is also a zoonosis, i.e. a disease transmitted between different animal species, which explains why the virus that caused it was so unpredictable. Here, then, are four objects and four animals, accompanied by information that might guide visitors through this exhibition.

## A. Objects

– *The respirator.* Covid-19 is a respiratory disease, which first infects the lungs, with secondary symptoms in the nervous system such as loss of taste or fatigue, grouped together under the term "long Covid." Patients with severe respiratory symptoms, such as choking, were treated in intensive care hospital wards, using respirators to ventilate them artificially. These machines, which involve heavy interventions on the bodies of patients who must be regularly turned over and may be placed in an artificial coma, require the constant presence of nursing staff at their side. In times of emergency, hospital space must be reorganized to accommodate these priority patients. These techniques take over from the "iron lungs" invented in Boston in 1928 to combat poliomyelitis, benefiting from advances in artificial respiration in aviation during the twentieth century. The production of artificial respirators, whether rudimentary or high-tech, was greatly accelerated by the Covid-19 pandemic.[1]

- *The mask.* Initially a protective tool for hospital staff, the "surgical mask" spread to the entire population to protect against the transmission of Covid-19 by capturing droplets from the mouth and nose. Mainly worn in public transport and enclosed public places, where it was sometimes imposed by governments through sanctions, it was also worn in intimate spaces, with some people reluctant to remove their mask in front of others for reasons of precaution or modesty. It has thus profoundly redefined what it means to be a person (the term *persona* designates the mask in Latin Antiquity) confronted with the threat of respiratory disease circulating in the atmosphere shared by humans. Manufactured industrially from plastic or more traditionally from textile, it has become one of the waste products of contemporary societies, raising new issues of recycling. An archaeologist of the future may find that the only trace of this pandemic is an increase in the layer of plastic produced by humans since the middle of the twentieth century. Indeed, thanks to the invention of the plastic surgical mask in the 1950s, this piece of cloth, introduced into hospitals in Europe at the end of the nineteenth century, and imposed in the public arena after the work of Chinese physician Wu Liande on pneumonic plague in 1910 and on the occasion of the Spanish flu of 1918, was transformed into an industrial product, in such a way that the stockpiling of masks for hospitals became a criterion for evaluating a modern state.[2]

*Opening* xi

– *The vaccine.* Covid-19 is an infectious disease caused by a virus called SARS-Cov2. In the absence of antiviral treatment for those who were already infected, and despite the hopes raised by advocates of hydroxychloroquine or artemisinin, vaccinating the uninfected population was the best public health strategy for curbing the pandemic, since it put an end to "stop-and-go" policies alternating lockdown and release of the population. The speed of vaccine production by pharmaceutical laboratories in Europe and North America, using the latest messenger RNA technology, surprised all observers and revived mistrust of vaccination, which has been a major trend on both continents over the last thirty years. The development of an inactivated vaccine by the pharmaceutical industries in Russia and China, less effective than messenger RNA vaccines but easier to distribute, and the World Health Organization's calls for international solidarity under the Covax initiative, making vaccines a "common good of humanity," have raised hopes on the possibility of sharing them with the countries of the South. The global distribution of a Covid vaccine offers a glimpse of a world in which SARS-Cov2 would be eradicated, but doses of vaccine would have to be manufactured regularly to respond to mutations in the virus. Two hundred and twenty years after its invention by Edward Jenner, and one hundred and forty years after its extension by Louis Pasteur, the vaccine, a pharmaceutical product supervised by the state and distributed to citizens as part of mass campaigns, has thus become an essential component of public health policies to combat pandemics.[3]

– *The cell phone.* This is a new public health tool linked to the digitization of contemporary societies, whereas the other three objects have been used to control epidemics for at least a century. Through applications containing barcodes, it can summarize data on individuals (their infection by the virus, their different doses of vaccine) and inform them about potential virus carriers in their environment. During the Covid-19 pandemic, this application enabled individuals to make more informed decisions about their travels, and it allowed public authorities to monitor these travels. As a dematerialized version of the tracing policy chosen by certain countries to limit the pandemic as an alternative to confinement and vaccines, it is indissociable from the more rudimentary materiality of the test, a cotton swab that individuals have to insert into their orifices to find out if they are carriers of the virus. These applications and tests found a particularly well-developed form in China's "zero-Covid policy," reinforcing measures to control the population movements and to measure "social credit" that were already in place before the Covid-19 pandemic.[4]

## B. Animals

– *The bat.* Coronaviruses very similar to those causing Covid in 2019 have been found among rhinolophids in southern China and Southeast Asia. While it had been known since the 1950s that bats could transmit rabies through their bite – which remains exceptional for certain so-called "vampire" species in South America – it was discovered in the 1990s that they were also transmitting new viruses called Hendra and Nipah to humans in Australia and Southeast Asia, through horses, pigs, or fruit they had infected. The emergence of SARS-Cov1 in China in 2002, causing the epidemic of Severe Acute Respiratory Syndrome (SARS), was explained with certainty by the transmission of a coronavirus – whose mild forms had until then been studied by veterinarians in pigs – from bats in southwest China to civets consumed in major cities such as Guangzhou. Two recent phenomena are mentioned to explain that new viruses are emerging in bats: deforestation, forcing bats to move to trees closer to human habitats, and new breeding practices for horses and pigs, bringing them closer to the forests and caves where bats breed, thus multiplying the number of intermediate species between bats and humans, and therefore the opportunities

*Opening*                                                          xiii

for their viruses to be transmitted to new species. Over the last forty years, it has been discovered that bats harbor a large number of viruses that are potentially dangerous to humans, due to their unique characteristics: they make up a quarter of all mammalian species, they live in dense multi-species colonies where they exchange large numbers of viruses that constantly cross species barriers, and they have developed immune defenses that enable them to withstand the metabolic cost of flight, notably a microbiota of restricted size and mechanisms for repairing the chromosomes carrying their genetic information.[5]

– *The pangolin.* The identification of bats as reservoirs of coronaviruses left aside the question of the intermediate animal that transmitted SARS-Cov2 to humans. In April 2020, Chinese authorities suggested that the pangolin might be the intermediate animal between bats and humans, after viruses close to SARS-Cov2 were found by Chinese researchers in Malaysian pangolins.[6] This discovery turned the attention of health authorities and the media to the international traffic of pangolins, whose scales are consumed in traditional Chinese medicine as a remedy for fevers. The International Union for Conservation of Nature banned the sale of Asian pangolins in 2000, which redirected international pangolin trafficking to Africa. The pangolin is thus an indicator of the transformation of a traditional hunting practice into a prestige consumption practice organized by an international market, which can go as far as new breeding practices of wild animals to supply new forms of traditional medicine. But the pangolin was an emblematic species for conservation in China for the last twenty years, which may explain that it was brought on the public scene at the start of the Covid pandemic.[7]

– *The mink.* Mink farms tested positive for the SARS-Cov2 virus in Holland in June 2020 and in Denmark in November 2020, presumably due to infection by humans working on the farms. Health authorities were less concerned about mink mortality in these farms, slightly increased by the presence of SARS-Cov2, than about the appearance of a viral mutation that could be transmitted to humans and compromise the undergoing vaccination campaign. Denmark, the world's leading producer of farmed mink for fur (with 28% of global production, followed by Poland and China), ordered the slaughter of twelve million mink using gas. As the decomposing corpses rose from the ground, farmers were forced to dig them up and incinerate them, sparking media images that travelled around the world. The European public discovered that mink had been farmed industrially since the 1850s in North America to compensate for the decline in beaver fur production by trappers, then introduced at the end of the nineteenth century in Northern Europe, where their fish-based diet was replaced by protein compounds. The mink was domesticated more recently than the ferret, which also belongs to the mustelid family and was prized in medieval Europe for its sociability, scent (musk) and ability to detect game, making it a companion species at court and for the hunt. More recently, ferret breeding has developed to provide laboratories with animal models for the study of respiratory diseases such as influenza, since ferrets sneeze like humans. An animal species that has long been involved in human social practices linked to hunting has thus been transformed into a commodity for a century, but the health crisis has once again made it a bearer of warning signals for humans.[8]

- *The deer.* While tests on dogs, pigs, poultry, and cattle have all been negative for SARS-Cov2, cats have been shown to replicate the virus, but not in sufficient quantity to cause transmission to humans.[9] In January 2022, an outbreak of Covid-19 was discovered in Hong Kong among humans who frequented a pet shop where Syrian hamsters had been imported from Holland: the slaughter of 2,000 hamsters in Hong Kong put an end to this route of disease transmission.[10] On the other hand, significant circulation of

*Opening* xv

SARS-Cov 2 has been discovered in white-tailed deer in the USA, with rates ranging from 30 to 40 percent depending on the states in which the deer population was tested. The origin of this transmission remains mysterious, whether it be infected carcasses or contaminated water, but such prevalence in wildlife precludes the use of eradication methods such as culling techniques applied to mink and hamster. Instead, the US wildlife authorities have launched an extensive program of regular deer sampling and a prevention campaign aimed at hunters to limit direct contact between humans and deer.[11] The discovery of cases of SARS-Cov2 in mink and deer thus qualifies Covid-19 not only as an emerging disease, in the sense that the virus would have crossed species barriers by passing from bats to humans via an intermediate species such as the pangolin, but also as a zoonosis, in the sense that the virus has the capacity to return to other animal species after passing through humans, in a permanent mutation mechanism that makes its definitive eradication impossible.[12]

# Introduction:
# Wild thought about biopolitics

Using the argumentation and documentation methods of social anthropology, this book aims to answer the following question: how do we think about the forms of critique and emancipation in the age of pandemic viruses? It opened with a project for an exhibition on the Covid-19 pandemic because exhibitions pose the same problem as argumentations, but with different documents. An exhibition involves a "curatorial" approach that aims to heal (*cure*) humans through attention (*care*) to the things between which it is necessary to sort (*krinein*) in order to make them visible in public space.[1] Since we have all suffered the Covid-19 pandemic as subjects of contemporary societies, we can respond to the concerns and questions it has raised by displaying the material traces this event has left in our memories, as museums have done for societies of the past. But it is also possible to make a retrospective diagnosis of this pandemic by reflecting on the categories through which we think more generally about zoonoses and, through them, relations connecting us to all living beings.

The Covid-19 pandemic threatened the ideals on which modern societies are founded because it gave rise to archaic fears associated with contagion. States adopted authoritarian measures of quarantine, lock-down and vaccination, undermining individual freedom. The extraordinary spread of the SARS-Cov2 virus among human populations revealed inequalities between human populations in their exposure to diseases and in their access to healthcare technologies. But this pandemic has also highlighted new forms of solidarity between humans, bats, pangolins, mink, and deer, since we have all been affected by the same zoonosis. While humans have reflected during the Covid-19 pandemic how they could emancipate themselves from constraining forms of power, they also realized they were exposed to the same diseases as other animals, who suffer from more violent forms of surveillance, vaccination, lock-down, and killing.

Therefore, the Covid-19 pandemic has questioned the relationship between life and power, in a way that forces us to ask what modern societies understand by "life" and "power," and to reset the modern project of emancipation on new foundations. What does it mean to "make live," "make die," "let live," and "let die," when human populations are locked-down in their homes for months to avoid contagion, sometimes dying alone for lack of access to healthcare, when citizens are encouraged to vaccinate themselves to contain an unknown virus, and can no longer access public places if they don't, when minks or hamsters are slaughtered to avoid viral mutations in their bodies, when bats are caught and bled to extract virus samples, when deer are kept away from domestic animals to prevent them from transmitting a virus that has already spread widely within their species?[1]

This book approaches these questions through the concept of biopolitics, coined in 1976 by the philosopher Michel Foucault to describe the formation over the last two centuries of a power to "make live and let die." Many commentators have used this term to describe the techniques of quarantine, containment, vaccination, surveillance, and anticipation that enabled public authorities to limit the spread of Covid-19.[2] Reflection on the "power" involved in these biopolitical measures could lead either to the denunciation of a globalized state manipulating populations into buying masks and vaccines, according to an updated version of conspiracy theory, or to the more subtle but also more discouraging questioning of a power that infiltrates social interactions through individuals' suspicions about the infectious potential of their neighbors,

*Introduction*                                         3

framed as a "capillary" view on power.[3] Conspiracy theory thus confuses two political registers, which Foucault aimed to distinguish: the sovereign register of the state, which acts through laws in the service of a people, and the biopolitical register of government, which acts through norms to protect a population. Noting the "capillary" extension of medical power into the beliefs and practices of modern individuals, conspiracy theory attributes to it a "deep state" that is more extensive than the forms of sovereignty. It is founded on the will to fight this invisible enemy, while it has not analyzed the conjunctural and reversible alliances between the state and government.[4] This book, by contrast, seeks to show that there is not a uniform biopolitics from which modern subjects should emancipate themselves, but several forms of the relationship between knowledge and power in modern and non-modern societies, which redefine the project of emancipation according to the ways in which humans domesticate animals. It thus seeks to include animals in the modern project of emancipation according to the techniques of knowledge and power in which they are caught up.

When the term "biopolitics" was introduced into the social sciences by Michel Foucault in 1976, it essentially concerned human populations in the face of diseases such as plague, which has been controlled in the modern age by a policy of quarantine imposed on persons and commodities, as well as smallpox, which can be controlled by vaccination because it is not regularly transmitted from animals to humans. It did not seem to apply to animal populations, even though the emergence of the Ebola virus in 1976 demonstrated the role of primates in the circulation of new pathogens. Discussions of biopolitics therefore lack any consideration of what animals do when they introduce new pathogens into the human population. The control and monitoring of pandemics concerns not only cities where humans live in close proximity to each other, but markets, farms, forests, caves, where humans live with animals. How is biopolitics transformed when it operates

4 *Introduction*

not in territories where populations are exposed to risks, but in infrastructures where disasters occur at the borders between species?

The notion of biopolitics appeared in public debate at the same time as the notion of zoonosis in the 1970s but, until then, they had rarely been brought together. The joint appearance of these two notions indicates that a transformation was underway in relations between the human species and its environment. On the one hand, health issues have played an increasingly important role in political organization, notably through risk insurance, to the extent that Michel Foucault defined man as "an animal whose politics place his existence as a living being in question."[5] On the other hand, the distribution of animal species has changed dramatically, with the mass extinction of a large number of wild species and the increase in domesticated species for human consumption, transforming the ecosystems in which microbes mutate.

Yet these two trends are conceived within quite different frameworks, which explains why they don't meet. The notion of biopolitics is conceived within the statistical framework of risk management, while the notion of zoonoses is conceived within the ecological framework of disaster anticipation. The conjunction between these two phenomena bears witness to a historical fact that becomes increasingly clearer today: while warning signals have multiplied over the last four decades about ecological disasters resulting from the extension of the industrial way of life, liberal societies thought of them as risks for individuals.

The founder of social anthropology in France, Claude Lévi-Strauss, posed the problem of disease control quite differently from Michel Foucault, using the term *pensée sauvage*, recently translated as "wild thought." By this term, Lévi-Strauss meant not "the thought of savages," but thought "in a sylvatic environment" (*à l'état sauvage*). When it finds itself in a forest rather than in a planned countryside, human thinking is not finalized by a performance objective, but elaborates a set of

## Introduction

classifications from animals and plants to solve all kinds of problems. According to Lévi-Strauss, Indian societies in the southeastern United States identify animals and plants in their environment to diagnose and treat disease: they "treat pathological phenomena as the consequence of a conflict among men, animals, and plants. Irritated by humans, animals send them diseases; plants, the allies of humans, counterattack by providing remedies."[6] This formulation of the biopolitical problem resonates strangely with some of the statements we have heard about the Covid-19 pandemic. Indeed, bats or pangolins have been said to "revenge,"[7] and mink corpses emerging from Danish soil after slaughter as well as deer carrying SARS-Cov2 across American forests have appeared as "ghosts" haunting humans to potentially transmit the pandemic virus.[8] The idea of animal vengeance is a very strange one for modern societies, who posit a separation between humans and non-humans in their intellectual capacities; it is closer to hunter societies, who attribute intentionalities to animals and plants to better mark the differences between specific materialities.[9]

When one says that "nature revenges itself," one explains the emergence of SARS-Cov2 by the intention of bats to send viruses to humans to punish them for deforestation, but this explanation makes little sense in the eyes of modern science, which emphasizes the random nature of biological mutations.[10] It is, however, the exact symmetry of the opposite thesis, according to which the emergence of SARS-Cov2 is caused by the intention of humans to manufacture biological weapons in order to frighten populations, and thus sell them vaccines protecting them against an evil manufactured by humans. This rather simplistic form of conspiracy theory attributes evil intent to humans, ignoring all the complications and uncertainties of manipulating biological material, just as the idea of bat revenge ignores the instabilities and complexities of the animal chain that led a coronavirus to travel from a forest in southern China to airports around the world. For ecologists who study the correlations between viral emergence

6                          *Introduction*

and biodiversity loss, the problem is rather to understand how the random mutation of a virus is selected and amplified by a change in the ecosystem, be it deforestation, climate change, urbanization, or industrial livestock farming.[11]

Organizing the encounter between Foucault's "biopolitics" and Lévi-Strauss's "wild thought" around Covid-19 means tying together two threads that were woven without intersecting between the 1960s and 1970s to think about this event: the random emergence of a new virus that crosses species barriers in a way that brings the global economy of human activities to a halt. When Foucault introduced the notion of biopolitics into the human sciences in 1976, it was the year of the publication of Gary Becker's book, *The Economic Approach to Human Behavior*,[12] which marked the extension of neo-liberal logic to all living beings; but it was also the year of the eradication of smallpox and the emergence of Ebola, which led international health authorities to anticipate emerging infectious diseases by monitoring pathogens that crossed species boundaries in animal reservoirs.[13] When Lévi-Strauss published *La pensée sauvage* in 1962, it was the end of the Algerian war, which put an end to France's colonial history, forcing anthropologists to invent new forms of collaboration with indigenous knowledges; but it was also the year of the publication of Rachel Carson's *Silent Spring* in the United States and the second edition of Frank Macfarlane Burnet's *Natural History of Infectious Diseases* in Great Britain, which warned of the effect of pesticides on the trophic chain of ecosystems in which humans live, and of influenza viruses circulating in wild birds and amplifying in domestic animals.[14] The neo-liberal revolution analyzed by Michel Foucault in the United States, which accelerated the global extension of capitalism by empowering individuals capable of taking risks, is inextricably linked to the failed reception of warning signals about the health consequences of ecological transformations, whether through the production of new toxins or the emergence of new viruses.[15] The Ebola virus emerging in 1976,

*Introduction*    7

followed by HIV/AIDS, Nipa, Hendra, avian and swine flu viruses, up to SARS coronaviruses, was the first of a series of such warning signals.

If we think about it through this double genealogy, the biopolitical problem posed by the Covid-19 pandemic can be clarified. What is at stake is certainly how we can construct a free, non-authoritarian relationship with these technical objects – respirators, masks, vaccines, and cell phones – and thus appropriate them subjectively in everyday use. But it is also how we can interact with viruses coming from the wild, for which we have no immunity, in ways other than treating them as enemies to be eradicated. Foucault poses the biopolitical problem as that of the liberation of the living, but leaves aside the problem of the domestication of the wild, which is much more central in the thought of Lévi-Strauss.[16] Foucault affirms the subjective power of truth against normative forms of power, but pays little attention to the ways in which living beings are conserved against exploitation by a standardizing power, which Lévi-Strauss analyzed in indigenous knowledges. How is the ideal of truth and justice that lies at the heart of the modern project of emancipation reformulated, when it no longer concerns only relations between patients, doctors, pharmacists, and police officers, but also relations between humans and bats, pangolins, minks, and deer mediated by virologists, epidemiologists, veterinarians, and ecologists? If statements about pandemic viruses constitute a form of globalized truth, for example about the number of deaths they have caused, or their various mutations after their emergence, how can relations between humans and the other animal species they unequally infect be oriented toward environmental justice to take care of the diversity of lives exposed to them?

Zoonoses have led to collaborations between microbiologists, immunologists, epidemiologists, physicians, veterinarians, and ecologists around microbes that become pathogenic when transmitted between species. In the same way, this book is part of a collective effort to pose this problem with the methods of the social sciences, combining philosophy, sociology, anthropology, and history, in order to understand how societies perceive, manage, and anticipate zoonoses. It approaches the notions of causality, immunity, and health used by veterinary medicine and planetary ecology through a broader questioning of the political formulation of medical issues in modernity and of the emancipation of living beings from modes of exploitation and domination. The first four chapters take up Michel Foucault's analyses of biopolitics, gradually introducing medical notions – endemic, epizootic, zoonotic, pandemic – and anthropological concepts – pastoral power, cynegetic power, cryopolitics. The last two chapters are more normative: they question the possibility of articulating these various medical concepts and modalities of power with ideals of truth and justice. The book concludes with a reflection on the form of solidarity between humans and other living beings that the international organization of planetary health represents, and with a call to study sentinels in the territories where they give rise to critiques of industrial capitalism, whose pathologies are revealed globally by zoonoses.

# 1

# Biopower:
# Disciplining individuals,
# regulating populations

When Michel Foucault proposed the notion of biopower in 1976 in his lectures at the Collège de France and in the first volume of his *History of Sexuality*, he was critically adopting a term that had been circulating in a normative way for half a century: biopolitics.[1] In 1920, the Swedish geographer and political scientist Rudolf Kjellen called "biopolitics" the science of competitive and cooperative relations between social groups, to emphasize that politics is not the result of the free wills of individuals, but of the collective life of a people.[2] He thus launched a project for strengthening the state over its vital space, which would be radically and destructively realized by Nazi Germany. The notion of biopolitics was reformulated after the Second World War in the context of growing ecological awareness of the limits imposed by the planet on the development of human activities. Dietrich Gunst defined biopolitics as the regulation of population and the protection of the environment, while Kenneth Cauthen saw it as a project for a planetary society that reinscribes man in a nature spiritualized by Christian joy.[3] In 1976, Michel Foucault takes up this notion reflexively and critically, to show how it differs from the classical definition of politics as a relationship between a sovereign and his subjects.

Foucault uses the notion of biopolitics as a weapon against the philosophy of law supposed by his two main opponents in his reflection on power: critical theory, formulated at the time by Herbert Marcuse in Frankfurt, and republican philosophy, expounded at the time by Quentin Skinner at Cambridge.[4] For

Foucault, to oppose the neo-liberal power being organized in the United States to a non-alienated subject, as in the Marxist tradition, or to a community of rights, as in the British tradition, is to ignore the norms that govern relations between living beings and the forms of subjectivation they give rise to. The discovery of life as an order of phenomena endowed with its own regulations, notably through the formation of biology as separated from other sciences in the eighteenth century, leads to a redefinition of politics as a set of modifiable actions on which it is possible to intervene, in particular with the clinic and the police as new institutions of power.[5]

The crucial point in Foucault's redefinition of biopolitics is his understanding of disease as both an individual and collective crisis. Disease is no longer perceived as a divine punishment, analogous to the sovereign's punishment of a crime, but as a simple deviation from the norm, which can be the object of clinical and statistical knowledge, aligning the patient back within the norm.[6] Whereas the classical state acted on individual wills through the form of the law, which defines an action on the basis of its sanction, the modern state acts, according to Foucault, through the norm, which conceives of action as regulable or modifiable. The State, says Foucault, is no longer justified by the figure of the people, resulting from the agreement of free wills, but by that of the population, an aggregate of living beings who reproduce regularly on a territory.[7]

Foucault takes up the notion of biopolitics as part of a general philosophical reflection on the relationship between power and knowledge. He asks what a body can do in a context where several forms of knowledge are in competition. At the beginning of the nineteenth century, the period of interest to Foucault in his reflection on biopower, three types of knowledge were competing: criminal law, public hygiene, and psychiatry.

## 1.a Public hygiene and mental health

Public hygiene emerged in Europe at the end of the eighteenth century among aristocrats concerned about the effects of the industrial revolution on craftsmen, but it was instrumentalized by the state at the beginning of the nineteenth century, when diseases caused by workers' labor appeared to be obstacles to economic growth.[8] It contributed to the formation of the social as a new field of phenomena when it showed how the spread of a disease could be slowed down or stopped, based on knowledge of the working and living conditions that favored its transmission. Following the cholera epidemic of 1832, Louis Villermé used figures to show that the poorest districts of Paris were more affected by the disease than the richest, while John Snow used maps of London to highlight the role of water in disease transmission, enabling the city authorities to act on the source of the epidemic.[9] Since they disagreed on the measures that should be taken, between closing and opening infected districts, between protectionism and liberalism, the hygienists failed to transform European societies in the nineteenth century by extending preventive measures to the local level. By the end of the century, they joined their forces with microbiology and they incorporated techniques of insurance and vaccination to anticipate and control epidemics, as part of what has been called a "risk society" and a "welfare state."[10]

According to Foucault, public hygiene re-configured the fear of epidemics, perceived as divine punishments through multiplied and imminent death, into a concern for "endemics, i.e. the form, nature, extension, duration, intensity of the illness prevalent in a population (. . .), Death was now something permanent, something that slips into life, perpetually gnaws at it, diminishes and weakens it."[11] The notion of endemic disease, which appeared at the beginning of the nineteenth century, was less the object of public hygiene than of tropical medicine. An endemic disease is transmitted in societies colonized by Europeans due to a different "climate." Medical writings of the nineteenth century say that yellow fever is "endemic" in the West Indies, that cholera is "endemic" in Southeast Asia, that a skin disease now known as leishmaniasis is "endemic" in the Biskra region of Algeria, or that a goiter called cretinism is "endemic" in the Alps conquered by France.[12] The notion of endemic thus presupposed a knowledge of environments, with a view to acclimatizing Europeans to an environment that is not their own.[13]

When he introduced the notion of biopolitics in 1976, Foucault didn't mention these territories then submitted to the process of colonization, but rather the notion of milieu "insofar as it is not a natural environment, that it has been created by the population and therefore has effects on that population."[14] Taking this notion from Georges Canguilhem, who saw it as the operator of a dynamic relationship between the living organism and its environment, Foucault analyzes the milieu as the object of a technique of government,[15] notably through the forms of urbanism that capture "the emergence of the problem of the 'naturalness' of the human species within an artificial environment."[16] But in defining public hygiene as "a technique for controlling and modifying environments,"[17] Foucault leaves aside the problem of the diversity of environments and climates, which is central to tropical medicine, human geography, and the ecology of infectious diseases.

If Foucault thinks about epidemics through the vision of public hygiene rather than that of tropical medicine, it is because this vision is symmetrical to psychiatry's views of mental illness. In fact, these two fields of knowledge are in competition when it comes to highlighting living organisms on different scales: hygiene focuses on populations in the name of public health, while psychiatry focuses on individuals in the name of mental health. In his lectures at the Collège de France from 1973 to 1975, entitled *Le pouvoir psychiatrique* (*Psychiatric Power*) and *Les anormaux* (*Abnormal*), Foucault, preparing his 1975 book *Surveiller et punir* (*Discipline and*

*Punish*), shows that psychiatry invented a form of modern subjectivity in the carceral spaces of prisons, barracks, and schools.[18] Through devices such as the timetable and the panopticon, the modern individual is situated, according to Foucault, under the gaze of a power that enters into the details of his or her daily life, in contrast to the sovereign power that only manifested itself to him or her in spectacular moments such as the torture of the condemned, as in the famous scene of *supplice* at the opening of *Discipline and Punish*. Psychiatry is this knowledge that gradually inserts itself into the courts, qualifying crime not as the result of an evil inclination that overwhelms the will, but as a mental illness that shapes subjectivity. The "crime without reason" becomes a "test" through which psychiatry competes with law to redefine sovereign power, i.e. to establish equivalences and prove causality.[19] Where law invokes "reasons," psychiatry invokes "instinct," through a series of figures such as the monstrous criminal, the incorrigible pupil, the masturbating child, and the degenerate patient, as it allies itself with new institutions: the school, the family, and medicine.[20]

Can we say, then, that public hygiene confronts the law in a test that would be analogous to that passed by psychiatry? Foucault doesn't say, but this is how we can understand the famous formula by which he defines biopower as a power to "make live and let die," in contrast to sovereign power, which aims to "make die and let live." Foucault defines biopower both by its object (it deals with the lives of individual and collective bodies, not just legal subjects) and by its test (it redefines causality and value on the basis of life itself). When sovereign power presents criminals in a court of law, biopower asserts, through the voice of psychiatry for the incarcerated individual and that of public hygiene for the population of a city: "we're not going to make them die, but on the contrary, we're going make them live, to transform them into modern subjects." The test is then reversed: it's not a question of giving the reason for the crime (like the diabolical desire of parricide or regicide), but of tracing the life of the individual or population in which the crime is part of a trend.

In a manner similar to Lévi-Strauss's structuralist method,[21] Foucault inverts binary oppositions (die/live, make/let) to generate a diversity of forms of power around the tipping point of modernity.[22] He writes: "This death that was based on the right of the sovereign (to defend himself or to ask to be defended), is now manifested as simply the reverse of the right of the social body to ensure, maintain it or develop its life."[23] When two technologies of power and knowledge confront the same object, the living body of individuals caught up in relations within a population on a territory, they tip over the whole of what Foucault calls a *dispositif*.[24] There is something in the living bodies of individuals that makes sense within the framework of biopower, and which sovereign power fails to grasp; but these two devices deal with the same living body, inverting its polarities to think about the possibility of its death. Sovereign power, says Foucault, orients these polarities toward a symbolism of blood, because it thinks of them in terms of killing, whereas biopower orients them toward an analytics of sexuality, because it affirms the proliferation of life.[25] Blood is a substance appropriated by the sovereign in the act of killing, while sexuality is both what modern individuals talk about to the psychiatrist in order to know their inner selves, and what the state controls through public hygiene in order to grow its population.[26]

This division of biopower between the individual and the population seems to provide a peaceful solution to the problem of war. War is both what spills blood in the killing, since torture is conceived as a war of the sovereign against the criminal who defies him, and what establishes alliances between noble families in the sharing of blood. By replacing the alliances of blood with the combinations of sex, biopower seems to put an end to war; and yet, war returns to biopower through racism, in the sense of an ideology asserting the domination of one race over another. As Foucault famously put it in 1976:

"Race, racism, is the condition for the acceptability of killing in a society of normalization."[27] Racism establishes cuts in the biological continuum of the population in order to legitimize the destruction of living beings by representing them as inferior species. It thus formulates in the terms of biopower – i.e. those of psychiatry and public hygiene – a problem that sovereign power had resolved through the "race war," which Foucault defines as a conflict between "two groups which, although they coexist, have not become mixed."[28] Foucault's analyses of this notion in the 1976 course, particularly those of the report written by Boulainvilliers for the Duke of Burgundy to criticize Louis XIV's centralizing project,[29] show that the race war is the basis of the right of conquest in the structure of power organized around sovereignty.[30] The real question, in this perspective, is not: how does the notion of race justify the killing of some humans by others? but: why do we justify the killing of living beings today in the name of the health of populations, when we used to do it in the name of race warfare?[31]

## 1.b Biotechnology, biosafety, and biolegitimacy

The notion of biopower proposed by Foucault in his 1976 book and course was revived in the late 1990s, after having disappeared from Foucault's work, interrupted by his untimely death. The two forms of biopower distinguished by Foucault were pushed to the limits of their theoretical possibilities by his readers, to the point of becoming incompatible and producing an oscillation, even a vertigo, as evidenced by the revival of the term during the Covid-19 pandemic. These revivals of the biopower hypothesis took place particularly between Italy and France, as Foucault's 1976 lecture circulated informally in Italian before being published in French in 1997.

On the one hand, Giorgio Agamben took up Foucault's idea of an "anatomo-politics of the individual," defining power as a structure for organizing and excluding the living. Drawing on Aristotle's distinction, taken up by Hannah Arendt, between

16                          *Biopower*

*bios* and *zoē*, Agamben noted that some living beings escape the grip of power, which he described as "naked life." He commented on a notion from Roman law, that of the *homo sacer*, defining an individual outlawed by society, whom anyone can kill but who cannot be sacrificed, according to a logical structure of rule and exception analyzed by Agamben as universal. Finding this figure in the concentration camps and refugee centers of contemporary societies, Agamben saw it as a trans-historical invariant, and explored its possibilities through meditations on animality and passivity, drawing inspiration from Walter Benjamin and Georges Bataille.[32]

On the other hand, Antonio Negri extended the idea of a "biopolitics of population." In two books published with Michael Hardt, he contrasted the figures of the multitude – defined as a community of singularities constituted by shared practices and affects – and the Empire – defined as a set of multinational corporations that exploit the productive capacity of the multitude.[33] Drawing on the analyses of Saint Augustine, Spinoza, and Marx, Hardt and Negri described the relationship between the multitude and the Empire as that of flesh to body, of naturating nature to naturated nature, or of living labor to parasitic capital.[34] For Hardt and Negri, the multitude is a positive figure of the population, analyzed by Foucault as an object of techniques of power in modernity.

Agamben's and Negri's diagnoses, therefore, overturn Foucault's concept of biopower: no longer does it describe a shift in modern societies at the end of the eighteenth century, but it is an archaic structure visible as early as Roman law according to Agamben, and, according to Hardt and Negri, it is a mode of production that emerged in the 1970s on the ruins of Fordist capitalism and in the wake of digital capitalism. However, all of them define power structures in opposition to life, whether the naked life of the individual or the creative life of the multitude, leaving aside the fact that life itself is structured as power. By building a model of the

*Biotechnology, biosafety, and biolegitimacy*  17

DNA (deoxyribonucleic acid) molecule in 1953, James Watson and Francis Crick made it possible for power to intervene in living beings at the molecular level, opening up the field of biotechnology.[35]

In the 1990s, Paul Rabinow and Nikolas Roze investigated how the "molecularization of life" was transforming public health and mental health in California, France, and Great Britain. If hygiene and psychiatry invented in the nineteenth century the figures of the monster and the degenerate through statistics and the clinic, new figures were appearing at the end of the twentieth century, such as patients with HIV/AIDS or myopathy or schizophrenia, who appropriated the vast amount of data produced by doctors and biologists to construct an active subjectivity.[36] In an article entitled "Biopower today," Paul Rabinow and Nikolas Rose propose an analysis of biopower showing how it is recomposed in new discourses on race, assisted reproduction techniques and forms of genomic medicine.[37] In their view, biotechnologies are moving in two directions: on the one hand, the constitution of individualities who assess the risks of their conduct through medical care, in a co-production of scientific norms by patients and doctors described as "biosociality";[38] on the other hand, the formation of closed communities through "biosecurity" measures, whose norms are developed to protect laboratories from the risk of accidents in the flow of biological material.[39] These two directions recompose human–animal relations in different ways: biosociality leads to recognition of the amount of genetic information that humans share with other animals – in the words of Arthur Rimbaud: "the poet is truly a thief of fire. He is filled with humanity, with *animals* themselves"[40] – while biosecurity leads to the genetic selection of animals in factory farms protected from all external infection. Paul Rabinow thus compares biopolitics to tinkering (*bricolage*) in the sense of Claude Lévi-Strauss: from a small amount of genetic information, it produces a set of life forms and collective values that vary according to context, and which, in their collaborations with biologists, anthropologists substantialize through the term "society."

Marilyn Strathern continues this reflection on biopower by showing what it means for the anthropology of "kinship". Following fieldwork among the Hagen people of Papua New Guinea, a society in which the exchange of pigs by men is perceived according to the same structure as the reproduction of children by women, Strathern studied the new forms of kinship in England based on the debates on assisted reproduction.[41] While biology tends to value the idea of genetic kinship, which excludes other forms of kinship from reproduction, Strathern shows that technologies such as the conservation of biological material and medical imaging are changing relations between men, women, and children. Biopower is thus described by Strathern as a redistribution of relations of alliance and descent between persons, based on the possibilities opened up by biotechnologies, which industrial capitalism fails to grasp because of its substantialist conception of property. An intervention on living beings such as artificial insemination, egg donation, in vitro fertilization, or maternal surrogacy is "artificial" but, Strathern writes, "far from creating an autonomous domain of enterprise (as in industrial production), it is presented as directly responsive to fundamental natural processes. Its power is a bio-power, replicating the (ideal) potencies of the body."[42]

This anthropology of biotechnologies questions, rather than answers, the demand for ethics that guides their development in modern societies: it analyzes how biopower reorganizes the subject around a reflection on life, by comparison with other ways of constructing moral values.[43] Dominique Memmi points out, for example, that for medical staff, the task of "make live" implies a whole set of procedures to "let die," through debates on abortion, euthanasia, or the "work of mourning."[44] Didier Fassin proposes the concept of "biolegitimacy" to describe the way in which undocumented refugees

## Biotechnology, biosafety, and biolegitimacy 19

have to tell doctors a narrative of suffering lives in order to obtain the right to asylum, whereas a narrative of political oppression justified this right in the aftermath of the Second World War. He shows that, in these spaces on the frontiers of sovereignty, humanitarian doctors have to manage the tensions of an action aimed at potentially saving all humans, while leaving some humans to die through formalized procedures such as "triage."[45] Fassin notes that in Foucault's texts, "the notion of biopolitics is not about life as such, but about population: it is in fact a demopolitics."[46] He thus opens up a new field of research into "life as such," in the gap between living beings and the lived experience (*le vivant et le vécu*), between the objective and the subjective, between the calculation of the value of life and the value that each individual gives to his or her life, between life expectancy and the hope of living. Such attention to the narrative capacities of "life as such" enables the anthropologist to criticize the "government by emergency" that tends to naturalize social and racial inequalities through its discourse about war on poverty or against epidemics.[47]

Memmi and Fassin, following in the footsteps of Pierre Bourdieu, understand this reflexive capacity of living beings to look at themselves in order to know themselves by comparison with their fellow creatures, as a socially constructed way of distancing oneself from one's own body, cultivated by the educational institution, and as a propensity to tell stories that justify inequalities, which is more particularly developed in humans. In this anthropology of ethics, very few analyses are devoted to the capacity of animals to bring the signs of their suffering into the public arena.[48] Yet the question became crucial at the end of the 1990s, when Foucault's texts on biopower began to circulate and be discussed in European and North American academia: to what extent could this concept be applied to animals, and in particular to the large-scale slaughters that took place in Europe and China to protect humans from diseases coming from cattle and poultry?[49] However, the courses following the 1976 one, and published in the 2000s, suggest such an extension of biopower analyses to non-human animals through the notion of pastoral power.

# 2

# Pastoral power:
# Watching over humans like sheep

## 2.a  A benevolent and sacrificial power

In his lectures at the Collège de France following those of
1976, Foucault no longer spoke of biopower, divided between
the individual and the population, but of liberal governmentality and pastoral power. These pairs of notions do not overlap: the first corresponds to a doubling of the same power
after the threshold of modernity, the second to an analogy
between two forms of power on either side of this threshold.
In fact, these courses read as if liberal government, whose
transformation Foucault observed in the United States in the
late 1970s, was prefigured by what Foucault calls pastoral
power, whose forms he explored in texts from Antiquity to the
Classical Age. How does this transformation allow us to think
about the place of animals in biopolitics?

In his lecture at the Collège de France in 1978 and in a
talk given at Stanford University in 1979, Foucault proposed
a genealogy of biopower based on pastoral power.[1] Using this
term to refer to the shepherd's care for his flock, he sees it as
a forerunner of the knowledge of living organisms and population management techniques that emerged in European
societies in the nineteenth century. According to Foucault,
the Hebraic and later Christian traditions modelled the relationship between the state and its citizens on that between
the shepherd and his flock. Indeed, the shepherd constantly
counts his flock to ensure that no sheep is missing, through
a knowledge of surveillance and a technique of vigilance. As

22                                    *Pastoral power*

this knowledge is aimed at the collective good of the flock and the individual good of each sheep, it is both benevolent and individualizing. The flock is conceived as a multiplicity on the move that must be constantly monitored, as it is constantly exposed to dangers such as falling into ditches or predator attacks. Pastoral power thus differs from sovereign power in that "the shepherd wields power over a flock rather than over a land."[2]

Foucault attributes the invention of pastoral power to the Hebrew tradition. In this tradition, kings are conceived as shepherds and God as the first shepherd, who delegates his transcendent power to kings. This relationship between God, the shepherd and his flock then passes into Christianity through the relations between the priest, the confessor, and the individual, who internalizes pastoral power by being encouraged to tell the truth about himself or herself for personal salvation. The generalized benevolence of the shepherd for his flock was extended in the Middle Ages to all levels of reality: it enabled clerics to think about the relations between God and humanity, but also the relations between humans within the Church.[3] The history of modern Christianity can thus be described by Foucault as a history of pastoral power, i.e. of revolts and challenges to the shepherd's mode of government over his flock in the name of greater benevolence. Criticism of the welfare state by neo-liberal thinkers then appears as a new stage in the history of pastoral power.[4]

The notion of pastoral power thus complicates the description of the relationship between life and death before the advent of modern biopower. Whereas sovereign power decides on life and death in a land through race warfare, pastoral power takes care of its flock to maximize collective life. Death is not justified in the same way in the two forms: sovereigns put to death those of their subjects who transgress the law on their land, whereas shepherds may decide to die by themselves to save their subjects, as the figure of Christ shows in Christian theology. "Pastoral power is not simply a form of power which

*Veterinary medicine and breeders' knowledge*   23

commands," Foucault says, "it must also be prepared to sacrifice itself for the life and salvation of the flock. Therefore, it is different from royal power, which demands a sacrifice from its subjects to save the throne."[5] The problem of killing in pastoral power thus takes on a paradoxical form, as it marks the failure of benevolence. Since power is distributed equally among all members of the flock, the shepherd may sacrifice the flock to recover a lost sheep, or sacrifice a sheep to maintain the unity of the flock, or even ultimately sacrifice himself to save the whole flock.[6] "What could be called the paradox of the shepherd: the sacrifice of one for all, and the sacrifice of all for one, will be at the absolute heart of the Christian problematic of the pastorate. (. . .) Over the millennia, Western man has learned (. . .) to see himself as a sheep among sheep (. . .) to ask for his salvation from a shepherd who sacrifices himself for him."[7]

## 2.b Veterinary medicine and breeders' knowledge

Foucault says nothing about the reasons why shepherds must sacrifice themselves for their flocks, i.e. the diseases that affect them and threaten their salvation. He devotes a few brief analyses to animal population management in the eighteenth century in a 1976 lecture on the crisis of medicine, where he points out that "the French Academy of Medicine was born out of an epizootic, not an epidemic. This shows that it was indeed economic problems that motivated the beginning of the organization of medicine."[8] Indeed, the notion of epizootic disease played a central role in the constitution of veterinary medicine in the eighteenth century, as it designated a disease that spread rapidly through a herd and diminished its value, either in horses, whose economic value increased with their military use in modern warfare and their equestrian use in royal courts, or in cattle, whose transformation into commodities traded and transported over long distances increased their vulnerability to disease.[9] The management of the first

# 24 *Pastoral power*

epizootics provided an opportunity to develop knowledge of animal populations through the observation of mortality indicators and their correlation with intervention methods. During its formative years, veterinary medicine oscillated between rural economics and social medicine.

The eighteenth century was marked by the controversy between Claude Bourgelat, esquire at the Académie d'Equitation in Lyon, who founded the first veterinary school in 1762, which became the École Royale Vétérinaire in 1774, and Philippe-Etienne Lafosse, who belonged to the elite farrier profession, and was a member of the Académie des Sciences in the rural economics section. He wrote in Diderot's *Encyclopédie* in 1775 the article "Haras (Art vétérinaire)," which ran as follows: "This article is by M. Lafosse, former king's farrier, known for his superior talents in his profession, excellent works, free courses in hippiatrics, and above all for the zeal with which he serves the State on the frequent occasions when the government has recourse to his enlightenment."[10] In the king's *haras* launched by Colbert, breeders fought against the degeneration of horse breeds by introducing new blood through the importation of "oriental thoroughbreds"; this set them apart from the British breeding school, which was more attentive to the possibilities of crossbreeding. The notion of breed enabled breeders in the eighteenth century to select animals on the basis of their conformity to an ideal model, in order to increase their performance or competitiveness, through a knowledge that came to be known as zootechnics.[11] In addition, as the requisitioning of horses for war led to the mixing of horses of different breeds and origins in places that were not suited to them, the sanitary control of epizootics mobilized naturalist discourse on the purity of breeds. Veterinary medicine thus appeared as a medical topography attentive to places, waters, and climates, and concerned with preventing epizootic outbreaks resulting from animal movements. Bourgelat, with the support of Vicq d'Azyr, head of the Société Royale de Médecine, prescribed the slaughter of

## Veterinary medicine and breeders' knowledge 25

horses to control outbreaks of anthrax, and demonstrated the contagious nature of horse glanders, winning over the King's approval in each case against Lafosse's advice.

Cattle plague (also known by its German name, *Rinderpest*) was the first epizootic disease to spread internationally as a result of increased animal transport. It killed around 200 million cattle in England between 1740 and 1760, and moved to East Africa at the beginning of the twentieth century as a result of colonial policies of free movement promoted by the British government, while foot-and-mouth disease, which appeared in England in the 1870s, spread rapidly in Argentina, where, without killing the cattle, it greatly reduced their productivity.[12] Henri Bouley, who came from a family of farriers and studied veterinary medicine at Maisons-Alfort (the second veterinary school in France built in the suburbs of Paris) and later became Inspector General of the Veterinary Schools, organized a slaughter campaign in 1866 that eliminated rinderpest from French territory, and supported the first law on contagious animal diseases the same year.[13] This sanitary and legislative success led to the creation of the Office International des Epizooties (OIE) in Paris in 1924, to coordinate the fight against animal diseases and promote veterinary training.

In his writings on the plague and vaccination, Foucault never discusses these issues of veterinary art and animal health, dismissing them on the grounds that they fall under the heading of rural economy, which was less central to him than urban economy. On several occasions, Foucault returns to the difference between leprosy and plague, considered to be the two great epidemics of the Classical Age. Whereas the treatment of leprosy involved the confinement of the sick, who were excluded as outcasts, the control of plague involved the surveillance of the potentially sick population.[14] Foucault precisely describes the layout of a city quarantined against plague, with its pyramidal and continuous organization "from the sentries (*sentinelles*) who kept watch over the doors of the houses from the ends of the streets, up to those responsible

26                          *Pastoral power*

for the quarters."[15] He never mentions the fact that rats dying before humans could also serve as sentinels to anticipate the transmission of the epidemic, probably because this knowledge was not shared until the end of the nineteenth century, when it led to the invention of multiple techniques for destroying rats.[16]

Similarly, Foucault leaves out the veterinary knowledge involved in vaccination. In 1978, he devoted his seminar to vaccination techniques, focusing on the debate that arose in Europe at the end of the eighteenth century over the inoculation of smallpox, a technique introduced in 1721 by Lady Montagu, wife of the English ambassador to Istanbul, and long known in India and China. Foucault notes that the mechanism of this technique is analogous to that used by economists to forecast food shortages.[17] Indeed, variolation was the subject of a controversy in 1760 at the Académie des Sciences in Paris between the Swiss mathematician Bernoulli, who calculated the increase in life expectancy of a city whose entire population was variolated on the basis of the technique's effectiveness (approximately one variolated person in 200 died after inoculation), and the French philosopher d'Alembert, who opposed him about the significance of life expectancy for the individual who took the risk of dying from the technique. But Foucault doesn't mention the fact that vaccination was systematized by Edward Jenner, based on his observation of milkmaids in the English countryside, who generally didn't contract smallpox. Jenner derived the hypothesis that cowpox, a disease similar to smallpox but only mildly affecting cows, protected humans against a disease which was fatal to them. The success of this hypothesis led European governments to impose compulsory, free vaccination against smallpox, first in Sweden in 1816, then in England in 1871, and Germany in 1874. In fact, smallpox, after ravaging Europe and America in the classical age, is one of the few epidemics to be eradicated in the human species, since it is only transmitted from other animal species in an attenuated form.[18]

*Veterinary medicine and breeders' knowledge*  27

In his lecture, Foucault seems to confuse variolation and vaccination, by focusing exclusively on the urban economy to the detriment of the rural economy. Whereas variolation was primarily a technique used by aristocrats and literati in salons, vaccination was first and foremost a technique used by veterinarians and breeders, who turned milking cows into a kind of open-air laboratory. The first opponents of vaccination were doctors who practiced variolation, as they were wary of a technique using animals and systematized by the state, and they defended the aristocratic model of person-to-person inoculation.[19] The variolation model is well suited to Foucault's interest in liberal governmental techniques, whereas vaccination relies on more authoritarian techniques, extending from the central state to remote countryside and colonized territories. France was one of the last European countries to impose compulsory vaccination, with the 1902 Public Hygiene Act, without any binding measures. But compulsory variolation was imposed in French Cochinchina in 1871, relying on the spread of this technique among Vietnamese elites and on a brutal colonial army. The International League Against Vaccination was founded in France in 1880, but for a long time it remained a movement of aristocratic doctors who defended variolation, before being joined by opponents of vivisection and environmental activists.[20]

Ignoring this rural dimension of vaccination, Foucault showed little interest in its extension by Louis Pasteur, who used it not only for smallpox, but also for other diseases transmissible between animals or between humans, or even from animals to humans, thus forging a new alliance between microbiology, social medicine, and the veterinary arts. Inoculation of cattle against plague had already been practised in England in the eighteenth century, and was the subject of debate among French veterinarians in the nineteenth century, who did not recommend it, preferring slaughter.[21] In 1877, Louis Pasteur wrote in a letter to Henri Bouley, who was to become his main supporter in veterinary schools: "Reading veterinary

28 *Pastoral power*

works makes my head burn."[22] In 1881, Pasteur declared at a congress of the Academy of Medicine in London that he had discovered vaccination for diseases other than smallpox, and he staged the success of his sheep anthrax vaccine in Pouilly-le-Fort, through a public demonstration of animal vaccine experimentation. As the success of his rabies vaccine led him to receive a large number of requests for vaccination, he founded the Institute that bears his name to meet this demand. The use of rabies vaccination ushered in a new era for this rural technique, as the rabies virus is transmitted from wild animals (foxes) to domestic animals (dogs) to humans. By inoculating rabbit spinal cord with the virus from a rabid dog, Pasteur believed he had observed a race between the virus and the vaccine to reach the patient's brain after a bite. By shortening the distance between the wild, the domestic, and the human in the laboratory, this speed race inside the laboratory multiplied its dangers. Pasteur was ready for any sacrifice to win this race: he proposed that the rabies vaccine be tested on death row inmates and then on himself, before inoculating a human for the first time – Joseph Meister, a young Alsatian bitten by a rabid dog on the French–German border.[23] Without any pun or glorification, we can say today that Louis Pasteur exercised a pastoral power in nineteenth-century France.

While he made no distinction between variolation and vaccination, neither did Foucault distinguish between epizootics (such as rinderpest or horse glanders) and zoonoses. The term was coined by German physician Rudolf Virchow, professor at the University of Berlin, in 1855 to describe the human transmission by a worm, called trichina, of a disease affecting pigs, trichinosis.[24] This worm had first been observed in 1835 by the English physician Richard Owen, in the muscles of an Italian patient declared dead of tuberculosis. In the 1850s, the thesis of the spontaneous generation of trichinae was discussed and criticized by European scientists, and the role of rats in their transmission from pigs to humans was incriminated. But this

## Veterinary medicine and breeders' knowledge 29

thesis was thrown into disarray when a health scandal broke out in Germany and France over the importation of salted pork from the U.S.A., which competed with domestic pork production by lowering the consumer price compared with fresh meat, because it contained trichinae. Virchow, regarded in Germany as the founder of social medicine and comparative pathology, demonstrated in his laboratory that trichinae ingested by an animal remained for a long time in its intestinal tract, where it multiplied and eventually passed into the muscles. In 1860, Friedrich Albert von Zenker, professor at the University of Dresden, revealed that trichinae can be transmitted from pigs to humans, where they cause more severe diseases than in pigs, and described the cycle of these parasitic worms in pig and human organisms. This laboratory research made it possible to examine different pork production techniques (salting, fumigation, cooking) in terms of the risk of transmitting trichinae to the consumer, which is undoubtedly the first use of microbiology to assess food safety. Henri Bouley wrote in a "Note on trichinosis": "Our country's immunity derives from our culinary habits. We cook meat for a long time.[25] In 1881, the excessive cost of microscopic inspections forced many governments to ban the import of American salted pork, thus creating a major crisis in free-trade relations; the United States threatened France in return with investigations into the quality of its wines. Uncertainty about the transmission of trichinella from pigs to humans, combined with American pressure, led European governments to lift the embargo on imported salted pork by imposing health certificates, taking into account color as an indication of food safety. The widespread use of cans at the end of the nineteenth century and the introduction of freezing in the twentieth century sent into oblivion this central health and economic crisis for the European meat market: trichinosis is no longer a public health or an animal health issue.

This is not the case for another zoonosis, tuberculosis, which has killed a billion people since 1800, and continues to be

30                         *Pastoral power*

transmitted latently among two billion people today, causing around 1.5 million deaths every year, a third of them in India. Described today as a "neglected disease," it was the social disease par excellence in the nineteenth century. Since it is transmitted in insalubrious dwellings, the fight against tuberculosis was often a war against the poor. It gave rise to the first criticisms of workers' housing and working conditions, and patients were treated in sanatoria, which in retrospect appear to have been ineffective institutions of confinement.[26] Robert Koch is famous for his method of regulating animal experiments in the laboratory, which in 1882 enabled him to identify the bacterium causing tuberculosis, known as *Mycobacterium tuberculosis*, or Koch's bacillus. Koch's followers observed a similar bacterium in cattle, called *Mycobacterium bovis*, which, as in humans, caused lesions (called tubercles) throughout the body by its toxic reproduction. Given the difficulty of diagnosing the disease and explaining its transmission in cattle, quantified estimates of its prevalence at the end of the nineteenth century vary widely, but the fear of its transmission to humans through meat consumption justified mass slaughtering of cattle, according to what may be called in retrospect a "precautionary principle."[27] While English epidemiologists statistically established that the consumption of cow's milk increased the risk of tuberculosis in humans, Robert Koch asserted that human and bovine tuberculosis were not the same diseases, as the bacteria do not objectively resemble each other under the microscope.[28]

This scientific and ontological controversy (what is tuberculosis, if it affects both humans and cattle?) was resolved with the introduction of vaccination. German physician Emil von Behring and French veterinarian Saturnin Arloing developed vaccines against bovine tuberculosis in the final years of the nineteenth century. At the Pasteur Institute, physician Albert Calmette and veterinarian Camille Guérin developed a vaccine bearing their name (Bacille Calmette-Guérin or BCG), which protected both humans and cattle against tuberculosis.

*Veterinary medicine and breeders' knowledge*     31

Their strategy was to demonstrate the vaccine's effectiveness by offsetting failures in cattle with successes in humans, and vice versa.[29] BCG vaccination reduced tuberculosis transmission in humans and cattle until the 1960s, when it was gradually abandoned by veterinarians who reverted to herd culling. When *Mycobacterium bovis* was discovered in badgers during sampling in England, British health authorities, fearing the transmission of tuberculosis to cattle, applied these culling measures to wild animals.[30]

If Foucault ignores the problem of animal diseases, which nevertheless played a central role in the development of technologies for intervention on living beings, this is not only due to his focus on urban knowledge to the detriment of peasant knowledge, but also to his use of pastoral power as a metaphor for the surveillance of humans among themselves, leaving aside the other animal metaphors through which techniques of power are expressed. When he discusses mental illness in the classical age in his course entitled *Abnormal*, taking up Michel de Certeau's analyses, Foucault points out that the convulsions of the possessed are an internal effect of Christian technologies of confession, both at their point of maximum intensity and their reversal, just as witchcraft was a form of resistance to the tribunals of the Inquisition.[31] According to Foucault, the convulsed body of the possessed observed by her confessor is transformed into the monstrous body of the criminal under the gaze of psychiatry in the nineteenth century. But this diabolical scheme of splitting reduces the richness of the animal imaginary through which the discourse of witches and possessed women is expressed.

Similarly, in his analysis of the race war in his 1976 lecture, entitled *Society Must Be Defended*, Foucault makes no reference to the animal coats of arms by which the various "races" in struggle were identified, and he makes no attempt to explain how this medieval bestiary was reconverted in the eighteenth century into a zootechnics that presented itself as a selection of animal breeds.[32] Surprisingly, in Foucault's

1977 course, the notion of pastoral power replaces that of "mystical possession" and "race war" put forward in the 1975 and 1976 courses. Foucault's courses read as if the war waged by individual subjects against the Inquisition, and the war waged by collective subjects against the rituals of sovereignty, had to give way to herd-counting techniques, as if the alliance between pastoral power and sovereign power in modernity – or between Church and State – enabled pastoral power to stabilize the war waged by individual and collective subjects against the techniques of sovereignty, by justifying the shepherd's benevolence with the overhanging viewpoint of the centralizing state.

This is certainly one of the keys to the genesis of biopower: the modern state integrates the singularizing potential of pastoral power through disciplinary techniques and knowledge of populations, so that land becomes territory and benevolence an offer of security. "Pastoral power," says Foucault, "must constantly duplicate itself through a 'conduct of conducts',"[33] foreshadowing modern government as the art of "not governing too much."[34] However, this reflexivity of pastoral power through surveillance techniques loses sight of the actual relations between shepherd and flock, and their tensions with other relations between humans and animals. In the Christian West, the benevolence of the sovereign over his land and of the shepherd over his flock is contrasted with another form of power: that of the hunter over his prey. Yet Foucault's genealogy of biopolitics strangely overlooks this cynegetic form of power.

# 3

# Cynegetic power:
# Catching the prey's perspectives

### 3.a Colonial slavery and hunting societies

The hypothesis of a cynegetic power, whose genealogy would complement that of pastoral power established by Michel Foucault, has been proposed by Grégoire Chamayou in a series of important works where he makes a diagnosis of contemporary societies. He defines this power and its test as follows: "Cynegetic power is exercised over prey, living beings that escape and flee, with a double problem: how to catch them? how to retain them once they are caught?"[1] Grégoire Chamayou finds the sources of this cynegetic power in the biblical story of King Nimrod, "mighty hunter before the Lord," who captured humans to build his city and refused the divine injunction to become a good shepherd. Whereas Abraham crosses spaces to care for his people considered as a flock, says Chamayou, Nimrod accumulates slaves in a territory to build his people. Nimrod thus appears in biblical tradition as the "bad king," not in the sense of a failing shepherd, but in the sense of "its inverted double,"[2] as he reveals the tendency of kings toward tyranny and exploitation. Chamayou writes: "Whereas pastoral power guides and accompanies a multiplicity in movement, cynegetic power extends itself, on the basis of a territory of accumulation, over a space of capture. Whereas pastoral power is fundamentally beneficent, cynegetic power is essentially predatory."[3] Chamayou notes that Thomas Hobbes made room for the pastoral power of the Church when he founded sovereign power on his theory

34            *Cynegetic power*

of the social contract, thus ruling out cynegetic power. Jesus, according to Hobbes, "said not to his Apostles, he would make them so many Nimrods, Hunters of Men; but Fishers of Men."[4] In pastoral power, men can be like sheep or like fish, but they cannot be like prey.

What makes cynegetic power particularly dangerous in contrast to pastoral power is that the hunter is not above his prey as the shepherd is above his flock: he is on the same level as his prey and can be killed by it. Unlike surveillance, hunting is a reversible relationship, so that hunting power must always fight to avoid being overthrown.[5] Therefore, while pastoral power condemns hunting power as that of "bad kings," it allies itself with it to better extend its control over living beings. Chamayou distinguishes between hunting for acquisition and hunting for exclusion, based on the ambivalence of the word "chase," which means both to pursue and to repel. The former is essential to cynegetic power, according to the biblical definition, while the latter is a form of cynegetic power mixed with pastoral power: when a sheep has strayed, it must be pursued, and, if it is sick or contagious, destroyed.[6]

The whole history of cynegetic power appears as an effort by hunting authorities to avoid coming face to face with their prey, by delegating their prerogatives and multiplying intermediaries through a series of heterogeneous alliances with pastoral authorities. Thus, according to Chamayou, the Inquisition trials can be understood as devices that enabled Catholic priests to avoid coming into contact with the bodies of witches and the rural knowledge they carried.[7] Similarly, when the Spanish conquerors used dogs and beaters to hunt Indians, it was not to integrate them into the social body like slaves, but to slaughter them like sick animals, thus basing incipient imperialism on the massacre of indigenous peoples.[8] When they discussed with contradictory arguments whether Indians had souls and could be converted to Christianity, Sepulveda and Las Casas challenged cynegetic power in the name of pastoral power, since they asserted that Indians

*Colonial slavery and hunting societies*     35

had the capacity to think and therefore to revolt against a power that dehumanized them. In their African trading posts, on the other hand, the Portuguese denied the humanity of the slaves they bought through the slave trade as commodities, a position taken up by Hegel in his philosophy of history, when he refused to allow the dialectic of master and slave to unfold in Africa. According to Chamayou, the stories of slaves' flights introduced a new motif into European literature: it is possible to take the slave's perspective, to feel what it means to be hunted down like prey.[9] The hunter pursues an animal whose movements he perceives as if they were his own, and thus confronts a death that could be his death. "Hunting is defined not as a battle to death, but as an execution temporally delayed."[10] Accumulating the body's slaves, therefore, is a way to capture an abundance of perspectives displaying the hunter's power.

Chamayou shows that the echoes between biblical tradition and debates on Spanish–Portuguese colonization still resonate through techniques of surveillance and control in modern and contemporary societies. Recalling that Alphonse Bertillon founded biological anthropology at the end of the nineteenth century on "a scientific police force in which all the technical information connected to manhunt will be brought together,"[11] he points out that the "scientific police force" combines the hunt for the poor, the hunt for foreigners and the hunt for Jews, conceiving movements of the crowd as the trajectories of a flock. Chamayou extends this genealogy to contemporary societies: he shows that the drones used for war indefinitely extend the distance between hunter and hunted, when the shooter aims at his target in the theater of operations from a computerized office in the U.S.A.[12] In his view, this distance between predator and prey in contemporary societies makes them "ungovernable": when biopower realizes that it cannot extend its control over all living things, it is panicked by the proliferation of counter-movements, and enraged by its own powerlessness to regulate them from above.[13]

36                                  *Cynegetic power*

Achille Mbembe has taken up the notion of cynegetic power to describe the situation in Africa after transatlantic trade and European colonization. These historical moments produced the figure of the "Negro" as a certain form of life in globalized capitalism, which Achille Mbembe proposes to critique, since it designates both a primitive energy that the world needs in order to regenerate itself, and an existence alienated in slavery that cannot achieve self-consciousness.[14] Through the plantation economy, the slave is indeed produced, according to Mbembe, as a form of mutilated life, a zombie modality of "death-in-life."[15] Slaves dehumanized by cynegetic power come back to haunt slaveholders, failing to challenge them with a fight to the death. Mbembe thus coined the term "necropolitics" by playing with the term "negropolitics": it is not just a power to cause death, but above all a power to split life into a ghostly form.[16] Mbembe strongly argues that, when viewed from the perspective of their African colonies, European states are in contradiction with their biopolitical objectives, since European governments experimented in these colonies with techniques of mass killing such as extermination camps, which they then applied to their own populations.[17] The figure of the "Negro" thus comes to haunt Europe as that of an inferior race that the government can put to death at the risk of tipping its biopolitical rationality toward generalized death.

According to Mbembe, cynegetic power is not limited to the colonial plantation economy, but also characterizes the post-colonial extension of capitalism through digital technologies, with its new forms of resource extraction, such as patents on genetically modified organisms. In his article on "necropolitics," Mbembe distinguishes two ways of reversing the cynegetic balance of power: the logic of survival, in which the prey kills the predator, and the logic of martyrdom, in which the prey kills itself in order to take the predator to its death.[18] In his *Critique de la raison nègre* (translated as *Critique of Black Reason*), Mbembe outlines a third, more optimistic path: the figures of Marcus Garvey, Aimé Césaire, Frantz

# Colonial slavery and hunting societies 37

Fanon, and Nelson Mandela prepare the advent of a new African community on the ruins of the predatory economy. This "emancipatory violence of the colonized" is described by Mbembe as a "politics of the sentinel," in the sense that some humans "on the lookout" perceive the signs of the advent of a new era that would put an end to the mortifying splitting of all signs by globalized capitalism, in order to explore its creative potential.[19] According to Mbembe, this "politics of the sentinel" is based on the constitution of "reserves of life," where a dynamic of restitution and reparation would close the infinite cycle of colonial debt.[20]

The genealogies proposed by Grégoire Chamayou and Achille Mbembe thus reintroduce the colonial economy of the plantation and the political form of slavery into Michel Foucault's genealogy of biopolitics. The latter is built against the Marxist analysis of the primitive accumulation of capital, according to which imperialism resolves the contradictions of the capitalist mode of production by constituting labor reserves in the colonies through the form of slavery.[21] Foucault notes that colonial power not only takes a repressive and alienating form, but also productively makes subjects through the control and surveillance of populations. Biopower thus takes up the archaic discourse of the "race war" through an opposition between a superior and inferior race, that leads colonized subjects to internalize their exploitation.[22] This explains, according to Foucault, that the colonies were testing grounds for techniques of power that were later applied in Europe, such as mass vaccination campaigns and prisoner concentration camps.[23] Slavery is thus analyzed by Foucault as a technique of subjugation through which individuals leave traditional forms of power to enter into formats of standardization and circulation of goods.[24] The genealogy of cynegetic power established by Chamayou and taken up by Mbembe shows that this power of surveillance, which conditions the primitive accumulation of capital in the colonies, is contaminated by the hunting techniques of colonized societies. Mbembe thus takes up the

38 *Cynegetic power*

term "animism," by which anthropologists have described the beliefs of colonized societies, to describe the "predatory" mode of operation of colonial and post-colonial capitalism.[25]

However, such a genealogy of cynegetic power through techniques of predation and accumulation does not provide a point of support for critique, as life or truth could be in Foucault's genealogy of biopower. Chamayou concludes his analysis of "ungovernable societies" with a call for self-management, and Mbembe ends his diagnosis of "necropolitics" with a eulogy of African sentinels, but they give no indication of how these forms and norms emerge from cynegetic power to contest it. In the same way that Agamben and Negri gave grand philosophical accounts of life, without showing how it is organized through technologies, Chamayou and Mbembe's analyses refuse to indicate how cynegetic power functions in societies where hunting is the main activity. As a consequence, they fail to distinguish between good and bad ways of hunting prey and accumulating perspectives.

Chamayou and Mbembe's analyses do not enter the machine of cynegetic power in order to derail it because they share with Foucault's analyses of pastoral power a metaphorical use of animals. The animal is for them a figure of dehumanization or commodification in a historical process, not a living being in relation to another living being in an environment or territory. These analyses thus miss what has been called the "ontological turn in anthropology" – sometimes also referred to as the "animalistic turn" – which enjoins anthropologists to describe animals not as symbols with which humans fabricate representations, but as real beings with which they interact.[26] This "turn" is often traced back to Eduardo Viveiros de Castro's writings on the relations between prey and predators in Amazonian hunting societies.[27] Indeed, the Brazilian anthropologist has showed that kinship systems and ritual ceremonies lead humans to take the perspective of the animals they hunt in order to follow their tracks, but that they must stop taking this point of view when they kill them, at

*Colonial slavery and hunting societies*     39

the risk of eating themselves – a view of the world and an ontology of relations Viveiros called "perspectivism." In these societies, diseases are interpreted as animals taking revenge on humans by transmitting pathogens, because humans can share the perspectives of animals when they are sick. These texts have played a founding role in recent transformations of anthropological theory, leading to a renewed analysis of predation, notably in the work of Philippe Descola.

But this "animalistic turn in anthropology" could just as easily be traced back to André-Georges Haudricourt's 1962 article, in which this specialist of Vietnamese languages compared relations between humans, animals and plants with relations between humans in Mediterranean and Asian societies.[28] Haudricourt described the techniques used by the Kanaks of New Caledonia to grow yams in their gardens as "negative indirect actions." In contrast, he described the movements that Mediterranean shepherds impose on their sheep when choosing where to graze as "positive direct actions." Instead of opposing animal husbandry in the West and plant gardening in the Asia-Pacific, Haudricourt compared different relationships to the space on which the action takes place. Tuber plants, indeed, require careful handling of the soil to allow them to reproduce, while seed plants, cultivated by pastoral societies, rely on selection to adapt them to different soils. According to Haudricourt, these modes of action determined different forms of government and navigation techniques between the West and Asia-Pacific. Such a distinction enables us to better understand what Foucault calls "faire vivre" (make live) in biopower, based on the techniques by which the shepherd acts on sheep and the cultivator on seeds in European societies. The notion of "negative indirect action" sheds light on what Foucault means by "let live" in his definition of sovereign power, as it seems to be based on the renunciation of sovereign power to act on living beings, giving way to new forms of territorial planning. What we might call "botanical power," by way of symmetry with "cynegetic power," was

40                        *Cynegetic power*

displayed in European royal gardens and in the first zoological parks.[29]

When analyzing the Greek sources of pastoral power, Foucault does not cite Haudricourt's analyses of Asia-Pacific gardens, nor does he cite the work of Pierre Vidal-Naquet and Alain Schnapp on hunting techniques in ancient Greece. According to these two historians, the space of power where Greek citizens spoke in public – the *agora* – was built in contrast to a wilderness (*sylva*) where young men had to return to confront their animality. In Sparta, hunting served as a "preparation for military life,"[30] introducing a tension between the collective order of the phalanx that it heralds and the disorder of individual feats that it magnifies. In the trag-edies of Aeschylus and Euripides, "the function of the hunt is both complementary to and opposed to that of sacrifice (. . .): the hunter is both the predatory animal and the possessor of an art (*tekhné*)" characterized by cunning (*mètis*), i.e. the ability to perceive the movements of living beings at the heart of wild spaces.[31] In the writings of Herodotus, the Greeks are confronted with a dual figure of cynegetic power: that of the Scythians and Amazons, who cunningly conceal them-selves, and that of the kings of Persia, who accumulate game.[32] Hence the ambiguity of kings-hunters, like Ulysses, goddesses-hunters, like Artemis, or heroes-hunters, like Hercules, when they serve as models for the initiation of the citizen. While hunting is a predatory activity based on the seduction of prey, it is also an apprenticeship of desire: the hunter must trick his or her prey to reverse the balance of power in his or her favor. The historical anthropology of ancient Greece thus reveals a tension between pastoral and cynegetic power that subse-quently permeated all European societies.

Chamayou's reading of the Bible, Haudricourt's hypotheses on Asia-Pacific as well as Schnapp and Vidal-Naquet's work on ancient Greece show that pastoral power and cynegetic power are not opposed as cultures developed in different parts of the world, but rather contrasted as ontologies of power that

*Colonial slavery and hunting societies*  41

coexist in all societies to justify the appropriation of living beings. I will leave aside the American and African continents, which I have briefly touched on, based on the hypotheses of Viveiros de Castro and Mbembe, and I will return to Asia-Pacific, where I situate my own ethnographic research.

In the "Middle East," power is justified in the name of protecting the herd (*reaya*) within a territory, but is exercised outside of the territory by logics of reciprocal predation.[33] In colonial India, the British government relied on the caste system to promote proper ways of handling animals, criminalizing as "impure" castes that practiced hunting.[34] In postcolonial India, the trade in body parts, like blood transfusion or organ trafficking, is part of a generalized surveillance of the population through digital technologies for classifying and tracing.[35] The Indian government uses this biopolitical rationality to control stray dogs and limit the transmission of rabies: it singularizes pet dogs within a logic of animal protection, while aggregating stray dogs as pests to be eradicated.[36] Anthropologists' reflections on "biocapital" – the accumulation of a "surplus" by a pharmaceutical industry betting on future diseases – apply particularly well to contemporary India, where capitalism takes on a form that is both deregulated and authoritarian.[37]

In classical China, the idea that the government manages its people like a herd is spelled out in a text from the fourth century.[38] But this agrarian conception has always coexisted in China with a ritualization of hunting practices by the sovereign, which was amplified under the Qing dynasty of Manchu origin.[39] When reformers of the imperial power at the end of the nineteenth century wanted to extend these pastoral techniques to the Chinese Empire, they came up against the circulation and display of corpses encouraged by the European media, who used these images to portray China as "the sick man of the East."[40] These reformers, like Liang Qichao, responded to Western criticism with a conception of the unity of the national body based on family genealogy

42                           *Cynegetic power*

and an urban architecture founded on public hygiene.[41] Mao
Zedong's Communist China internalized these hygienist policies through the fight against epidemics, based on the mobi-
lization of the masses against an enemy, and the one-child
policy, oriented toward the goal of improving "worker quality"
through birth control.[42]

The pneumonic plague in Manchuria, which killed around
60,000 people between October 1910 and April 1911, can be
seen as a tipping point in the connexions between pastoral
and cynegetic power in China. A Malaysian-born Chinese
physician who trained at Cambridge University, Wu Liande,
demonstrated that this respiratory disease was transmitted to
humans by marmots. Noting that the plague followed the railroad tracks used by coolies, migrant workers sent to Manchuria
to harvest marmot fur, Wu Liande hypothesized that the
intensification of the fur trade through the construction of
the railroad had upset the ecological balance between the
marmots (called *tarbagan*) and the native hunting populations
(Buryats and Mongols), as the latter knew how to perceive the
signs of the disease, notably when marmots shouted. Because
coolies replaced hunters in the development of Manchuria, a
plague bacillus that had previously circulated among marmots
without causing an epidemic was transmitted to the rest of
China and potentially to the world.[43] Following Wu Liande,
the hunting techniques of North Asian shamanistic societies
provided intellectual resources for criticizing the extension of
cynegetic power by modern capitalist societies.[44]

Moving on to Southeast Asia and Australia, we find similar compositions of pastoral and cynegetic power. Anna
Tsing worked with a "shaman" in a Borneo tribal society,
the Meratus Dayak, finding in her songs the capacity of
this society to engage in peasant mobilizations against the
expropriation of the forest.[45] She then went on to study the
forms of resistance or "friction" manifested in environmental
mobilizations in Indonesia, when the natural entities they
defended could not pass through the scale of capitalist glo-

*Colonial slavery and hunting societies* 43

balization, what she calls their "inscalability."[46] This is why she has turned her attention to the *matsutake* mushroom, which traditionally grew in the shade of Japanese pines, and is now found in the forests of Yunnan and Oregon. This mushroom cannot be cultivated in the colonial plantation form, but is the subject of harvesting practices developed by hunter-gatherer societies. Following Laotian refugees from the Vietnam War, some of whom, the Hmong, carry with them the values of hunting, while others, the Mien, display vegetarian Buddhist values, Tsing shows that these mushrooms symbolize for them the freedom conquered on American soil. But the same mushrooms, when sold in a Japanese market, elicit passionate comments from gourmets, who perceive them as symbols of past aristocratic practices. The pastoral power that standardizes plantations thus fails to make collecting forms and gastronomic practices "scalable" in the *matsutake* market, which produces opposite symbols at its two poles: freedom in Oregon and discipline in Japan. Anna Tsing, even if she doesn't use the term coined by Grégoire Chamayou, describes the practices observed in the forests of Oregon as a dispersed, heterogeneous form of cynegetic power, which she imagines as "rhizome," the term by which mycologists describe the growth of mushrooms.

On the Australian continent, groups of hunter-gatherers have for millennia developed ways of relating to non-humans very far from those of European societies, which anthropology has theorized a century ago under the term "totemism."[47] But more recent work has shown how this form of cynegetic power has come into tension with the pastoral power of European settlers over the past two centuries. Working with Aboriginal communities in northern Australia, and supporting their claims to their land against mining companies, Elizabeth Povinelli has coined the term "geontopower" to bring an Aboriginal perspective to debates on biopower. She poses the question: how is the Foucauldian description of biopower transformed if it includes accounts of the earth as alive?[48] In

44         *Cynegetic power*

the "totemistic" conception of the Australian Aborigines, the land bears the traces of beings of the Dreaming time, who are mobilized in narratives about the movements of ancestors, justifying the millennia-old occupation of this land. In these narratives, according to Povinelli, European figures of biopower – "the hysterical woman, the Malthusian couple, the perverse adult and the masturbating child; the camps and barracks, the panopticon and solitary confinement" – are replaced by "new figures: the Desert, the Animist, the Virus."[49] These three figures challenge the opposition between life and death on which biopower is based:[50] "the Desert" is a space where life was but is no longer, "the animist" is a human who attributes life to inanimate things, and "the virus" is a piece of information that replicates itself by hijacking a cell's nuclear material.[51] If capitalism mobilizes these three figures by prospecting for materials in the desert, investing in valuable commodities and representing viruses as terrorists, Povinelli's anthropological investigation aims to explore other possibilities for these figures, by collecting the narratives of hunting societies around geological events.[52]

Povinelli's indications on "geontopower" open up a research program for following hunter-gatherers in Australia, tracing their relations with the land and understanding their confrontations with capitalist modernity. Anthropologists can thus study how Aboriginal communities perceive dingo dogs, with which they have forged millennia-old relationships and which the government wants to isolate in parks;[53] dromedaries, imported from Afghanistan and Pakistan by the British and now vessels of the Australian desert;[54] cattle, monitored by Aboriginal communities and slaughtered by Department of Agriculture when not vaccinated;[55] bats, which the municipal authorities chase out of towns to prevent them from transmitting viruses, even though the Aboriginal communities have been consuming them for thousands of years as a source of vitality.[56] Indigenous Australians have traced paths with their animals on their land, which often abruptly cross the projects

*Colonial slavery and hunting societies* 45

of capitalist modernity, guided by the benevolence of pastoral power and the violence of sovereign power.

In reformulating Tsing and Povinelli's researches through the distinction between cynegetic power and pastoral power, I depart from the interpretation that has been given to their works in an oft-cited article on "multi-species ethnography."[57] The authors of this article, Eben Kirksey and Stefan Helmreich, worked with naturalists in Papua New Guinea and microbiologists in the Pacific Ocean.[58] By this label, which played a unifying role in the U.S.A. comparable to that of the "ontological turn in anthropology" in Europe to integrate non-humans into human collectives, Kirksey and Helmreich designate work that "studies the hosts of organisms whose lives and deaths are linked to human social worlds."[59] Drawing on the seminal texts of Lewis Henry Morgan on the ethology of the beaver in North America and Harold Conklin on the ethno-zoology of Austronesian peoples at Yale University,[60] they aim to take up the questions posed by women studies to decentralize the figure of the human and question its impact on the planet and on other species through a "symbiopolitics."[61] Helmreich and Kirksey rely on bio-art to organize a "tactical biopolitics," which subverts the disciplinary strategies of biopower through the ability of microbes to "para-site."[62]

A contribution to the issue of *Cultural Anthropology* on "multi-species ethnography" illustrates the orientation of this current of thought, based on the case of bird 'flu in Indonesia in 2003. Under the title "Viral clouds," Celia Lowe shows that the figure of the "cloud" can be used to describe the dispersal of viruses in farms and markets, where poultry move in the open air, but also the shape of the virus as a folded protein in permanent mutation, as well as the shape of the Indonesian archipelago, which makes it impossible to control the potentially pandemic epizootic from a centralized biosecurity power.[63]

My own research into bird 'flu in southern China led me to pay less attention to the rhizomatic dimension of assemblages,

46 *Cynegetic power*

in the vein of Gilles Deleuze and Félix Guattari as claimed by proponents of "multi-species ethnography,"[64] and more to the thresholds crossed by living beings when they are transformed, in a method closer to the structuralism of Lévi-Strauss and Foucault. I have worked with virologists who take samples from wild bird reserves or poultry farms and transport them to laboratories to sound the alarm in the event of the emergence of a zoonotic virus. Borrowing from Grégoire Chamayou's notion of cynegetic power, I have described these virologists as "virus hunters" because they use viruses as signs to take the perspective of animals on chains of viral contagion, in a way that can rival or, on the contrary, ally with pastoral and sovereign forms of power, notably when the government decides to slaughter domestic animals or close wild animal reserves. Taking as a starting point the tensions between cynegetic power and pastoral power when viruses cross species boundaries, rather than opposing one to the other as a rhizomatic power and a hegemonic power, I propose to study what are the good and bad predation techniques applied to zoonoses, and how they can give rise to internal forms of critique. While multi-species ethnography highlights the rhizome versus the grid by opposing a good and a bad form of biopower, I analyze how the biopolitical practices of virologists transform "disease reservoirs" into virus reserves in order to understand the ideals that guide them. To do this, I need to retrace the history of the notions of virus hunters and disease reservoirs, which has escaped the genealogy of biopower constructed by Michel Foucault.

### 3.b  Virus hunters and disease reservoirs

The term "microbe hunters" was coined by Paul de Kruif in 1926 in a book with the same title. Translated into eighteen languages and featured in two Hollywood films, this book contributed to the popular diffusion of microbiology. Paul de Kruif was born in 1890 in the Dutch community of Michigan, which

*Virus hunters and disease reservoirs*   47

may have prompted him to set up Antoni van Leeuwenhoek as the founder of microbiology, for his invention of an enlarging lens apparatus in Holland at the end of the eighteenth century.[65] De Kruif fought in France during the First World War, where he met disciples of Louis Pasteur, before joining the Rockefeller Institute in New York. He then left bacteriological research to write popular works on medicine, starting with a book entitled *Our Medicine Men* and later advising Sinclair Lewis on his novel *Arrowsmith*.

*Microbe Hunters* is a series of fourteen portraits of microbiologists making glorious discoveries about the role of bacteria in vital processes such as fermentation and infectious diseases. Some of them were contemporaries of the author, who didn't recognize themselves in the portrait he painted. For de Kruif, the term "microbe hunters" indicates a violent confrontation with a wild world and a tenuous attempt to control and master this world. The notion of hunters doesn't point to the killing of microbes as prey, but rather to the destruction of the animals on which they are collected and manipulated. De Kruif recounts the routinization of this hunt as the power of the early discoverers is distributed in a more procedural science: "The hunt for microbes has always been a funny business. A janitor with no proper education (Leeuwenhoek) was the first man to see microbes; a chemist (Pasteur) put them on the map and made people properly afraid of them; a country doctor (Koch) turned the hunting of them into something that came near to being a science; to save the lives of babies from the poison of one of the deadliest of them, a Frenchman and a German had to pile up mountains of butchered guinea-pigs and rabbits. Microbe hunting is a story of amazing stupidities, fine intuitions, insane paradoxes."[66]

One might think that the term "hunter" refers exclusively to male figures asserting their superiority over microbes by taking advantage of the domineering effect of the microscope. Indeed, the 1926 book closes with the figure of Paul Ehrlich, who found a "magic weapon" against microbes (the first

48 *Cynegetic power*

synthetic drug against syphilis), and whom de Kruif compares to "primitive blacksmiths clawing at metal to find the material for their swords."[67] But in another book, *Men against Death*, De Kruif tells the story of Alice Catherine Evans, who in 1917 demonstrated the role of bacteria in the transmission of brucellosis through the milk of cattle and sheep, while working for the U.S. Department of Agriculture. De Kruif points out that her discoveries met with misogynistic resistance, but were confirmed by other bacteriologists in the 1920s and led to major reforms in the dairy industry.[68]

The term "hunters" is justified by the fact that the microbiologists described by de Kruif identify with the microbes or vectors they track, seeing nature through their movements. Microbes are endowed with agency by biologists, who take their place through imagination to understand their chain of transmission across species. Ronald Ross thus wrote to Patrick Manson, giving voice to the microbe that causes malaria: "I find that I exist constantly in three out of four mosquitoes that feed on birds infected with the disease."[69] De Kruif describes Battista Grassi as the true discoverer of the role of anopheles mosquitoes (called *zanzarone* in Italy): "He knew as much about the manners and customs and traditions of the *zanzarone* as if he were a mosquito himself."[70]

De Kruif also emphasizes that both "microbe hunters" and animal breeders see different animal species as ecological niches for microbes. At the beginning of the twentieth century, hunters, who took the perspective of microbes, and breeders, who took the perspective of animals, used the same techniques of surveillance. Theobald Smith is described as "watching the disease as closely as possible, just as the breeders did. It was a new form of microbe hunting, following nature and changing it by the smallest tricks."[71] Theobald Smith, who taught comparative pathology at Harvard, is considered the founder of parasitology for his discovery of the tick's role in the transmission of bovine fever. He proposed an evolutionary vision of parasitism as a relationship in which parasite and host find mutual benefit. According to him, this relationship must be the subject of a quasi-mathematical study of all the parameters involved to explain the conditions under which it becomes pathological. For example, importing cattle from the North of the United States upsets the cohabitation between ticks and cattle from the South, and favors the spread of bovine fever.[72]

Theobald Smith generalized the concept of the "animal reservoir" in microbiology. The term appeared in Pasteurian medicine to designate populations in which a pathogen is identified before causing an outbreak of disease. In 1905, the brothers Edmond and Etienne Sergent thus explained an outbreak of malaria in Algeria: "the virus reservoir was represented by Europeans who were already infected and by the natives, who were very often infected without any morbid manifestations."[73] The notion of reservoir plays on the analogy with an apparently quiet body of water whose dikes can break. It blurs the distinction between the natural and the artificial, since a reservoir is built by humans but threatens to overflow in ways they cannot predict. We find the term again in 1922 in the writings of Louis Tanon, who conducted with the Préfecture de Police in Paris a survey of plague-infected rats, and, out of 5,000 rats he had caught, found thirty of them carrying the plague bacillus, while they had no symptoms of the disease. "The rat, he wrote, appears to be a reservoir of the virus because it can preserve, over the years, the bacillus in its bodily organs, transmitting it from one generation to another in a less virulent form, until, under the influence of secondary causes, the bacille slowly resumes its activity, causes an outbreak among its hosts and then attacks man via the flea."[74] Concern about the role of rats as plague reservoirs extended beyond the realm of colonial medicine, as rats have an ability to move anywhere following humans, and can therefore invisibly spread a plague outbreak worldwide.[75]

Theobald Smith extended the concept of animal reservoir from rats and mosquitoes, which can be eradicated by massive

50         *Cynegetic power*

sanitary campaigns, to domestic animals, whose cohabitation with humans is necessary. In 1928, he wrote: "Animals that contribute to human disease can be divided into useful and noxious species. From a scientific point of view, the distinction is of no value. It becomes, however, very significant when we endeavour to suppress the disease. We may make continuous, relentless warfare against rats and mosquitoes, but the problem becomes more complex when we have to deal, for example, with cows as reservoirs of human disease. Medical literature abounds in references on the possibilities of harm lurking behind animal diseases, and in nearly every epidemic of the past, animal diseases have been reported as precursors."[76] Theobald Smith pointed out that transmissions of pathogens from animals to humans are rare, and the conditions under which they occur remain mysterious: hence the need, he argues, to investigate the mechanisms of parasite change to see diseases before they appear. "The ancestry," he wrote, "might be directly before us, in our midst, in fact in some animal disease, but we may fail to see it because of the irreversible process that has brought the change about."[77]

Karl Friedrich Meyer, who studied under Theobald Smith at Harvard, developed the concept of animal reservoir in connection with the new science of ecology.[78] Trained in veterinary medicine in Zurich and professor of public health at UC Berkeley, Meyer developed contacts with ranchers and industrialists in California, which enabled him to discover the role of soil spores in the transmission of botulism, or that of squirrels in the transmission of plague. He also investigated "parrot fever," or psittacosis, which infected 139 people, 33 of whom died, in the U.S.A. in 1930. Meyer discovered the symptoms of psittacosis, notably lesions in the bile, in parakeets that did not appear to be sick. He suggested that parakeet breeders in Los Angeles test ten percent of their parakeets by inoculating mice with their serum, which revealed a high incidence of the disease. Meyer corresponded with Australian microbiologist Frank Macfarlane Burnet, who had found the psittacosis virus in Australian cockatoos, and showed that they excreted the virus without symptoms. Burnet deduced that the virus circulated naturally among birds in Australia, and that it had become pathogenic as a result of the concentration of birds on ships bound for Europe and America. From his practice of nature observation, Burnet retained the idea of a natural circulation of the virus, which becomes pathogenic when it leaves its ecosystem.[79]

In their correspondence, Burnet and Meyer discuss Charles Elton's conceptions in *Animal Ecology* (1927), according to which disease intervenes in population cycles that involve predators (microbes) and prey (the animals that harbor them).[80] For Elton, diseases reveal an imbalance in these predatory relationships, and they regulate populations by bringing them back into balance, notably by destroying invasive species that threaten the stability of ecosystems.[81] In his view, we need to take the microbes' perspective to understand that what is bad for living beings is good for the whole they form, whose size cannot exceed a certain limit. The microbe literally appears as a parasite when we realize that it infects a population in order to reproduce, because it cannot destroy its host through disease. Only by following the evolution of a microbe can we understand how it moves from a state of symbiosis with its host to one in which it produces pathological symptoms. When it maintains the parasitic relationship to its advantage, the microbe only gives rise to a "latent infection," which can be reversed to disease if ecological conditions change. In his 1941 review of Burnet's book on the natural history of infectious diseases, Meyer writes: "Those who, of necessity, have been compelled to interpret the dangers of infection emanating from the vast reservoir of the Animal Kingdom fully acknowledged the guiding hand in the ecological concept of the epidemics produced by population regulators – the microbian or virus parasites."[82] Such a conception of the animal reservoir, inspired by the liberal model of the "invisible hand," limits human intervention to the control of invasive

## Cynegetic power

species that pass from one ecosystem to another and transmit pathogenic microbes.

At the same time, another concept of animal reservoir was taking shape in the Soviet Union, which gave greater prominence to human intervention.[83] It developed in the 1920s to 1930s under the name of "natural foci theory," and spread to the United States with the publication in 1966 of a translation of Evgeny Pavlovsky's *Natural Nidality of Transmissible Diseases*. Pavlovsky taught zoology at the University of St. Petersburg (then called Leningrad), from where he organized expeditions to Central Asia. In 1952, he was elected President of the Geographical Society of the Academy of Sciences and awarded the title of Hero of Socialist Labor. The theory of natural foci enabled him to explain the transmission of plague by marmots and rodents, as well as its persistence in burrows and caves. Pavlovsky spoke of "biocenosis" or "parasitocenosis" to describe the way in which an organism, conceived as a habitat for microbes, became part of a secondary environment made up of the relationships between animals, plants, climate, and soil, where an invisible chain of transmission takes place, such as the steppe, taiga, or desert. This dynamic community of organisms forms a nest (*ochag*) for microbes, conceived by Pavlovsky as an unstable equilibrium requiring constant environmental monitoring. Such a theory of nidality justified the development of Soviet agriculture: its aim was to cleanse landscapes by liquidating the components of the outbreak, including the removal of human populations that could contribute to disease transmission, according to a colonial land-use practice that ignored local conceptions of interactions between humans, animals, and microbes.

A third conception of animal reservoir has been developed in France midway between the "Anglo-Saxon" conception developed by Smith, Meyer, and Burnet and the Soviet conceptions developed by Pavlovsky. Louis Pasteur's pupils were undoubtedly the first to use the term, but it was Charles Nicolle, director of the Pasteur Institute in Tunis from 1903

## Virus hunters and disease reservoirs

until his death in 1936, who gave it a more general meaning. After unsuccessfully trying to demonstrate the transmission of leprosy by fish, Nicolle discovered the role of lice in the transmission of typhus, and went on to describe the animal vectors of brucellosis, leishmaniasis, and malaria.[84] In an article published in 1911 with Ernest Conseil on typhus in Tunisia, he wrote of disinfection against lice: "These prophylactic measures must be particularly directed against persistent reservoirs, even before the epidemic spreads. Knowing these reservoirs and their usual locations in winter will facilitate the application of rigorous measures that will make the epidemic disappear."[85] In 1919, he coined the concept of "inapparent infection" to describe diseases that circulate asymptomatically before causing infectious outbreaks, and to alert "civilized countries" that typhus could be transmitted from southern countries through population mixing at the front.

In *Naissance, vie et mort des maladies infectieuses* (*Birth, Life and Death of Infectious Diseases*), published in 1930, Nicolle foresaw the appearance of "new diseases" and prescribed a form of solidarity between humans and animals who are exposed to them in common with different physiologies. He wrote: "Knowledge of infectious diseases teaches men that they are brothers and sisters. We are brothers because we are threatened by the same danger, and we are in solidarity because contagion most often comes from our fellow human beings. We are also, from this perspective, whatever our feelings toward them, in solidarity with animals, especially domestic animals."[86] According to Nicolle, the birth of an epidemic has two components: the virulence of the microbe, which he defined as "a mosaic of antigens," and social and environmental conditions, which amplify the invention or mutation capacities of microbes according to their "genius." His work on the ecology of infectious diseases – although Nicolle did not use this term – was continued by his students, such as Edouard Chatton, who described marine microbes in Banyuls,

## 54                    *Cynegetic power*

and Hervé Harant, who focused on mosquito populations in Montpellier.

In 1933, geographer Maximilien Sorre analyzed "pathogen complexes" as "areas of extension," where infectious agents "haunt both man and other animal species."[87] This expression takes seriously the role of zoonoses in the long history of domestication: if domestic animals transmit diseases, the house where they cohabit with humans (*domus*) becomes a haunted place, where animals are potential carriers of viruses that can drag them to their deaths, forcing humans to multiply gestures to keep away from other living beings and protect themselves from them. Historian Gil Bartholeyns uses this term to describe breeders and veterinarians as "ghost hunters."[88] He notes that, in the biosecurity interventions that are the daily lot of farms in the era of pandemic viruses, it is unclear whether the farmer haunts his or her animals by perceiving the virus behind their movements, or the sick animal haunts the farmer by reminding him or her of the poor conditions in which it was raised. Haunting, here, appears as the reverse side of solidarity: the consequence of breaking a quasi-domestic contract, whereby humans exchange care with animals in exchange for food.[89] This idea is echoed in the environmentalist commitment of French bacteriologist René Dubos, who made his career in the United States, where in the 1960s he sounded the alarm on the capacity of bacteria to resist antibiotics, based on his observation of soils he conceived as "terroirs." Dubos is famous for his phrase: "Nature strikes back, we have to run to stay in the same place." It means that terroir responds to external interventions by mutating its inner balance, forcing humans to constantly invent new techniques to re-establish it.[90]

From the 1930s onwards, we can thus distinguish three lines to follow viruses in animal reservoirs: the English-speaking approach, focusing more on government regulation of the flow of goods and animal trafficking, the Russian-speaking approach, relying on state intervention to develop rural areas, and the French-speaking approach, insisting on solidarity between living beings to contain their mutual fears. These lines correspond neither to national cultures nor to disease ontologies that would develop dialectically: they are biopolitical legacies experienced in different colonial spaces, where linguistic structures (English, Russian, and French) are variably linked to techniques for managing non-humans, and thus to relationships between the state and collectives of humans and non-humans. In these three conceptions of collectives, the virus hunters must learn to perceive the environment through the microbes that circulate between living organisms. The concepts of nature, nidality, and terroir refer to three ways of orienting this perception in terms of possible interventions, and thus of criticizing virus hunters for their mistakes or erring ways in this perception.

Molecular biology transforms these conceptions of shared environments between animals and microbes by redefining the virus as a mutant piece of information. As we have seen in the quotations from Sargent and Tanon, the Pasteurians initially used the notion of "virus" in the etymological sense of "poison" to designate the pathogenic effect of a microbe; but, as they observed infectious diseases that were transmitted even when they found no microbes, they came to define viruses as pathogenic agents that could not be filtered out in the laboratory. The invention of the electron microscope in 1931, which bombards the sample with electrons instead of light, and the discovery of the DNA molecule in 1953, which reduced the diversity of living organisms to a universal genetic code, made it possible to visualize these viruses, which do not form cells like bacteria, but must insert their genome into cells in order to reproduce.[91] Reporter Greer Williams entitled his 1960 popular science book *Virus Hunters* in homage to Paul de Kruif. In it, he points out that microbe hunters no longer simply look at a bacterial cell under a microscope to find a medical treatment, but must also become chemists, physicists, and geneticists to describe the forms taken by

56                          *Cynegetic power*

these much smaller and more unstable entities.[92] While the discovery of antibiotics enabled health authorities to control diseases caused by bacteria, Greer Williams takes a detailed look at the technological innovations of vaccines to track the viruses that cause polio and influenza.

At the end of his book, Greer Williams quotes microbiologist Joshua Lederberg: "We do not know how many kinds of antibodies there are."[93] We could as well say: "We don't yet know what a virus can do," as an antibody, since the term was coined by Paul Ehrlich in 1891, can be defined as the trace left by the virus in the organism it occupies.[94] Lederberg was awarded the Nobel Prize in 1958 for his work demonstrating the role of viruses called "bacteriophages" in the exchange of genes between bacteria. He launched a vast molecular biology research program to map the different forms of microbes and the reactions they provoke in the human organism. A major player within American scientific institutions, he has imposed the term "emerging infectious diseases" on public debate in the 1990s to describe the mutations in pathogens that are accelerated by international transportation and that increasingly bypass antibiotics and vaccines.[95] In 2000, he defended the ecological conception of infectious diseases through the perspective of the virus hunter: "It is time," he wrote in *Science*, "to abandon the old metaphor of a war between germs and humans and replace it with a more ecologically informed metaphor, which includes the germ's eye-view of infection."[96]

New books appeared in the 1990s on these emerging infectious diseases, signed by virologists themselves and not by reporters. Robert Gallo pointed out that Paul de Kruif could not have known that viruses cause communicable cancers in animals by inserting their genetic code, such as the AIDS virus, of which Gallo was one of the discoverers after Françoise Barré-Sinoussi and Jean-Luc Montagnier.[97] Joseph McCormick and Susan Fischer Hoch narrated for their readers how the Ebola and Lassa viruses moved from the jungle to the hospital to a laboratory from their reservoirs in Central

African primates.[98] More recently, Robert Webster, in a book entitled *Flu Hunter*, looks back on a career in which he identified the role of waterfowl as a reservoir for influenza viruses. Working in the 1970s at the Department of Microbiology at the University of Canberra in Australia, founded by Frank Burnet, Webster identified influenza antibodies in a dead bird, which led him and his colleague Graeme Laver to undertake a campaign of sampling birds from the Great Barrier Reef. Chemistry and genetics enabled him to model protein variations in the influenza virus circulating in birds, and to explain its pandemic emergence in humans.[99] Webster then set up an influenza virus bank at St. Jude's Hospital in Memphis, U.S.A., to bring together strains collected in Australia with those he collected from migratory birds in North America from a site in Delaware Bay. He describes this strain bank as a "gold mine of influenza viruses."[100] When warning of the risks of an influenza pandemic in 2003, Webster wrote: "The main issue in controlling influenza is the sheer size of its animal reservoir."[101]

Robert Webster's book, as an ultimate transformation of Paul de Kruif's book published a century earlier, aptly describes the forms of cynegetic power exercised by "virus hunters." The molecularization of living organisms through chemistry, physics, and genetics has enabled microbiologists to replicate within the laboratory the diversity of viral strains they collected in nature, and to conserve them outside the high-visibility moments of epidemics. Webster draws an analogy between the animal reservoir outside the laboratory and the virus reserve inside. Just as the animal reservoir is a place of "latent infection" that can be triggered at any time, the virus reserve is a "latent life" that can be used to identify new viruses. In the "mine" that virologists transform into a "bank," each virus takes on its value by comparison with other viruses for which it reveals a valuable variation. Whereas for the first virus hunters, the animal reservoir was a space with blurred contours, it becomes increasingly delimited when it is duplicated in a virus bank for experimentation. We could thus say that the cynegetic power of the "virus hunters" becomes "cryopolitics" when it is exercised in the frozen space of laboratory. The problem posed by zoonoses is no longer how to properly hunt the microbes that cause them, by perceiving the environment from their perspective, but how to properly conserve them, by building reserves where these microbes are accumulated and classified. The microbe hunter-gatherer becomes a cold chain technician and a museum collector.

# 4

# Cryopolitics: Conserving collections in nature reserves

## 4.a The mutations of influenza viruses

If avian influenza has played a paradigmatic role in contemporary thinking about zoonoses, by contrast with other zoonoses we have discussed so far (trichinosis, tuberculosis, psittacosis, plague . . .), it is because mutations in the influenza virus force "virus hunters" to return regularly from the laboratory, where the virus is studied in terms of its structure and pathogenicity, to the "animal reservoirs," where it mutates constantly. This specific capacity for mutation has made it the focus of a particularly developed "cryopolitics," which seeks to synchronize in the laboratory the transformations of relations between living beings, in a way that resonates with other forms of synchronization of living beings through the cold chain.

The influenza virus is composed of eight proteins, including hemagglutinin and neuraminidase, which determine its entry and exit into the cell it infects. George Hirst identified hemagglutinin in 1941 from the observation of chicken embryos inoculated with human influenza virus, following a technique introduced by Frank Macfarlane Burnet a few years earlier. As the blood vessels on the surface of the embryo stained red, suggesting "blood agglutination," Hirst devised a test to describe the structural variation between influenza viruses as a function of the quality of staining on chicken embryos. A few years later, neuraminidase was identified, along with its role in virus exit from the cell, enabling virologists to classify influenza viruses using the letters H (for hemagglutinin) and

60                          *Cryptopolitics*

N (for neuraminidase). The 1918 pandemic influenza virus was thus called H1N1 and the 1957 pandemic influenza virus was called H2N2.

Molecular biology and genetic sequencing explain the great variability of influenza viruses by the fact that they are composed of a single molecule of RNA (ribonucleic acid), and have no mechanism for correcting replication errors like the double strand of DNA. All it takes is a few mutations in the hemagglutinin, or a few breaks in these strands through a mechanism known as "reassortment," to radically change the behavior of the virus, i.e. its ability to enter the cell by attaching to a receptor. Hence the need for 'flu specialists to track mutations and reassortments of influenza viruses across the globe in order to anticipate the emergence of pandemic viruses. Molecular biology thus moves microbiology from the paradigm of infection, with health policies aimed at containing the epidemic at home, to the paradigm of mutation, in which global health aims to monitor viral variations across the planet to detect by early warning signals those that are potentially pandemic.[1]

This conceptual shift from infection to mutation is linked to the technological possibility of synchronizing mutations in the laboratory so as to anticipate infection in nature. A crucial player in this transformation was the French surgeon Alexis Carrel, who took Ross Harrison's methods for growing nerve cells from frogs at the Rockefeller Institute for Medical Research in 1907, and applied them to heart cells in chicken embryos, earning him the Nobel Prize in Medicine in 1912.[2] Carrel invented artificial feeding techniques, enabling him to create a living environment in the laboratory so that the metabolism of living tissue is stopped and then reactivated, producing a regenerative effect that postpones death indefinitely. With this invention, cell proliferation in the laboratory becomes as controllable as the movements of a herd under the watchful eye of a shepherd. Each cell finds its singular place in a whole, whose growth is synchronized: the laboratory

## The mutations of influenza viruses 61

space regulated by the experimenter's surveillance.[3] As early as 1928, Carrel highlighted the possibility of cultivating viruses on cells in the laboratory, so that "a chicken embryo crushed to a fine pulp is capable of producing as much vaccine as a calf."[4] But it was really with Jonas Salk's production of polio vaccine in 1951 from immortalized human tissue (the cell line that became known as HeLa, after Henrietta Lacks, the person from whom it was taken) that the technique met with industrial development. This application resulted from Christopher Polge's 1949 discovery of the ability of glycerol to freeze chicken sperm, which was first applied in industrial cattle breeding, where it made possible artificial insemination and genetic strain comparison as a new breed selection technique, before being used in biology laboratories.[5]

These cryobiological techniques have influenced influenza research in a way that distinguishes its overall management from that of other zoonoses. In the 1930s, English microbiologists realized that the 1918 pandemic had not been caused by bacteria, as the German physician Pfeiffer had claimed, but by viruses. In 1933, Wilson Smith, Christopher Andrews, and Patrick Laidlaw infected an animal in the laboratory for the first time with a sample from a human who had influenza illness, and showed that ferrets displayed the same symptoms as humans when infected with influenza. In particular, ferrets sneeze when they have the 'flu, making them excellent experimental models, compared with mice or guinea pigs, which display no such symptoms for this disease. Isolating the influenza virus from humans and ferrets then enabled microbiologists to requalify a range of diseases which, while not displaying the same symptoms as human influenza, are indeed caused by the same pathogen. "Fowl plague" was reclassified by English microbiologists as "avian influenza," even though birds infected with influenza had digestive rather than respiratory problems, while "hog cholera" was reclassified as "swine influenza."[6]

These different identifications of the same causal agent in England in the 1930s led to George Hirst's project in the

U.S.A. in the 1940s to compare the antigenic variations of different influenza strains across the globe. Such a project relied on a range of techniques enabling human or animal samples containing influenza viruses to be dried or frozen and sent to reference laboratories in England or the U.S.A. In this way, influenza ceases to be perceived as a cyclical seasonal disease, studied clinically when it causes epidemics, and becomes a phenomenon that can be reproduced in the laboratory at any time of the year.

Cold preservation of viral samples, using ice or nitrogen, is a recent technique. At the end of the nineteenth century, bacteriologists preserved their samples in alcohol. In the mid twentieth century, influenza virus samples were dried before being sent to the World Health Organization, where the influenza reference center regularly reactivated them by passing them through eggs.[7] Today, the global comparison of influenza virus mutations is based on inventory classification work, to ensure that each sample is kept at the right place and at the right temperature (between −80 and 4°C), and on bioinformatics sequencing work based on a digital data policy, which keeps the genetic sequences of viral strains in a particular laboratory available to researchers worldwide.[8]

Thanks to freezers full of samples and banks of digital viruses sorted into genetic sequences, biologists observe the mutations of influenza viruses in their laboratories as shepherds monitor the movements of their flock. Virologist Edwin Kilbourne describes a sample from an influenza patient as "a statistical consensus of a genetically heterogeneous population in constant flux."[9] Such a pastoral view of influenza samples leads virologists in turn to conceive of nature as a laboratory in which viral strains are constantly mutating, so that they need to be caught up by ever faster sequencing work.[10] In a state of constant vigilance, assisted by computers that never stop sequencing samples, teams of biologists take turns to run as fast as the "gene teams."[11] Such a computerized process eludes the opposition between "natural mutations" and "cul-

*The mutations of influenza viruses* 63

turing life": it is an overheated planetary metabolism of which viruses are the signatures.

In the mid 1990s, this worldview of a nature constantly producing viral mutations that need to be anticipated in the laboratory resonated with the "global war on terrorism," following a paradoxical sentence that became common sense among 'flu specialists in the early 2000s: "nature is the greatest bioterrorist threat." Such a formula can be understood when related to two events that struck international public opinion: first, the defection in the mid 1990s of bacteriologists from the former Soviet Union, alerting the U.S. government to the possibility of the ex-Soviet republics selling their "biological weapons" to "rogue states," second, the attacks of September 11, 2001, followed by the "anthrax letters" episode and the U.S. war against Iraq aimed at ending its biological weapons program.[12] The U.S. government, knowing that there were only two strains of smallpox left in the world frozen in laboratories in the American territory and in the Soviet Union after the successful global eradication of smallpox, organized exercises simulating smallpox attacks in New York subways in the late 1990s, and stockpiled smallpox vaccines for fear that the American population would no longer have immunity to smallpox thirty years after the last vaccination campaign.[13] When the H5N1 virus crossed from Asia to Europe, prompting a pandemic alert from the World Health Organization, the Bush administration declared war on bird 'flu. U.S. media portrayed the virus as a terrorist capable of "hijacking" the cell's means of replication, just as terrorists had hijacked airplanes to attack New York. The pastoral power of microbe farmers was then subordinated to the sovereign power of "homeland security."

One of the most famous stories of "virus hunters" is inscribed in this sequence. At the end of the 1990s, several teams of biologists searched the 1918 pandemic influenza virus across the frozen lands of the Far North. Kirsty Duncan, a geographer from the University of Toronto, led an expedition

64 *Cryptopolitics*

to the Svalbard region of Norway; but the six bodies of miners she had identified were not preserved deep enough in the permafrost, and the samples she brought back did not contain a sufficient quantity of virus.[14] Johan Hultin, a Swedish microbiologist, searched a cemetery at Fort Brevig in Alaska from 1951 for the influenza virus. In 1998, he discovered the body of a young Inuit woman whose obesity had protected her lungs, and whom he named Lucy. Jeffery Taubenberger, a microbiologist working in the armed forces in Washington, was then able to amplify the genetic sequence of the viral strain taken from Lucy's body and compare it with the one he had already established from the lung tissue of soldiers preserved at Fort Jackson in North Carolina.[15] This research led him to the reconstruction of the entire 1918 H1N1 pandemic virus using a technique known as "reverse genetics." Its DNA was transcribed into protein-producing RNA, then the virus was assembled and injected into a chicken embryo, before being transmitted to ferrets and mice, which developed virulent 'flu symptoms. When the journal *Science* published this research in 2005, the article reporting the discovery in the *Washington Post* commented: "It is quite conceivable that the resurrected 1918 flu could someday be used as a bioterrorist agent."[16] Peter Palese, a virologist working in Jeffery Taubenberger's team on influenza mutations at Mount Sinai Hospital in New York, criticized this excessive use of the precautionary principle in the American media. He argued that what was being published was genetic information – the sequence of the H1N1 virus – and not an active virus.[17]

In 1976, Michel Foucault had already seen that sovereign power might want to control the biopolitics of viral populations. In his lecture, he referred to the possibility of "ultimately build[ing] viruses that cannot be controlled and that are universally destructive" as a "formidable extension of biopower [. . .] beyond all human sovereignty."[18] This brief, rarely commented-on passage is perhaps an allusion to the H1N1 'flu virus that circulated among humans between 1918

*The mutations of influenza viruses*  65

and 1957, and then was replaced by the H2N2 virus, before reappearing as "swine 'flu" in 1976 in the United States, possibly through its circulation among pigs. Experts at the U.S. Center for Disease Controls discovered the virus in an influenza outbreak at the Fort Dix military post, and launched a vaccination campaign that was halted by too many side effects.[19] A year later, another H1N1 influenza virus, more closely related to the 1918 virus, accidentally emerged from a Soviet laboratory where it had been stored for experimental purposes, and spread to the Chinese population without causing a fatal epidemic.[20] However, in describing the anticipation of emerging viruses as a return of sovereign power within biopower, Foucault misses the work of "virus hunters" transporting viruses from "animal reservoirs," where they are tracked and collected like prey, to laboratories, where they are cultivated and synchronized like a herd.[21]

The work of "virus hunters" was particularly visible in Vietnam and China, where post-Communist authoritarian governments became heavily involved in controlling their avian populations after 2005 to assert their central role in global health. The Vietnamese government benefited from the SARS crisis, as its strict policies limited the epidemic to 63 cases in a single hospital. It then responded to the fears of international health authorities about the transmission of the H5N1 virus from Asia to the rest of the world with an equally strict surveillance and control policy on poultry, making it a model in the management of avian influenza and the main beneficiary of international funds for the fight against this zoonosis.[22] Poultry farming is a major source of income in Vietnam, with two-thirds traditional and one-third industrial in the early 2000s. To control the rapid transmission of the H5N1 avian influenza virus in 2005, with a lethality of 70 percent when transmitted to humans, the Vietnamese government slaughtered 66 million poultry and launched a massive vaccination policy. Prevention campaigns warning Vietnamese people about the right way to behave toward poultry in markets or on

66 *Cryptopolitics*

farms were based on a set of military slogans: don't touch suspect animals, report cases, accept sanitary measures, protect the community.[23]

As the management of bird 'flu redefined relations of power and knowledge, veterinarians climbed the hierarchy of Vietnam's bureaucracy by taking on issues central to human health. But they were criticized both by medical elites, who took a dim view of the rise of an often despised profession, and by the peasant communities from which they were often drawn. The latter perceived them as corrupt officials in the service of the government, and challenged their authority at the risk of severe sanctions. The peasant who hid poultry to avoid slaughter or vaccination was described by the government as an enemy of the people, or a monkey on the verge of humanity.[24] In the daily life of farmers, these spectacular measures were refracted into a multiplicity of expert knowledge, aimed at producing statistical data on human and animal populations, and disciplinary techniques, such as prevention and vaccination, often ignoring local knowledge. Indeed, relations between humans and poultry on the farm produce values that are not only economic, but also ethical and aesthetic: raising a quality chicken that is not only healthy, but also beautiful and tasty at the end of a good life, implies a set of criteria that escape the governmental logic of infection control.[25]

Avian influenza viruses were displaced from poultry farms in Vietnam to laboratories in England and the U.S.A. to simulate their behavior at the molecular level and limit their pandemic potential. At the University of Cambridge, researchers genetically modified chickens to introduce a gene that would act as a "decoy" for the attached influenza virus, diverting it from the cells of the digestive tract where it replicates. They then bred these chickens with pigs to see how this gene reacted to mutations of influenza viruses resulting from cross-species contact, and to check that this gene was not passed on to pigs, with unpredictable consequences. The value of these genetically modified chickens is questionable, whether from a public

## The mutations of influenza viruses

health perspective (since they risk triggering mutations of the virus), from an economic perspective (since the geneticists own a patent on the modified gene) or a cultural perspective (since European consumers are reluctant to eat genetically modified organisms), which explains the lack of success of this experiment. The sovereign logic of limiting bird 'flu by slaughtering or vaccinating poultry is circumvented here by a logic of competition between biologists, who intervene directly at the molecular level of virus-cell interactions using cynegetic techniques to lure viruses.[26]

Similarly, a Japanese researcher, Yoshi Kawaoka, used avian influenza viruses collected in Vietnam to produce a "mutant H5N1" in a Wisconsin laboratory. He introduced five nucleotides from the H1N1 virus that had caused the 2009 pandemic into the H5N1 virus, in order to simulate a virus as contagious as H1N1 and as lethal as H5N1. His results converged with those of Ron Fouchier at Rotterdam's Erasmus Medical Center; he had used a more rudimentary method closer to that of Pasteur and Koch to pass the H5N1 virus between several ferrets, who transmitted it from cage to cage by sneezing. When Fouchier and Kawaoka sent an article to *Nature* and *Science* in 2011 showing that this "mutant H5N1" could emerge "in the wild," and in particular within poultry farms and markets in China, it triggered a controversy similar to that generated by Taubenberger's reconstruction of the H1N1 virus in 2005. The American authorities who had funded the research referred the article to the National Scientific Advisory Board on Biosafety (NSABB): these experts in ethical procedures questioned the two biologists about the laboratory conditions under which they had produced the results. They authorized publication on condition that the genetic sequence of the "mutant H5N1" remained confidential, and called for a moratorium on "gain-of-function" research, which genetically modifies viruses to vary their lethality or contagiousness.

This authorization was given after an investigation showing that the conditions under which the influenza viruses had been transported from farms to laboratories were trustworthy. Officials from Vietnam's Institutes of Public Health were happy to send samples to Kawaoka, as they had established a long-standing relationship with him, but they refused to send samples to biologists requesting them for laboratories in South Korea, as they were unsure of the biosafety conditions in these laboratories. Kawaoka's colleagues inoculated ferrets with the modified influenza viruses and recorded their symptoms using a sick/non-sick coding system before euthanizing them.[27] Their research showed that the mutant H5N1 virus was much less lethal in ferrets than in poultry, although much more contagious than the "wildtype" H5N1 virus. At stake in the controversy surrounding Fouchier and Kawaoka's work was whether "virus hunters" could simulate in the laboratory the behavior of viruses "in the wild" to anticipate future pandemics, thereby invisibilizing the death of ferrets, reduced to mere models of human death. The question was whether Fouchier and Kawaoka were good "virus hunters" when they simulated the next pandemic virus through their "mutant H5N1," or whether they had simply been lured by their prey. For Fouchier and Kawaoka, this research was justified by the size of the animal reservoir for influenza viruses in southern China, where they mutate in wild birds before being transmitted to poultry, pigs, and humans in such a complex way that a "target" must guide the hunter.[28]

Such a virus-hunting strategy followed the hypothesis formulated in 1982 by Kennedy Shortridge, head of the microbiology department at the University of Hong Kong, and Charles Stuart-Harris, one of the key players in virological research on influenza in England and the U.S.A., that China constitutes an "epicenter of influenza pandemics" due to the dense relationships between humans, pigs, domestic poultry, and wild birds in the rice paddy ecology.[29] This hypothesis led Shortridge to sound the alarm about the H5N1 virus when, in 1997, it was detected in Hong Kong among 5,000 poultry found dead on the territory's farms, 20 percent of the poultry

# The mutations of influenza viruses

sold in markets, particularly ducks, whose infection rate was sixteen times higher than that of other poultry, and twelve people, eight of whom died.[30] This public health crisis, in the context of military and environmental fears linked to Hong Kong's handover to the People's Republic of China after two centuries of British colonization, led Hong Kong's new governor, Tung Chee-Wah, advised by his Director of Health, Margaret Chan, by Agriculture Director Leslie Sims, and by U.S. Center for Disease Controls representative Keiji Fukuda, to order the slaughter of all poultry reared in Hong Kong territory – 1.2 million chickens and 400,000 ducks, geese and quail. "We didn't cull, we conducted a slaughter," Shortridge retrospectively admitted.[31] To avoid a repetition of these massacres, particularly painful for citizens who had immigrated from the rural provinces of Guangdong and Fujian, and who saw backyard poultry not only as sources of protein in times of shortage, but also as companions in daily life, the Hong Kong government set up surveillance techniques to monitor the circulation of avian influenza viruses among wild birds and domestic poultry, in anticipation of the emergence of an H5N1-type virus highly pathogenic to birds and humans.

These technologies were transferred to mainland China when the H5N1 virus spread throughout Asia, then to Europe and Africa in 2005. Vincent Martin, a French veterinarian who headed the Beijing office of the Food and Agriculture Organization of the United Nations (FAO) between 2006 and 2020, set up the Emergency Center for Transboundary Animal Diseases (ECTAD) to encourage the Ministry of Agriculture of the People's Republic of China to communicate its cases of bird 'flu, on the model of the transparency policy (*touming*) adopted by the Ministry of Health after the SARS crisis in 2003.[32] He developed a method for mapping animal markets, following supply networks and species sold, and he collaborated with ecologist Marius Gilbert, who modeled the ecosystems in which wild birds exchanged viruses with domestic poultry.[33]

70 *Cryptopolitics*

Among these, Lake Poyang, located in Jiangxi province, south of the Yangtze River, was particularly monitored by influenza specialists. Not only is it the largest lake in mainland China, home to some 350,000 migratory birds of around a hundred species, but since the 1980s it has also been the site of an industrial duck farming producing an estimated fourteen million ducks, three times more than duck production in the whole of the U.S.A.[34] Marius Gilbert modeled H5N1 cases on Poyang Lake according to the movements of wild and domestic birds, and showed that they were more numerous where domestic ducks were raised in the open air, and therefore in contact with wild ducks.[35] The breeding practice known as *fangyang* (free grazing) helps to offset the effects of the increase in farm size promoted by the Chinese government under the name *guimohua* (climbing the ladder). As factory farms become increasingly vulnerable to highly pathogenic influenza viruses, breeders adopt strict biosecurity measures in enclosed buildings intended for sale, and keep ducks in the open air for local production, presumed to be of better taste and more resistant to disease. The distinction made by duck farmers between "large-scale" (*guimo*) and "dispersed" (*sanyang*) farms does not, therefore, overlap with the distinction made by virologists and ecologists between sectors of Lake Poyang according to the risk of infection, since these two types of farming are close to each other and are sometimes combined by the same farmers to manage the threat of sanitary culling of some of their ducks. Moreover, some "special farms" (*tezhong yangzhi*) are under the supervision of the Ministry of Forestry rather than the Ministry of Agriculture, which allows them to avoid compulsory vaccination, as they involve wild geese in order to cultivate "external genes" *(wailaide jiyin)* that are supposed to strengthen the potential of domestic geese against diseases.[36] The paradigm of the "virus hunter," who collects samples from "animal reservoirs" and transforms them into sequences that can be used in the laboratory, is here overwhelmed by an entanglement of breeding and caring

## The mutations of influenza viruses

practices, where expert knowledge interbreeds with local knowledge in a way that escapes the "epicenter of pandemics" hypothesis.[37]

A detour through Vietnam and China reveals a multiplicity of "virus-hunting" practices, depending on the knowledge that breeders and veterinarians develop about poultry diseases. What then explains the global hegemony of the perspective of "virus hunters," which imposed itself when the H5N1 avian influenza virus spread from southern China to the rest of the world? Why has their way of seeing influenza viruses as a set of mutations in an animal reservoir been instituted as the best perspective on the complex ecology through which wild birds, domestic poultry, and humans live together in this part of the planet? Such a hegemony comes from the fact that they can assert that the same virus is circulating in different parts of the planet, and sound the alarm about a potentially pandemic virus in any part of the globe, by contrast with the response of Chinese experts, which remains local. The strength of such a statement lies in its inscription within a singular infrastructure: the conservation of viruses in freezers enables virologists to exchange them between different points on the globe to compare their genetic sequences. Thus, Robert Webster, during a visit to the Chinese countryside organized by the Ministry of Agriculture in 1968, and Guo Yuanji, a member of the Institute of Virology in Beijing, in 1981, declared that the People's Republic of China could not collaborate with the World Health Organization in monitoring influenza mutations because it lacked the refrigerators to store samples.[38] This critical argument – "China cannot enter the techno-scientific modern world because it has not mastered the cold chain" – has undergone a singular transformation in the debate on the origins of SARS-Cov2. After recalling the controversies sparked by influenza mutations, we will now turn to this more recent and still sensitive controversy, in order to examine its implications for the politics of zoonoses.

## 4.b The cold chain in markets and laboratories

The debate over the origins of the virus causing the Covid-19 pandemic can be seen through the different forms of power we have distinguished following Foucault. It pitted nation-states against each other over "viral sovereignty":[39] the United States, represented by its president Donald Trump, accused the People's Republic of China of manufacturing a "Chinese virus" and refusing to share samples to hide its misdeeds. It also pitted pastoral (Western media blamed "the Chinese" for mismanaging the trade in bats, pangolins, or mink),[40] disciplinary ("the Chinese" were allegedly not sufficiently educated in modern hygiene) and biopolitical powers (according to Western public opinion, the Chinese government imposed control measures on its human population that denied individuals' attachment to freedom). But the main interest of this controversy for thinking about the politics of zoonoses is the way it pitted "virus hunters" against each other over the right ways to use the cold chain.

Peter Daszak, founder of the U.S.-based Ecohealth initiative, teamed up with Shi Zhengli, director of the P4 laboratory in Wuhan, to carry out "gain-of-function" research on bat viruses collected in southwest China. The aim of this research was to modify the furin site of the spike protein, which allows coronaviruses to enter cells, in order to study the conditions under which this virus would become transmissible between humans. A growing number of virologists, notably in France and the United States, accuse this project of leading to the escape from a Wuhan laboratory of a highly contagious strain of bat coronavirus for which humans had no immunity.[41] The gain-of-function research carried out in Wuhan was indeed focused on a coronavirus that appeared in 2013 in a cave in Mojiang, where miners had fallen victim to pneumonia after coming into contact with bat guano. Virologists have highlighted the similarities between the virus discovered in Mojiang and SARS-Cov2, using phylogenetic models that trace

*The cold chain in markets and laboratories* 73

the evolution of viruses based on the proximities between their sequences. A laboratory accident appears on these phylogenetic trees through a particularly long branch, as the evolution of the virus is "frozen" when it is kept in the cold and resumes when it escapes into the environment. Virologists were thus able to trace the re-emergence of a bluetongue virus in 2015 that had been eradicated in Europe in 2010, then stored in a laboratory from which it probably escaped.[42]

In response to these accusations, which first took the form of suspicions and then gradually became supported by evidence, Daszak and Shi supported the hypothesis of an emergence at the Wuhan seafood market, where the first Covid clusters were detected in December 2019, and where wild animals such as raccoon dogs, which could transmit coronavirus, were sold alongside numerous fresh and frozen products.[43] But this hypothesis is undermined by samples taken by Chinese experts from 80,000 wild and domestic animals sold in markets in 31 provinces of China, which revealed no trace of SARS-Cov2.[44] The World Health Organization report that made these data public described the hypothesis of animal-to-human transmission of SARS-Cov2 at the Wuhan market as "highly probable" and that of a laboratory accident as "highly improbable." But it was then criticized by the Western members of the WHO delegation to China in February 2021, as they had not had access to all the necessary data, and in particular to the strains kept in the Wuhan laboratories, whereas the genetic sequences of SARS-Cov2 were rapidly released in January 2020.[45]

Chinese health authorities then put forward a third hypothesis: SARS-Cov2 could have been imported via frozen products from Europe and the U.S.A. In the summer of 2020, Chinese experts detected traces of coronavirus on cutting boards used for salmon imported to Beijing's Xinfadi market, followed by American pork in Qingdao, shrimp from Saudi Arabia, and beef from Brazil and New Zealand.[46] This argument seemed credible when scientific publications were appearing on biological samples stored in Italy, attesting to the presence of SARS-Cov2 outside China before December 2019, the date of the first case reported in China.[47] The Chinese authorities were thus responding to Western accusations: it was not the lack of cold chain control in laboratories and markets in China that was the cause of the emergence, but rather its lack of surveillance in Europe and the United States.

Thus, distracting international attention from laboratories to markets was part of an internal discussion within Chinese society about the need to modernize the cold chain that runs from industrial slaughterhouses to supermarkets. Indeed, Chinese consumers continue to buy live animals that are slaughtered in front of their eyes in markets, despite the health risks of this "traditional" practice, because they don't trust the cold chain in supermarkets and they prefer to check for themselves the freshness of the animal they are about to eat. In Chinese, the notion of freshness (*xinxian*) refers less to a measurable temperature than to visual and gustatory qualities perceptible in the interactions between living things.[48] The Covid-19 pandemic thus pitted two uses of the cold chain against each other: that of the Chinese government, which aims to modernize its food economy, and that of citizens, who defend their own conception of freshness.[49]

It is therefore more relevant to study the Covid controversy through the technical issues surrounding the use of the cold chain than through the moral values mobilized to contrast governmentality in China and the West (security, public health, freedom), since we are dealing here with the infrastructure through which living beings (humans, animals, plants, and microbes) are preserved and exchanged across the planet. Discussions on the management of cadavers and vaccines, which have both emotional and legal aspects, should also be analyzed in terms of cold chain practices. The end of the Chinese "zero-Covid" policy in January 2023 caused a saturation of morgues, which had to freeze corpses awaiting incineration, but a comparable scandal broke out in France in

April 2020 over a building at the Rungis market transformed into a morgue, which had already been used to store corpses during the 2003 heatwave.[50]

Similarly, the international race to produce vaccines in 2020 gave the advantage to laboratories using recombinant RNA techniques such as Pfizer or Moderna, but this new technique required vaccines to be stored at very low temperatures: −20°C for Pfizer and −70°C for Moderna. Chinese companies such as Sinovac then put forward their virus inactivation technique, which enabled them to store vaccines at between +2 and +8°C, particularly in the face of competition from countries in the Global South. Here again, a failure to control the cold chain was strategically turned to an asset in the circulation of biological materials. The Chinese government has established agreements with Indonesia and Brazil for clinical trials in exchange for the supply of free vaccines manufactured in China. In February 2021, Chinese Foreign Minister Wang Yi accused Northern countries of stockpiling large quantities of Covid-19 vaccines and blocking supplies to Southern countries.[51] But when China had to open its borders after three years of zero-Covid policy, its health authorities recognized that the elderly had been less vaccinated than the rest of the population, even though they were the most vulnerable to Covid.[52] This resistance to vaccination, at a time when the Chinese government was offering its vaccines to the global South, may be explained by a greater reluctance on the part of the elderly to take biomedicine preserved in refrigerators, by contrast with traditional medicine preserved in the form of dried or powdered animal or plant products.

Controversies over the use of the cold chain in laboratories, markets, and pharmaceutical companies in China during the Covid-19 pandemic can be compared to those that took place in the U.S.A. a century earlier, when this technique was introduced in the city of Chicago. Historian William Cronon has described how the cold chain transformed the relations between humans and their environment at the end of the

# 76                        *Cryptopolitics*

nineteenth century, and in particular the growing disconnection between the city and its "hinterland" in the Great Plains of the North America. The forty million bison that lived there in the wild were killed by American pioneers as part of the genocide of native peoples and the conquest of the West, then replaced by cattle brought from Texas and popularized in the image of the "cowboy" who transformed the plains into pastureland. Railroad construction led to the relocation to the city of hogs and cattle raised in the southern and western states of Illinois, sparing them the loss of energy and weight involved in grazing. The railroad also enabled butchers to bring blocks of ice from the Great Lakes region, thus preserving meat for longer. Beef, which Americans prefer to eat as steak, in contrast to the salty, packaged products of pork, benefited greatly from the technological revolution of transporting meat in refrigerated trains. Meat consumption no longer depended on the seasons: up until then meat had been eaten mainly in spring and summer, as animals lose weight during the winter. Meat could now be consumed all year round, and exported throughout the country in packaged form, at a much lower price than transporting live animals.

Butchers initially opposed this new industry of cut and chilled meat, arguing that slaughtering animals in their stores allowed inspectors to better control the health of the carcass. But the meat manufacturers lowered prices to such an extent that Chicago butchers were forced to close their private slaughterhouses in the 1890s. This victory favored the centralization of slaughterhouses and refrigerated meat storage in a few city districts, whose environmental pollution was denounced by many observers. Cronon quotes the defense of the meat packers by their wealthiest representative, Philippe Armour, in the Vest Report in 1889: "they are making beef more palatable, attractive and wholesome, by a proper and advanced system of refrigeration, than it was when the small slaughterer butchered a steer during the night and hung the still warm carcass in the market next morning, and are distributing this beef

The cold chain in markets and laboratories 77

throughout the country at the lowest charge for the service rendered."[53]

The sequence analyzed by Cronon can be summarized by saying that the cynegetic power of the buffalo hunters was replaced by the pastoral power of the cowboys, and that the latter made possible what can be called the cryopolitics of the meat industry, This, in turn, conditions the disciplinary power of consumers, when they read food safety labels, and the biopolitics of public health risks put in place by governments in the twentieth century, thus jeopardizing the sovereign power of European states which, in the nineteenth century, tightly controlled the meat market.[54] Such a sequence is then repeated with variations in the contemporary controversy over the biosafety of markets and laboratories in the city of Wuhan, often referred to as the "Chicago of the East" due to its central position in the Chinese economy.[55] In the wake of the SARS crisis, competition arose between Hong Kong and Wuhan to sound the alarm on emerging diseases in East Asia, similar to the competition described by Cronon a century earlier between Chicago and St. Louis to capture the flow of people and goods in North America.[56] Following the work of Australian virologists made in Hong Kong since the 1970s, Wuhan's virologists, relaying the injunctions of the Hubei provincial government and the Beijing regime, have been implementing since 2003 a new way of controlling living beings through their preservation in the cold chain. In the same way, the cold chain in Chicago turned Indian knowledge of hunting and preserving bison meat into an outdated tradition.[57] All the controversies surrounding zoonoses in southern China can thus be traced to the transformation of infrastructures caused by the introduction of the cold chain. While drying and salting techniques have long been used by human societies to preserve bodies and slow down their deterioration, modern freezing techniques have introduced a new relationship with living beings, since the frozen body can be brought back to life by a process that is both gradual

78                              *Cryptopolitics*

and reversible: this is the starting point for what we can call "cryopolitics."

## 4.c Storing living beings in reserves and museums

If "virus hunters" take the perspective of animals to map the reservoirs in which pathogens mutate, they impose this perspective on the global level through their use of the cold chain in laboratories. This shift from local to global perspectives can be described as a transformation of cynegetic power into cryopolitics. "Virus hunters" are not content to imitate the animal and postpone its death: they seek to keep living beings alive and to postpone their natural death.

The notion of "cryopolitics" is a conceptual transfer from the history of climate to the history of science. Using this term, Michael Bravo and Gareth Rees have described the strategies of the great powers aimed at appropriating Arctic resources to anticipate climate change, in an economy of standardization and accumulation that takes no account of the interests of fauna, flora, or indigenous populations.[58] Anthropologist and science historian Emma Kowal and Joanna Radin have extended the term to include laboratories, museums, zoos, and nature reserves, where what they call "latent life" is preserved, suspended between life and death.[59] Kowal and Radin ironically open their book *Cryopolitics* with ice cores cut from Arctic and Antarctic glaciers: these ice cores provide indicators of climate change from gas bubbles trapped in the ice at geologically distant times, but they themselves contribute to climate change, since they are part of an energy-intensive infrastructure, the *U.S. National Ice Core Laboratory* based in Denver, Colorado.[60] Moreover, the preservation of these ice cores causes fears that pathogens stored in the permafrost may escape, as has already been the case with the anthrax bacillus in Siberia released by the thawing of permafrost.[61] As cryopolitics involves regulating this "latent life" in low-temperature infrastructures and networks, it raises the question of the responsibility and purpose of this regulation.

Such problems have become popular through the imaginary of cryonics, mobilized by private companies to offer affluent consumers the dream of the resurrection of their bodies, or at least parts of them, which could be frozen while awaiting technologies to bring them back to life after death.[62] This future goal, financially unattainable and technologically improbable, reveals operations already underway in the present, through a range of techniques for preserving tissues or parts of living organisms in biobanks.[63] Refrigeration, designed at the beginning of the twentieth century to transform heat into cold according to the laws of thermodynamics, has evolved in such a way that it can preserve living matter at any temperature, down to $-200°C$ for certain liquid gases.[64] Taking up the formula with which Michel Foucault characterized biopolitics, Emma Kowal and Joanna Radin define cryopolitics as a paradoxical way of acting so that living beings are frozen: "suspended animation and action – that produces a zone of existence where beings are made to live and *not allowed to die*."[65] They quote the 1976 lecture in which Foucault analyzes the announcement of Franco's death a year earlier, when the Spanish dictator's coma was prolonged for several months.[66]

Kowal and Radin hesitate between two ways of taking up the Foucauldian definition of biopolitics: since "not letting die" is logically equivalent to "making live," cryopolitics can be defined as a power that "*makes live* and *does not let die*" or as a power that "*does not let die* and *lets die*."[67] Such a paradoxical structure of biopolitics thus opens up investigations into the thresholds at which it is decided which living beings will die and which will not. "Cryopolitics, then, is a politics of the liminal. It inheres when life is phantomatic, vacillating, and ambiguous: when life is not itself."[68] The beings that are preserved in cold storage are not just archives of the past or indicators of the future, like the ice cores used to measure climate change over time, but living beings awaiting a second life, whose "first life" is the object of a knowledge of conservation.

Cryopolitics thus blends environmental pessimism and technological optimism into a teleological imaginary of the future. Driven by a "cruel optimism," it can only postpone death, if not eliminate it, while awaiting the materialization of a better life and an indefinite extension of the end. Kowal and Radin write: "Lowering the temperature of optimism does not diminish its cruelty; it merely numbs the pain."[69] The anthropologist and historian of science argue for a democratization of cryopolitics that includes indigenous peoples and native communities in a discussion of the recombinations between life and death through the globalization of new cold technologies.[70] In this way, they extend cryopolitics from climate sciences, cryonics companies and biobanks to zoos and nature reserves, as well as museums of natural history and anthropology, because the inclusion of indigenous communities in cryopolitics also opens it up to the animals and plants whose knowledge they carry.

Matthew Chrulew has studied the "frozen ark" project piloted by the University of Nottingham in England, on the model of the "Frozen Zoo" in San Diego, California, and reinscribed it in a cryopolitical history of zoological parks. These projects, modelled on plant seed banks, the largest of which is preserved in Svalbard in northern Scandinavia, with seeds from all over the world,[71] anticipate the effects of a mass extinction of biodiversity by saving living specimens in the form of seeds. The progress made in breeding "acclimatized" animals in captivity in the 1970s, after two centuries of mass animal deaths in zoos based on an economy of capture and import, made it possible to establish a new science, conservation biology, based on the birth and death statistics of animal populations, the refinement of species classification through the study of their genomes, as well as the collecting and freezing of their gametes, exchanged between zoos and used for artificial insemination.[72]

*Storing living beings in reserves and museums* 81

Chrulew notes that this archive of frozen gametes splits captive animal populations in zoos between their current existence and a virtual one, whereas these parks were already conceived in the nineteenth century as splitting the exotic fauna observed and captured in the colonies within European capitals.[73] He emphasizes that these successive duplications are designed to avoid risky contact with wild animals and the costs of their conservation. In these "frozen ark" projects, biological life, in the sense of a life framed by a network of institutions and a plan to safeguard species, is privileged over animal life, in the sense of the encounter between exhibited species and visitors in the space of the zoo. Research and conservation functions are added to the educational and leisure functions of zoos, which aim at communication, imitation, or play between humans and animals.[74] "In their technological utopia, frozen zoos save life by bypassing the hazardous, aleatory, and agonistic dimensions of living itself. (. . .) Faced with the qualitatively amplified threat of extinction, of species death, cryopower strives to secure life against *living itself*."[75]

Cryopolitics thus complements biopolitics with technologies in charge of conserving animals. The hope of redemption they offer in the face of the threat of mass extinction of living species is an extension of pastoral techniques to save individuals from disease, while at the same time relying on techniques of sovereignty that justify the killing of animals within the confines of the zoo.[76] Just as Foucault saw in carceral knowledge and governmental knowledge a way of constructing the subjectivity of modern individuals by attributing to them a "soul," so conservation knowledge makes it possible to attribute to animals a genetic identity that singularizes them by preserving the species of which they are sometimes the only representatives.[77] Chrulew writes: "If Foucault understands biopower as the proliferation of pastoral power beyond the ecclesial laboratory that took as its model the relation of human shepherds with their animal flocks, this power today has abundantly returned to animal lives, concerning itself in-depth interest with non-human bodies and souls, whether as individuals or as representatives of their species. From national parks and reserves to zoos and labs, from urban centers and domestic homes to rural fringes and the ocean's depths, from conservation and rehabilitation centers to factory farms and abattoirs, animals are today governed according to the same goals of this-worldly salvation as the human population, such as 'health, well-being, security, protection against accidents'."[78]

Chrulew opens up the possibility of resistance to this "cryopolitics." Since it is constituted by a series of duplications, from colonies to metropoles, from captive animals to their frozen gametes, this leaves open the possibility of a remnant analogous to what the subjectivity of the possessed woman was for Foucault. Chrulew cites Heini Hediger, director of the zoos in Bern, Basel, and Zurich, who introduced the reflections of ethologist Jakob von Uexküll into the knowledge of life in captivity. Hediger observed that captive animals create their own territory within the space of their cages, which must be enriched qualitatively and not just fed by calculating the rations necessary for survival.[79] He understood the repetitive behaviors of zoo animals as questions addressed to visitors, referring them to their own experience of confinement in urban spaces, with animal pathology in turn questioning human living standards. In his view, temperature, humidity, ventilation, and light were all variables to which the zoo director had to pay attention in order to transform the cage into a habitat.[80] At the end of his life, Hediger criticized the advent of freezing techniques in zoos as an extension of laboratory science into zoos, to the detriment of knowledge derived from caring for the lasting relationship between subjects. "Everything that is based on tradition is lost in pure refrigerator breeding," he wrote in 1986, "and this is no doubt no small thing."[81]

The way of thinking described by Hediger as "traditional", and by Churlew as "pastoral," considers the animal as a subject through an intersubjective relationship possible in zoo captivity. It leaves aside, however, the hunting techniques by

*Storing living beings in reserves and museums* 83

which animals are captured and staged in parks. This is why I propose to see in cryopolitics not a transformation of pastoral power – it is rather the role of biopolitics that "sustains populations" – but of cynegetic power, in order to grasp what kind of subject appears there in modernity. This hypothesis seems to me to be confirmed by the ethnography of nature reserves and natural history museums.

Indeed, environmental ethics usually criticize these two spaces as forms of confinement, thus reducing them to the enclosed space of the zoo, where the animal is considered a subject under the gaze of the director and an object under the gaze of the visitor. Philosopher Thomas Birch wrote in 1990: "Areas designated as wilderness become prisons, where the imperium incarcerates the savage who rebels against assimilation, in order to complete its work, to finalize its reign."[82] In a more subtle way, William Cronon showed in 1996 that the notion of wilderness was deeply linked to the conquest of space by American settlers, who constantly pushed back a frontier beyond which they anticipated an eternal nature, which they sought either to exploit or to conserve, thus ignoring the presence of indigenous peoples before this conquest.[83] To the imaginary of nature controlled either by domestication or confinement, which is the aporia of "deep ecology," Cronon opposes the daily observation of one's environment to follow the beings with which it is populated and their transformations by capitalism. But, while this method is very useful for studying the chains of interdependence between the countryside and the city, in Chicago or elsewhere, it does not allow us to study what is happening in nature parks, nor their extension to a large number of societies through the globalization of nature protection standards and the domestication of the "wild."[84]

More recently, Guillaume Blanc has proposed the study of nature parks as places of "symbolic violence," in which the state exercises sovereign power by drawing borders from which it defies anyone who crosses them, and by imposing a

84 *Cryptopolitics*

definition of nature that reinforces its national imaginary.[85] The parks studied by Guillaume Blanc in France, Quebec, and Ethiopia were defined in the 1970s, in a moment when conservation of nature as heritage "froze" the history of the hunting and fishing societies that lived there, which led them to be expelled without being able to construct alternative narratives.[86] In the French Cévennes National Park, shows Blanc, hunting is regulated and geared toward "the protection of wildlife and the hunting herd," and the conservation of cultural traditions can be considered a "museification enterprise."[87] The Ethiopian Simien Mountains National Park was emptied of its inhabitants to protect an endangered goat species, the *walia ibex*, but above all to comply with international conservation standards and attract foreign tourists, in a form of "eco-racism" and "green colonialism."[88]

This analysis is relevant to paternalistic, authoritarian environmental policies from the center outwards, such as those applied in national parks in France, Quebec, and Ethiopia, but less so when we examine nature reserve policies in Ontario and South Africa. These follow the British model of indirect rule, emphasizing negotiation between stakeholders, and focus more on environmental health as a component of human health. James Harkin, the founder of Canada's National Parks, was a journalist turned bureaucrat in 1896, who arbitrated between the interests of potentially conflicting groups to preserve natural areas from industrial and urban development in order to promote the health and tourism impact of "nature." Far from the American model of wilderness, which separates "reserves" from "civilization" by means of violent expulsion, Harkin encouraged the construction of roads that would enable visitors to visit the parks from the large adjacent towns, and he managed to interest the native communities in this development policy.[89] Thus, in the development of Pointe Pelée National Park in 1918, situated on Lake Erie next to the city of Detroit, Harkin played the role of intermediary between ornithologists' associations, who protected wild birds

*Storing living beings in reserves and museums* 85

on their migration paths, wealthy hunters' clubs, who came from the city to kill ducks, and poor trappers' groups, who lived on the spot and caught muskrats.[90]

In South Africa, after two outbreaks of bubonic plague in the interior of the country in 1920, twenty years after a plague epidemic in major cities such as Cape Town and Durban, Austin Roberts, zoologist at the Transvaal National Museum of Natural History in the capital Pretoria, was commissioned to detect the rat populations responsible for these outbreaks. He opposed the zoologist Frederick FitzSimons, who had opened a natural history museum in Port Elizabeth, and showed that the wild bird species slaughtered by settler farmers as pests played a central role in the destruction of rats, and thus in the balance of South Africa's rural ecosystem. Drawing on indigenous knowledge, FitzSimons recommended that farmers create feeders and reservoirs for hawks and owls, and install scarecrows to keep them away from crops. Roberts argued for the introduction of dogs and cats into rat-infested settler farmland, based on a map of plague outbreaks showing that land occupied by native farmers was not infested. In 1925, the first law protecting wild birds from export was passed in South Africa, but a year later, a project extending this ban to hunting throughout the country failed, leading the Pretoria government to open the first national parks protecting birds from hunting.[91]

This controversy shows that the protection of public health was an important argument in South Africa for the protection of wildlife, thus building a bridge between the sanitary concept of "disease reservoir" and the ecological concept of "nature reserve." The term "reservoir of disease" was introduced to South Africa in 1905 by the colonial physician David Bruce, at the same time as it was introduced into French colonial medicine by the Sergent brothers, in connection with an epidemic of trypanosomiasis called "nagana" in Zulu, a term designating a body left by spirits, and attributed by the Zulus to the tse-tse fly.[92] Bruce claimed that the reservoir of the disease

86 *Cryptopolitics*

was wildlife, based on an observation that tse-tse flies disappeared from livestock when wild mammals were killed. This statement aroused the ire of the Society for the Protection of the Wildlife of the Empire (SPWFE), which opposed excessive hunting in the colonies.[93] The controversy lasted thirty years, and was then forgotten in the archives of the British Empire. Trypanosomiasis was intensively fought in East and South Africa in the 1960s, reaching fewer than 5,000 cases a year in 1965, before skyrocketing again in the 1970s. According to the World Health Organization, it is now back under control, with fewer than 10,000 cases a year, and the role of wildlife in its transmission to livestock has still not been established.[94]

It is remarkable that these controversies over nature reserves in South Africa pitted colonial doctors, who often hunted as a hobby, against naturalists working in museums, who preferred collecting to hunting. Naturalists have played an essential role in the history of nature reserves, no longer seeing them as hunting resources, but as places where living organisms can be stored and where degraded nature can be restored. In this respect, it could be said that naturalists brought the imaginary world of natural history museums to animal reserves. If collecting, like hunting, leads to the killing of animals, it is not in their eyes to destroy harmful individuals, but on the contrary to save species threatened with extinction by showing their place in the harmony of an evolutionary tree. The nature reserve thus transforms the cynegetic power of colonial powers aimed at accumulating wealth into the cryopolitics of global conservation institutions.

Jean Dorst, professor of ornithology at the National Museum of Natural History in Paris, which he headed between 1975 and 1985, wrote in his famous book, *Avant que nature meure (Before Nature Dies)*, published in 1965, two years after the translation of Rachel Carson's *Silent Spring*: "Strict nature reserves thus appear as sanctuaries where strains that would have disappeared long ago without these conservation measures are preserved, and as reservoirs from which arise new

*Storing living beings in reserves and museums* 87

'servants' of man, new genetic combinations, or simply breeding stocks transported to degraded areas that we can hope to restore through a natural equilibrium."[95]

The first ornithological curator employed by the National Museum of Natural History in Washington in 1879, Robert Ridgway, was as passionate about birding through the barrel of a gun as he was about reading naturalist books. John Muir, founder of the first great national parks in the United States, said of him that he had "wonderful eyes, which contained all the birds of America."[96] By comparison with John James Audubon, who was primarily interested in observing and drawing North American birds in their habitat, and could kill them massively to do so, Ridgway was obsessed with classification and conservation in museum space as a way of justifying the killing of birds. He spent his life making taxidermy, classifying them according to Darwin's evolutionary tree, and exchanging them with other museums to fill the gaps in his collection, until his death in 1929. Bird collecting was increasingly criticized in the course of the twentieth century, leading to the opening of nature reserves after the Second World War. Frank Chapman, curator in the ornithology department of New York's Natural History Museum, responded in *The Auk* to the Marquise of Tavistock's accusations against "the ruthless and excessive destruction of rare birds by the American Whitney expedition" in the Pacific Islands. He argued that collecting was not a threat to birds, and that bird specimens were better protected in a museum than in the wild, as they found their place and meaning within an evolutionary framework.[97] The "ghosts of nature" pursued by hunters were thus fixed in the tidy, enclosed space of the museum, then in the open but equally controlled space of the "wildlife reserve."

In 2008, in the reedition of *La pensée sauvage* for the Bibliothèque de la Pléiade edition of his works, Claude Lévi-Strauss wrote: "Whether one deplores it or rejoices in it, zones are still known in which wild thought, like wild species, is relatively protected. Such is the case of art, to which our

88 *Cryptopolitics*

civilization gives the status of a national park, with all the advantages and disadvantages attaching to such an artificial formula."[98] This statement should not be read as a conservative stance prescribing the confinement of beings in protected spaces to remove them from the grip of time, but rather as a call for the creation of spaces where living things can express all their possibilities outside any imperative of yield. In his last lectures at the Collège de France, Lévi-Strauss was interested in the monkey parks on the outskirts of Japanese cities, where humans could interact with apes in the wild.[99] These parks escaped the opposition between the national park, created far from cities to protect a nature separate from humans, and the zoological park located in the heart of cities, like a museum or laboratory, to provide the cultural spectacle of nature. Instead, they should be conceived as reserves in which modes of interaction between humans and non-humans are preserved at the boundaries of human collectives, with a view to replenishing them when they become exhausted.

Lévi-Strauss describes "wild thought" – thought that is constituted by the names given to beings in nature, rather than by mathematical models like "domesticated thought" – not as a rigid, arbitrary symbolic order, but as a classificatory dynamic that extends toward the universal and the particular. It is a thermodynamic machine that absorbs the contingency of events to cool them down by giving them a necessary place in a pre-existing classification system. With regard to proper names among the Tiwi, who forbid certain names in order to recharge them with energy, Lévi-Strauss writes: "Many names are thus kept in reserve, constituting a kind of onomastic fund on which it is praiseworthy to draw."[100] Lévi-Strauss's comparison between national parks and museums becomes clearer in the light of this passage: we can conceive of them as "banks" in which living beings are "kept in reserve" in a "sacred" form to produce more energy when they are introduced into ordinary classifications. This interpretation sheds light on the often misunderstood assertion that the hunter-gatherer societies anthropology deals with are "without history" or "cold."[101] As Eduardo Kohn writes, ". . . what is 'cold' here is not exactly a bounded society. For the forms that confer on Amazonian society this 'cold' characteristic cross the many boundaries that exist both internal to and beyond human realms."[102] Parks and museums "cool time" in the sense that they sequence the linear arrow of time, characterized by acceleration and warming, to recode it within other timelines stored in their reserves.

Disturbingly for us today, anthropology museums were built at the end of the nineteenth century on the model of natural history museums, i.e. by another transformation of cynegetic power into cryopolitics. European travellers collected objects from non-European societies and brought them back to Europe to produce a fixed image of human history. In this image, taken from Darwin's evolutionism, European mankind is at the end of evolution as its most advanced branch, and so-called "primitive" societies are conceived as branches in the process of extinction, to be preserved as testimony to human diversity. Anthropology museums have accumulated objects used in daily life or for ritual purposes, human tissues, skeletons, and skulls, most often without clear distinctions between the unity of "nature" and the diversity of "cultures." Following the Berlin Conference, which led European states to divide up the African continent in order to create colonial empires, a traffic in ethnographic objects was organized between Europe and the rest of the world, with a particular predilection for skulls, which were not only convenient scientific objects to transport, measure, and compare, but also fascinating war trophies to behold.[103]

Emma Kowal and Joanna Radin have extended the term "cryopolitics", from its use in the climate sciences to other contexts where the living is "frozen", to think about the situation in anthropology museums. Joanna Radin has studied a moment in the history of biological anthropology in the United States dubbed "freezer anthropology," as the industrial refrigeration techniques available during the "Cold War" enabled anthropologists to preserve blood samples taken from a large number of human societies pending their genetic sequencing for comparative purposes. Today, these collections of frozen blood are embarrassing for curators, who wish to destroy them or return them to their communities of origin, while some biologists argue in favor of their preservation in the name of as yet unknown analysis techniques that would produce new knowledge.[104] Emma Kowal has worked with Indigenous communities in Australia to develop protocols for reclaiming the remains of their descendants from museums and sharing the benefits of biological research made on these remains. Questioning what is "good science" in the times of genomic research and post-colonial debates, she follows the fate of Walter Baldwin Spencer, considered the founder of Australian anthropology for the survey he carried out in the Aboriginal communities of the Central Desert with administrator Francis Gillen in 1901–1902. Spencer was director of Melbourne's Victoria Museum between 1899 and his death in 1929, to which he bequeathed 1,500 ethnographic objects, 900 manuscripts, films, and recordings. In 2000, an exhibition entitled "Bunjilaka," meaning "the place of the eagle's descendants," was presented to this museum by anthropologist John Morton, a specialist in the Aboriginal communities of the Central Desert. A statue of Spencer was made for the occasion and displayed in a showcase among the ethnographic objects collected by Spencer in Australia's Central Desert, with the caption: "Thus the collector was collected." Emma Kowal describes this form of exhibition as "decolonial," since it turns the collector's gaze toward the object collected, in a characteristic reversal of cynegetic power when the hunter becomes the prey, by contrast with a "post-colonial" approach, more inclined toward multi-vocality. Investigating the trajectory of Spencer's statue, Kowal notes that it entered the Victoria Museum's storerooms without an inventory number, as it is devoid of value to both the art market and Aboriginal communities. In the cryopolitical rationality of the museum, which

*Storing living beings in reserves and museums* 91

"freezes" objects by assigning them a place in the reserves with an inventory number, Spencer's statue thus appears as a ghost embarrassing the history of the collection.[105]

The work of Emma Kowal and Joanna Radin is foundational for an approach to museums and parks that is no longer based on the opposition between nature and culture, but that takes as its starting point the technologies for collecting and conserving living beings. It raises the question of what can and cannot be exhibited to the public as a result of the colonial past. When the cynegetic power analyzed by Grégoire Chamayou and Achille Mbembe is transformed into cryopolitics, the question is not what can escape and what must be chased back, but what can be preserved and exhibited for the salvation of humanity, what must remain hidden in reserves and what should be restituted to communities of origin. If cynegetic power is the dark or cursed side of the modern project to extend rationality through techniques of capture and accumulation that amplify those of hunter-gatherer societies, cryopolitics is its luminous and emancipating side, since it accumulates objects for all humanity in order to escape the grip of time and death. Michel Foucault thus talks about "heterotopias," a term that encompasses for him museums, libraries, cemeteries, and vacation villages: "The idea of accumulating everything, the idea of constituting a kind of general archive, the desire to enclose in one place all times, all eras, all forms, all tastes, the idea of constituting a place of all times that is itself outside time, and inaccessible to its bite, the project of organizing in this way a kind of perpetual and indefinite accumulation of time in a place that would not move, well, all this belongs to our modernity."[106]

How, then, does cryopolitics enable us to reformulate the project of emancipating living beings that lies at the heart of modernity? How can subjects appear within the norms of this new power? If disciplinary power and biopolitics, extending into modernity the techniques of sovereign power and pastoral power, aim to subjugate living beings in such a way as to rationalize their spirit – the soul of the disciplined individual and the collective consciousness of the population – cryopolitics instead produces ghostly doubles of living beings kept in the cold of storage rooms, thus extending the techniques of cynegetic power by which valuable forms are taken from living beings perceived as prey. Whereas cynegetic power splits the bodies of slaves into ghosts that haunt their masters in order to turn colonial violence against them, in the way that the prey can sometimes kill the hunter, cryopolitics instead produces a set of virtual entities – genetic sequences and inventory numbers – that enable living beings to be preserved beyond their "natural" death through a scientific work of inscription.[107] While cynegetic power delegates the killing of animals to supernatural entities – the Master of the Forest is considered to be the cause of the death of animals in hunting societies – cryopolitics postpones death through a process that is both natural and technical – freezing in the cold chain. In cryopolitics, the thresholds between life and death, between nature and culture, between the wild and the domestic, which play a central role in the control of sovereign power over its territory, are blurred in such a way that living beings enter a metabolic machine – the storage room of a museum or a park – where virtual entities proliferate. The separation between cryopolitical spaces and their outside are not conditions for a power that maximizes its utility within its borders, as is the case with biopolitics, but thresholds for a lowering of temperature in a metabolic cycle that allows death to be deferred. Differences in temperature levels between the external and internal environments are the prerequisite for the proliferation of differences of nature within the conservation space.

In this sense, the subject of cryopolitics is neither the disciplined individual nor the surveilled population: it is the collection, defined as a set of objects that comes to life through being kept together.[108] Whereas disciplinary power aims at preserving the mental health of individuals and biopolitics

*Storing living beings in reserves and museums* 93

aims at maintaining the public health of populations, cryopolitics aims at conserving what is now called "planetary health", by considering living beings through the form of the collection. This way of justifying the care given to living beings, including humans, animals, plants, and microbes, raises the central question for cryopolitics: which subjects will receive priority care according to their relationships with other living beings, and which will be set aside to "let them die," as waste that makes no sense in this format, or to "make them die," as enemies of sovereign power?[109] In this sense, the test of entry into the laboratory, nature reserve or museum no longer aims to recognize the free subject behind the disciplined individual, nor the statistical trend behind the aggregate of the population, but the collected form behind the aggregate of objects or the decomposed organism. The threshold through which living beings enter collections, exposing their vulnerabilities, becomes the site for new practices of emancipation.[110]

The controversies surrounding mutant H5N1 or the origins of SARS-Cov2, which I have analyzed as cryopolitical problems rather than as problems of political sovereignty or biosafety ethics, can be rephrased as follows: how, among all the viruses that can be kept in the laboratory, can we justify that some of the objects are of special interest, to the detriment of others? To this question, "virus hunters" answer: because research into virus mutations in the laboratory enables global health authorities to prepare for the emergence of pandemic viruses. We need to take this justification seriously, and question it in the light of the ideal of truth and justice it involves. I will show that the ethical stakes involved in the politics of zoonoses imply thinking up a new form of solidarity between living beings, and extending socialism to a renewed form of ecology. Michel Foucault did not raise this question in his analysis of biopower, because he assessed it through the requirement of freedom, which is one of the forms of the ideal of justice. This is why he characterized his method as an "anarcheology,"[111] in the sense that the genealogy of different forms of power through dispersed historical series enabled him to challenge the centrality of the sovereign power of the state and open up possibilities for human freedom. If we evaluate cryopolitics in terms of the form of solidarity that the social sciences carry into the order of academic knowledge, we can contrast Michel Foucault's anarchist genealogy with a socialist one. In what sense do zoonoses, diseases shared by humans and other animals, bring animals into the city, the people or humanity? This question, posed today by a "zoo-political" philosophy,[112] will be addressed here using the methods of social anthropology, which aims to "repopulate the world" with animals.[113]

# 5

# Planetary health:
# Anticipating disasters with animals

In 2004, as the H5N1 virus was being transmitted by birds from Asia to Europe and Africa, members of three international organizations were brought together in New York by the Wildlife Conservation Society (WCS), founded in 1895 to manage the Bronx Zoo: the World Health Organization (WHO), created in 1945 in Geneva to monitor the health of refugees after the Second World War, and whose great success was the global vaccination against smallpox in 1978; the World Organization for Animal Health (OIE/WOAH), set up in 1924 in Paris to coordinate animal health monitoring systems by veterinarians, and which was soon to declare rinderpest eradicated through vaccination; the Food and Agriculture Organization of the United Nations (FAO), set up in 1945 in Rome to support agricultural production in the "Third World." The "Manhattan Declaration" formulated a set of principles known as "One Health," which emphasized the need to look after the health of animals, in particular by ensuring the quality of the water and land where they live and migrate, to avoid zoonoses affecting human health.[1] Between the epidemics controlled by WHO and the epizootics controlled by OIE, zoonoses opened up a space for coordinating surveillance networks at global level, given the impossibility of controlling their spread through slaughter or vaccination.

In October 2019, the same associations and international organizations met in Berlin to update the Manhattan Declaration, adding antibiotic-resistant bacteria and the effects of climate change to the factors amplifying zoonoses.[2]

96 *Planetary health*

Since 2005, the "One Health" principle had been criticized as an overly veterinary and paternalistic approach to animal health, which failed to take sufficient account of the local knowledge of livestock farmers.[3] Promoters of the "EcoHealth" notion, relying more on mathematical modelling, defended the interdependence between humans, domestic animals and wild animals in ecosystems,[4] while Earth system specialists spoke of "planetary health," following a report published in 2015 by the Rockefeller Foundation and the *Lancet* journal, in support of solidarity between all living beings within the limits of the planet.[5] The notion of planetary health clearly underlines the need to link the health of humans and other animals to that of the planet as a whole, by monitoring its internal regulations as disrupted by human activity. In this new way of thinking about health on several scales, from the local knowledge of breeders living on territories to expert systems modeling the Earth's equilibria, the relationships between humans and animals play a key role in generalizing care practices and giving meaning to catastrophic events.[6] Such an approach, revived by zoonoses such as bird 'flu and Covid-19, profoundly transforms the concept of biopolitics, extending it to all living beings exposed to transformations in the planetary balance, and making it necessary to invent a new form of solidarity.

### 5.a Responsibility: from pandemics to global warming

In the wake of the Covid-19 pandemic, citizens around the world asked themselves: after this ecological catastrophe, what will be next, and what lessons will we have learned from it? Many observers then noted that the effects of global warming over the next century would be on the same global scale, with a greater number of victims and more complex problems of infrastructure and government to pose and resolve. Hence the question: is the same causality at work in the pandemic as in global warming, and how does the pandemic experience prepare us for the effects of global warming?

## Responsibility 97

If it is addressed to virologists, epidemiologists, and ecologists, this question elicits a variety of answers, depending on the biological causality involved. It has been observed that the emission of greenhouse gases by human activity is leading to an overall increase in global temperature, with extreme weather events such as heatwaves, droughts, fires, or floods, all of which have an impact on animal populations carrying viruses or bacteria, particularly wild mammals (primates, bats, rodents) and insects (mosquitoes, ticks, lice, fleas). These climatic changes reduce the specific diversity that attenuates the virality of pathogens through a "dilution effect,"[7] and bring animals closer to human populations, to whom they transmit new pathogens for which the latter have no immunity. It has also been pointed out that higher temperatures in factory farms (pigs, poultry, cattle) increase animal stress, and thus the consumption of antibiotics, which weakens their bacterial diversity and immune response, thus favoring the transmission of new, potentially pandemic pathogens.[8] It is even conceivable that the melting of the permafrost could lead to the re-emergence of forgotten pathogens, such as anthrax, or even microbes that had never been in contact with the human species, because they were frozen before it appeared.[9]

These three arguments mobilize biological causality in different ecosystems, which can be characterized by the terms wild, domestic, and arctic. But they still say nothing about the sociological causality involved in these phenomena. How do interactions between humans, or between humans and non-humans, affect the risk of new pathogens emerging as a result of global warming? What measures can humans take to limit the effects of global warming, along the lines of those they took to control the Covid-19 pandemic? How, in other words, are humans responsible for global warming and zoonoses, in the dual sense of a past causality and the need to respond in the future?

Such a question mobilized social scientists, who noticed that measures long advocated against global warming (banning international transport, reducing mobility within the country, increasing teleworking, suspending construction activities, paying attention to biodiversity, making free medical treatment available) were being adopted very quickly by a large number of governments, in order to reduce the number of deaths caused by Covid-19. This new zoonosis confirmed what observers had known since the SARS crisis in 2003: in an age of accelerated exchanges of people and goods, a pandemic can bring the global economy to a halt, thus fulfilling the dream of general strike formulated as a political program a century ago by the socialist movement.[10] Does this mean that bats have revolted against the reduction of their habitats by humans, just as workers have mobilized against their working conditions, and should we include these virus-carrying non-humans in the symbolic figure of the proletariat or the people? The question of causality here is broader than that of responsibility in the modern sense: it leads us to imagine that animals act through the form of viruses when they cause pandemics, and thus to consider them as actors in a new conception of solidarity in the face of future ecological disasters.[11]

This question was tackled with great clarity by a Swedish geographer, Andreas Malm, in a book written in Berlin during the first months of lockdown, entitled *Corona, Climate, Chronic Emergency*. Malm is also a militant environmentalist, supporting the method of sabotaging large polluting companies.[12] In his view, the difference between a pandemic and global warming is not that the former is a rapid, visible catastrophe in the series of cases of contagion, while the latter is a slow, invisible catastrophe due to the gradual rise in temperatures. Both processes lead politicians to enter a "chronic emergency," which scientists have warned about for half a century. But, whereas global warming mainly affects the populations of the global South, who are not responsible for the production of greenhouse gases, the Covid-19 pandemic mainly affects the populations of the global North, and particularly the elderly, even though it began in the countries of the global South, and

*Responsibility* 99

particularly in China – which, indeed, plays a mediating role between these two poles. This chiasmus structure explains why Northern countries have taken measures against this pandemic that they would never have dared to take against global warming. The strategy proposed by Andreas Malm aims to resolve a problem of environmental justice: how can we ensure that populations exposed to global warming benefit from measures taken by the global North against pandemics, and are not accused of encouraging the transmission of emerging diseases? To do this, we need to look beyond the effects of pandemics and global warming, and go back to their causes: we need to shift from social vulnerabilities to their ecological roots.[13]

Following Marx, Malm analyzes the causality common to the various ecological catastrophes as that of capital, understood as a dynamic of accumulation that produces value and inequality by appropriating natural resources and rendering the effects of production invisible. If pathogens emerge in China or Central Africa, it is, according to Malm, because these are places of capital accumulation that intensify the mutations of microbes. Capital favors both the production of greenhouse gases, by harnessing fossil fuels to control cheap labor, and the emergence of pathogens, by bringing living beings into dense places where value is produced. The Covid-19 pandemic and global warming thus have the same cause, the accumulation of capital, which becomes visible at different degrees, through a sudden "global sickening,"[14] or through a gradual rise in temperatures. Malm writes, quoting economist Robert Wallace: " 'opening the forests to global circuits of capital' is in itself *'a primary cause'* of all this sickness. It is unrestrained capital accumulation that so violently shakes the tree where bats and other animals live. Out falls a drizzle of viruses."[15]

If viruses are side-effects of capital accumulation, then capital can present itself as a regulatory driver for the viruses it generates. Here, Malm sketches out a path for a biopolitics "of capital as metavirus and patron of parasites."[16] He thus borrows a classic Marxist argument: capital operates as a parasite that pumps workers' energy to inject them with a disease that alienates them.[17] In Malm's view, pharmaceutical capitalism extends this parasitic dynamic by selling modified viruses as commodities, on which it has established a property right. Pharmaceutical companies are described by Malm as "unconscious," because they do not address the causes of climate change and pandemics. Indeed, as we have seen, they are guided more by a "cryopolitics," when they paradoxically cool down viruses and vaccines in a world whose fever they pretend to cure.

Malm therefore plans instead "effective strategies of conscious intervention"[18] that would act directly at the root cause, rather than remedying disease by increasing the number of viruses stockpiled around the world. Citing Vladimir Lenin's 1917 text *The Impending Catastrophe and How to Combat It*, which sets out the collectivization of the means of production, the electrification of factories and the protection of ecological communities, Andreas Malm proposes limiting monoculture plantations and installing negative-emission machines that convert $CO_2$ into pure carbon dioxide.[19] While the "war on the virus" metaphor was often criticized during the pandemic, Malm assumes it in the name of a "war communism" that would re-establish good distances between humanity and a nature preserved in national parks and seed banks.[20] He quotes a slogan by which philosopher Daniel Bensaïd sums up Leninist politics: "Be ready! Be ready for the improbable, for the unexpected, for what happens!"[21]

This injunction to prepare for pandemics and climate change, which sounds like a declaration of war against an invisible enemy, is part of assumed authoritarian form of ecological engineering. The radical left, says Malm, must be prepared for the seizure of power caused by the defeat of government parties in the event of a major ecological catastrophe, and for that it must accelerate its acquisition of expert

*Responsibility*　　101

knowledge. Malm thus leaves aside the dynamics of participation through which different actors cooperate over time around viral emergences and extreme weather events, with heterogeneous knowledge requiring procedures of translation and diplomacy. This explains why Malm projects onto China's ecological situation a Marxist–Leninist schema that misses the history and geography of Chinese ecosystems. It is false to say that the emergence of SARS-Cov2 is directly caused by deforestation, since the Chinese government, in conjunction with international organizations such as the World Wildlife Fund, has pursued a policy of massive reforestation over the last fifty years, following the ecological disasters caused by Maoist policies.[22] It is equally false to say that a policy of nature parks based on the Leninist model would put an end to zoonotic emergences, as social science research has shown that nature parks exert a form of real and symbolic violence on the human and animal populations living there, and must make compromises with these inhabitants if they are to be accepted in the long term, as showed by the example of Taiwan.[23]

At the end of his book, Andreas Malm criticizes Bruno Latour's sociology for giving microbes the power to act. This paradoxical position leads Bruno Latour and his followers to take seriously the idea of a "revolt of nature," making health crises an opportunity for natural beings to enter politics. Malm regards this idea as absurd and compares it to a suicide attack by terrorist animals, thus missing the Latourian proposal of mediations by a "Parliament of Nature."[24] For Malm, who cites the founders of the Frankfurt School,[25] only humans can act as subjects because only they are conscious of the consequences of their actions, so that "defending wild nature against parasitic capital is now human self-defence."[26] Malm thus takes up a paternalistic scheme in which humans help animals to defend themselves against the alienation imposed on them by capital.

Although Bruno Latour's diagnosis of the ecological crisis is the same as Andreas Malm's, it is based on radically different premises and leads to equally opposite prescriptions. During the three years of the Covid-19 pandemic, which he knew would be the last three years of his earthly life as he was suffering from an incurable disease, Bruno Latour intervened in the public arena, through lectures, TV and radio broadcasts, and books, to make sense of the pandemic event and place it within a global socio-history. The author of *Politics of Nature* has shed a masterly light on this pandemic in the light of his hypotheses on the "politics of nature." Bruno Latour has long expressed distrust of the notion of biopolitics revived by Michel Foucault, since in his eyes it implied a theory of modernity marked by the emergence of life as an object of power.[27] Even if he wrote *Politics of Nature* as a response to the "mad cow crisis," he was little interested in zoonoses or emerging infectious diseases, as he proposed a sociology of actors in which the experience of disease is evacuated in favor of an alliance between humans and non-humans such as animals or microbes.[28] The term "politics of nature" he coins refers to the "risky attachments" between objects and subjects: the hybrids between nature and culture, who proliferate in modern societies precisely because they claim to separate nature and culture, need the work of representation (in the sense of spokesperson rather than cognitive category) to form a common world.[29]

Bruno Latour has given a theological twist to this ontology of relationships between humans, animals, plants, and microbes, by taking up James Lovelock and Lynn Margulis' concept of Gaia, in order to think about the solidarities between living beings revealed by the ecological crisis and global warming.[30] The English geochemist and the American microbiologist have shown that all these relationships form a single organism with its own atmosphere, telling the story of planet Earth as the result of these relationships over time. Latour then proposed to determine the status of this new kind of entity, i.e. how it might interact with other actors.[31] This is why he resorted to the vocabulary of war: Gaia puts humans at war with each other, as she manifests herself in a cry for help, pitting humans against each other between those who hear her and those who don't, between those who "face her" and those who turn away.[32]

Latour uses the Marxist vocabulary of class struggle to describe how this war pits an "ecological class," called "Anthropocene Earthlings," against a "globalizing class," called "Holocene Humans."[33] As for Marx, these actors clash with conflicting interests, unaware of the conditions that make these interests compatible. However, according to Latour, the outcome of this class struggle will not be decided by a revolution, i.e. a seizure of power aimed at occupying the state in order to dissolve it, but by a simulation, i.e. a theater in which all human representatives of non-humans will map out their attachments.[34] For example, if an employee clashes with an environmentalist over the construction of a shopping mall that damages the reproductive conditions of the land on which he lives, a simulation of the ecological catastrophe should make him aware of the vulnerability of his habitat. This virtual class struggle should emancipate humans, not by building a society separate from nature, but by making them aware of the limits of their earthly condition.[35]

Latour takes up Foucault's notion of biopolitics to describe this shift from revolution to simulation as a model of class struggle. He notes that "if there is one subject where the change in sensibility is manifest and had become almost universal, it is the understanding of living beings."[36] But biopolitics has failed, according to Latour, because it has only addressed health issues, on which the state has developed expertise through an administration, whereas for ecological issues, expertise has developed outside the state and its administration. Latour thus distinguishes two forms of biopolitics, depending on whether they serve "social classes," which are in legal conflict over forms of production and property, or "geosocial classes," which are in existential conflict over conditions of engendering and habitability.[37] The former

104 *Planetary health*

is coordinated by the state and relies on the knowledge of populations, while the latter is constructed by citizens as they become aware of their living conditions. Latour thus takes up the Marxist vocabulary of class consciousness, but without resorting to the state as a collective subject capable of acting on the primary cause. Instead, he suggests an inquiry into how citizens are attached to their living conditions, as second causes that enable them to participate in politics horizontally and democratically rather than vertically and authoritatively.

In the 1980s, science studies showed that science was the result of controversies and compromises between humans to stabilize the recalcitrant power of the non-human entities enlisted in their devices. Thus, Latour showed that Pasteur, far from "discovering" microbes against the advocates of spontaneous generation, had "enlisted" them in his war against disease, through alliances with hygienists, veterinarians, poultry or silkworm breeders, colonial administrators . . . This conception, which has become known as "actor-network theory," has led science studies promoters to support a participatory approach in "hybrid forums," where experts discuss with non-experts the entities they want to bring into the city, as was the case in Europe around Genetically Modified Organisms.[38] In the context of the ecological crisis revealed by the pandemic and global warming, Latour transforms these hybrid forums into "books of complaint" (*cahiers de doléances*), where citizens can describe to those in power the territories to which they are attached, and thus defend them.

The aim of this collective inquiry, according to Latour, is to define a common metric that will enable these attachments to coexist in a just society, where the profits of the earth are not monopolized by a few to the detriment of many others. The ideal of a just society is carried by the various actors in this collective inquiry, without being realized by any one of them in particular, as the state pretends to do when it governs the biopolitics of the population with a view to security.[39] Whereas the pandemic is dealt with by a "first biopolitics," which defends territories against emerging viruses, climate change is the subject of a "second biopolitics," in which viruses are taken as signals of more radical ecological transformations. This is why Latour calls on every citizen to establish "barrier gestures" against climate change, similar to those the state asked them to take to limit the effects of the pandemic. Linking the pandemic to climate change allows us to move from questions of health and safety to questions of social and environmental justice. It leads us to build up, "one step at a time," something akin to the collective consciousness of an ecological class, analogous to the contagion effects Durkheim described as constituting those of "society." The animals, plants, stones, and microbes to which humans are attached are now part of this collective consciousness, whereas they had been excluded from society, either as biological threats or as mere carriers of symbolic representations.[40]

In Latour's view, this expanded awareness of the cosmic joy of all living beings is opposed to the nihilistic awareness of globalists, who "necessarily know that they have lost"; they content themselves with "fleeing the planet" and accelerating growth, when what we really need is to slow down and land on Earth.[41] However, for Latour, this expanded cosmology remains linked to a concern: the virus is not a microbe like any other, a sign that can connect with other signs in limitless alliances; it is an alarm signal making us aware that our mode of production has limits, and that we need to move to another cosmopolitical regime to maintain the Earth's habitability.[42] The virus is not an actor endowed with autonomy and agency, but an ambivalent microbe: it must hijack the means of cell replication, and yet is necessary to life in its regulation. To wage war on the "Humans of the Holocene" with viruses, for the "Earthlings of the Anthropocene," is therefore to be attentive to the warning signals perceived at the frontiers of threatened territories.

Malm and Latour thus see the Covid-19 pandemic as an opportunity for humans to prepare for global warming, but from this vision they draw radically different consequences for their relations with other animals, because they interpret differently the collective awareness produced by the lockdown of spring 2020. Malm proposes a dialectical and revolutionary way of thinking, which identifies the primary causality common to both the pandemic and climate change – capital – in order to occupy the state and radically reverse its deadly orientation. Latour, on the other hand, proposes a semiotic and simulationist way of thinking, organizing assemblies in which citizens map out their attachments, waiting for the whole human race to join them, and letting the "globalizers" leave the planet in a nihilistic and desperate trajectory. Through this form of second causality or "second biopolitics," it is not the state that is occupied, but Gaia who manifests herself by withdrawing. For Malm, the lockdown of 2020 is an opportunity to accelerate the seizure of ecological power, while for Latour it is, on the contrary, an opportunity to slow down and reflect on the attachments between humans and non-humans. Malm's model is the Russian revolution, while Latour's model is pre-revolutionary assemblies in France. Malm moves toward communism of the means of production to control energy resources, while Latour wants to "invent a socialism that contests production itself,"[43] drawing on a theology of engendering.

Malm and Latour finally evacuate the event of the French Revolution itself, even though it was a founding event for the social sciences in France. The question that French socialism had to answer at the end of the nineteenth century, taking over from reactionary and liberal thought, was: how could a human society that had reached the pinnacle of the Enlightenment revert to a state of animality and violence, and what then should we make of the ideals of truth and justice that it formulated in a moment of effervescence?[44] French sociology has answered this question by transfiguring society into a new kind of reality, which constitutes itself by the sacrifice of the sensitive interests of individuals, by formulating the categories and rules of life in common. Hence a problem that occupied French sociology throughout the twentieth century: how to think about the forms of life that emerge below sacrifice, in the multiplicity of ordinary interactions between individuals and affective attachments between the living? How can we understand that individuals prepare for sacrifice without these operations being finalized by it? This is where we can return to the legacy of the French Revolution to think about disaster preparedness differently from how Malm and Latour do, avoiding the opposition between pre- and post-revolutionary assessments to situate ourselves in the event itself, or rather on the thresholds it traces between living beings.

The current ecological catastrophe indeed repeats the revolutionary event, in its threefold economic, political, and ideological dimensions, distributed, as Marx clearly saw, between England, France, and Germany. If the political revolution in France repeats the economic revolution in England, and if it is ideologically thought out in Germany – which justifies Marx's making the reverse journey from Germany to France and England – what type of consciousness emerges from this triple revolution, and what horizon of emancipation does it open up? We are still faced with this question two centuries after Marx posed it, but in the meantime, the industrial revolution has extended to animals and plants: it no longer concerns only human workers exploited in factories, but also pigs, poultry, and cattle, who get sick on factory farms. We are living through a moment of suspension of our attachments to living beings through pandemic viruses, which is analogous to the revolutionary moment at the end of the eighteenth century, but this forces us to stand within the moment itself, not before it as Latour does, nor beyond it as Malm does. How can the collective consciousness that emerges from health crises caused by zoonoses (mad cow disease, bird 'flu, swine fever) integrate the signs of ecological catastrophe that humans perceive in their relations with other animals? How can these signs enable living beings to prepare for catastrophe

108 *Planetary health*

in ways other than by sacrificing themselves to a collective consciousness yet to come? In what sense can animals participate in the ideal that emerged from the Revolution, and be emancipated from their exploitation by globalized capitalism? Malm and Latour missed this question because they thought of a first causality – that of capital – and a second causality – that of signs – without questioning how pandemic viruses make us shift from the second to the first on the occasion of zoonoses.

### 5.b Participation: the ideal of justice through war

The discussion between Malm and Latour on the diagnosis of the environmental crisis shows the need to think in terms of an "ecology of war"[45] to prepare humanity for global warming, drawing on the lessons of the Covid pandemic. Malm and Latour describe this generalized state of war through the Marxist schema of class struggle, which they broaden by reading Lenin for the former, and Lovelock for the latter. Malm proposes a new figure of the militant, who intensifies war to accelerate its emancipatory potential, while Latour proposes a figure of the diplomat, who negotiates the terms of peace on the basis of forms of attachment to territory. I would like to explore another way of thinking about war in social democracy in the United States and France, which places greater emphasis on citizen participation in disaster preparedness. War, in this dual context, doesn't oppose one social class against another, but one nation-state against another. By committing all its resources to war, the nation-state must reflect on its vulnerabilities and rebuild its ideal of solidarity. This is why the state enlists scientists in the war, but in return, scientists enlist citizens to demand new rights from the state. In contrast to the figures of the militant and the diplomat, who aim to intensify or slow down war in order to build a common good, the figure of the sentinel aims to prepare citizens for war through their participation to an ideal of truth and justice.

Following Michel Foucault's method and Paul Rabinow's indications,[46] Stephen Collier and Andrew Lakoff have proposed a genealogy of preparedness in the emergency government of the United States. This notion must be distinguished from that of pre-emption, which relies on the emergent nature of threats to proliferate them.[47] For example, the Bush administration's attack on Saddam Hussein's Iraq was a pre-emptive operation, because even if there was no proof that Iraq was manufacturing biological weapons, by intervening on Iraqi soil, the U.S. army realized the threat in the name of which the intervention was justified. As each threat leads to another by the very fact of intervention, pre-emption is justified by its effects rather than by its cause. The power of pre-emption thus produces a form of terror by identifying itself with what it fears.[48] In contrast to this pre-emptive logic, through which a state fabricates a threat to legitimize its power, Collier and Lakoff show that the idea that a state's citizens must be prepared for an impending catastrophe in order to mitigate its consequences can be traced back to the Roosevelt administration's anticipation of an attack on its territory during the Great Depression of the 1930s. They thus trace a genealogy of preparedness in social democracy, since this set of techniques was passed down through various administrations during the Second World War and the Cold War, who shared a constant concern for their compatibility with the democratic ideals on which the United States is founded.

Collier and Lakoff quote President Roosevelt in 1939 on the subject of the Reorganization Act, which prepared the United States to enter world war alongside the Allies: "keeping the tools of American democracy up to date, the plan had one supreme purpose – to make democracy work – to strengthen the arms of democracy in peace and war."[49] In 1955, an exercise simulating a nuclear attack called Operation Alert provided President Eisenhower with the scenario for the destruction of sixty American cities by sixty bombs, killing eight million people on the first day and eight million within

110 *Planetary health*

six weeks of the attack. Eisenhower decided to declare martial law for the first time, which prompted intense legal work to verify that it was compatible with the civil liberties guaranteed by the Constitution, and led lawyers to go back to Abraham Lincoln's decisions during the Civil War.[50] These scenarios for simulating catastrophe were the result of strong discussions in the expert circles advising the federal government as to whether deterrence should be based solely on the logic of "going to extremes" – the state launching nuclear war endangers its own existence – or whether it should involve the population in imagining the "nuclear winter" that would follow an attack between the United States and the Soviet Union. Herman Kahn, who supported the second option, invented disaster scenario planning using simulation techniques that involved fiction and theater professionals.[51] Disaster simulations are thus an opportunity to exercise criticism before the disaster itself, since they engage citizens in imagining themselves as actors in the catastrophic situation.[52]

At the end of the Cold War, these "contingency planning" techniques, designed to justify emergency government, were applied to a whole range of "generic threats," from natural disasters – hurricanes, earthquakes, and floods – to terrorist attacks and new epidemics. At the same time, they have spread beyond the borders of the United States through a range of actors such as international organizations and philanthropic foundations, notably the Bill and Melinda Gates Foundation, aiming to intervene on an emergency basis in threatened territories to protect "global health" when states are failing.[53] In the process, these techniques have lost their normative anchorage, clearly asserted by Presidents Roosevelt and Eisenhower: expert firms have moved from the federal government to the offices of the Gate Foundation or the World Health Organization, without asserting a unifying principle.

Collier and Lakoff propose to clarify this normative anchorage by distinguishing prevention from preparation. Whereas the welfare state based its population biopolitics on statistics that made it possible to predict the course of an epidemic, calculate exposure risks and intervene through vaccination, "global health" actors seek to prepare citizens for an epidemic by organizing simulation exercises, because new epidemics, due to their zoonotic origin, have become unpredictable events with catastrophic consequences. It is not possible to vaccinate populations against smallpox or influenza if new strains of these viruses can be transmitted from animals: this is why exercises designed to simulate the effects of a smallpox or influenza virus are organized in New York or Hong Kong. Governments find it hard to accept the logic of preparedness, as it does not provide the tools for protecting the population offered by the welfare state, but it aims to protect the conditions of social life itself.[54]

While many observers criticize disaster preparedness as a return of the sovereign state to disciplinary forms of biopower, Collier and Lakoff rather analyze it as a "reflexive biopolitics."[55] They emphasize that the techniques of government no longer focus solely on the population, conceived as an entity that can be regulated by statistics, but on the vital conditions of social activities, such as the infrastructures for communicating information, circulating goods and transporting people that support human and non-human collectives. If, they write, "the very systems that were invented to ensure health and well-being, and to manage the vicissitudes of life, have themselves become sources of vulnerability for catastrophic disruptions,"[56] it is through increased reflexivity that disaster management experts can justify protecting not just populations, but the "critical infrastructures" that make this protection possible.[57] However, this new kind of reflexivity no longer involves calculating risks in a national space, but imagining disasters in a global space.

To understand how imagination can become a resource for collective reflexivity, I proposed another genealogy of disaster preparedness, based on the history of socialism and the

112 *Planetary health*

social sciences in France. I returned to the figure of Lucien Lévy-Bruhl, founder with Marcel Mauss and Paul Rivet of the Institute of Ethnology at the University of Paris in 1925, to trace a family genealogy of experts at the service of the French state through knowledge such as law, economics, and epidemiology. Between 1914 and 1917, after the assassination of Jean Jaurès, the founder of French socialism, Lucien Lévy-Bruhl worked for Albert Thomas, a socialist deputy close to Jaurès who had been appointed Minister of Armaments, to assess the overall forces that France could commit to war factories against Germany.[58] The sociologist Maurice Halbwachs, who was also involved in this statistical work, noted in 1914: "War poses a host of problems that we are not prepared to solve, because it requires a sum of knowledge and a series of reflections that it has not yet been given to us to gather and make."[59] In a note entitled "Unpredictability" written in 1917, Lévy-Bruhl described his action as follows: "expect the unexpected, and prepare everything to channel and direct it."[60] After the First World War, Thomas defended workers' rights, notably at the International Labor Office, of which he was the first director, while Lévy-Bruhl promoted Jaurès' heritage by organizing an international network of philosophers in the service of peace. In 1934, the foundation of the Vigilance Committee of Antifascist Intellectuals, in which Lévy-Bruhl actively participated, continued Jean Jaurès's gesture of organizing a vigilance committee in 1898 to unify the Socialist Party after the Dreyfus affair.

Lucien Lévy-Bruhl's socialist commitment sheds light on the singular type of reflexivity he describes, following Émile Durkheim's sociological method, in his work on "primitive mentality," which played a central role in the constitution of social anthropology in France in the twentieth century.[61] Drawing on the philosophy of Henri Bergson, Lévy-Bruhl studied the techniques of dream interpretation and divination used by the societies observed by ethnologists and missionaries to explain past crimes and anticipate the future. Witchcraft, he

*Participation* 113

says, relies on vigilant attention to the signs that distinguish a situation from the ordinary and explain it by the action of a sorcerer. Similarly, divination uses techniques such as playing cards or sticks, whose configuration indicates a direction for the future, for example whether to plant a field or go to war. Lévy-Bruhl asserted that these techniques escape the principle of contradiction, which is taught in republican schools and used by colonial administrators in trials where individuals are accused of witchcraft, and that they are based on a principle of participation, which makes it possible to assert that a subject can be both himself and other than himself.[62]

This analysis of participation is inscribed in Durkheim's sociological reflection on solidarity. The term appeared in the Third Republic debate to describe the ties binding individuals in the face of an evil that affects them in common, notably in the "solidarist" movement launched by Léon Bourgeois.[63] The Durkheimian school of sociology took up this term, following in the footsteps of Charles Renouvier's Kantian philosophy, to develop a formal conception of solidarity. Durkheim analyzed variations in the forms of societies to compare their emotional reactions to crime according to their demographic size and division of labor, as well as differences in their religious practices and representations. But, whereas Durkheim related these variations to an invariant, which is the "elementary form" of the court or temple in which punishment or sacrifice takes place, Lévy-Bruhl studied instead how they are experienced by individuals in feelings of participation. Whereas Durkheim related social variations to the categories of sacrifice, which give rise to the state as collective consciousness through the separation of the sacred from the profane, Lévy-Bruhl studied these variations for themselves, describing their "mystical" aspects, in the sense that they express "a force imperceptible to the senses and yet real."[64] Lévy-Bruhl thus foreshadows Grégoire Chamayou's and Achille Mbembe's analyses of cynegetic power as a capacity to see double entities in order to act on ghosts, while Durkheim prefigures Foucault's analyses

114    *Planetary health*

showing how the constraint of sovereign power is doubled by a pastoral power of benevolence.

Marc Bloch, who referred to Lucien Lévy-Bruhl when he and Lucien Febvre founded the "history of mentalities," also took up his concept of participation when, in June 1940, he analyzed the reasons why the French army was so ill prepared for the German attack.[65] This historian of the Middle Ages, who was enrolled in the French army as a supply, cantonment, and fuel distribution officer, took part in Resistance activities before being arrested and shot by the German army. Calling for "a great sweeping of the atmosphere," Bloch appealed to young people "to reform the intellectual preparation of the country, as well as the command of its armies."[66] For Bloch, the notion of atmosphere refers to the way in which a society thinks through ritual practices, such as the medieval rite known as *écrouelles* whereby the king cured the sick simply by touching them, or false rumors, such as those that circulated at the front during the First World War.[67] Preparing for war meant for Bloch perceiving the signs in a mental atmosphere polarized by the presence of the enemy, who may appear at any moment in unpredictable ways. "What a gift of imagination," writes Bloch, "would it not take to constantly keep in mind the realities underlying these signs (. . .) What gymnastics of cerebral flexibility, above all, would it not take to make the unforeseen, i.e. the enemy, a sufficiently large part of the picture?"[68] According to Bloch, the French army failed because it tried to predict the arrival of the enemy, by erecting barriers behind which the national territory would be protected. Preparing for war meant, on the contrary, perceiving the unpredictable through an effort of imagination and an attention to signs, because these go beyond the instituted forms of representation of the enemy.

Marc Bloch's *L'étrange défaite* (*The Strange Defeat*) can be compared with the book written by Léon Blum a year later, entitled *À l'échelle humaine* (*On a Human Scale*). The Socialist MP, disciple of Jaurès and President of the Front Populaire

## Participation 115

government in 1936–1937, was locked up in prison by the Vichy government led by Philippe Pétain. He prepared his arguments for the trial, which took place in Riom in 1942 and was interrupted by Adolf Hitler, marking Blum's triumph over Pétain. While the Right accused the Front Populaire of having ill prepared France for war by promoting paid vacations and a society of leisure rather than work, Blum showed that the Front Populaire had actually improved France's military situation, because it modernized an army maintained by Pétain in old patterns, thus responding to Jaurès' call to forge a "new army" facing social challenges. As early as 1941, with the entry of the United States and the Soviet Union into the global conflict, Blum foresaw the defeat of Hitler's Germany, and thought about the social organization of France after its liberation. But to do so, he had to confront a question: why couldn't the Socialists reorganize France after the defeat of 1941, as the Republicans had done under Gambetta's leadership in 1870, or as the "sacred union" had done in 1914 after the death of Jaurès? Blum refused to accept personal responsibility, and he responded to anti-Semitic and virilist accusations that blamed him for France's "weakness" in the face of Germany's "brutal" attacks. He declared at the Riom trial: "I see that I have prepared minds in France for this conception of French unity, which could have been, which should have been, as beautiful as it was during the first months of the 1914 war."[69]

According to Blum, who echoed Bloch's analyses, France's defeat in 1940 was due not only to errors of military strategy – a slow, heavy army retreated behind a wall, while a fast, light army broke through the barriers – but above all to a social and historical reason. The bourgeoisie, which fulfilled the revolutionary ideal in the nineteenth century by replacing the aristocracy in the leadership of the government, lost this guiding role, because it was so afraid of the workers that its fear of the German enemy was merely the by-product of this more fundamental fear of the class enemy. But the workers, instead of taking power, also gave in to fear by voting for reactionary or

116 *Planetary health*

conservative parties. According to Blum, what was needed was a moral regeneration of the workers, so that after the war they could regain their leading role through their legitimate representative, the Socialist Party. Only this party (then called the SFIO, Section Française de l'Internationale Ouvrière) could remain faithful to the spirit of the French Revolution, whereas the Communist Party, separated from the SFIO at the 1920 Tours Congress, was presented by Blum as a "foreign party," taking its orders from Moscow and defending the legacy of the Russian Revolution of 1917. The role of the Socialist Party, according to Blum, was to participate in government to prepare for the advent of a fairer social regime and to respond to the siren calls of fascism, a role that it continues to play in the face of the challenges of ecological transition and the rise of the far right in the social democracies.[70]

Claude Lévi-Strauss's analyses of "wild thought" can be understood as a response to this political problem of preparation, renewing analyses of participation with a new science of signs. Lévi-Strauss came from a conservative family who remembered Jaurès' involvement in the Dreyfus affair, and he was influenced by the planning ideas of Belgian socialism when he campaigned to be elected as a socialist deputy in the Landes region before the Second World War.[71] Claude Lévi-Strauss's entire intellectual trajectory can be read as a response to Bloch and Blum's appeal at the start of the war, as he drew on the sciences developed in the United States to rebuild French society after the war.

Cybernetics, on which Lévi-Strauss based his analysis of kinship systems, aimed to prepare American society for catastrophe by seeing each event as an opportunity to repeat a pre-existing order. Such a program is at the root not only of the cognitive sciences, as a project to reduce the diversity of human societies to the structures of the brain, but also of management techniques called "contingency planning," which ritually reaffirm the principles of a social organization at a time when they are questioned by the event.[72] This plan-

## Participation 117

ning vision of social order is based on the use of perforated maps representing cities in terms of their potential targets, enabling the construction of urban knowledge based on the computerized comparison of vulnerabilities in cities.[73] Lévi-Strauss used this method to transform his drawings on the social organization of Amazonian societies into cards that could be compared with those of other societies in a large paper database, now digitized.[74] He used statistics, then in full transformation, to formalize complex kinship systems and propose a unified theory of social order based on the "structural unconscious."[75]

Lévi-Strauss's shift from the analysis of kinship systems to that of myth groups led to a singular inflexion in his anthropology. Whereas the study of kinship aimed to describe a form of group aggregation that would be the equivalent in unwritten societies of what statistics produce (hence a pre-modern form of biopolitics), the study of myths aims to formalize a "logic of the sensible" that can be read in the classifications of animals and plants by indigenous peoples, which had been devalued by Western science. This marks a major turn in Lévi-Strauss's thinking, from cybernetic positivism to catastrophist skepticism. The problem is no longer how to involve indigenous peoples in the socialist ideal of the French Revolution, according to the conception shared by Lévy-Bruhl, Bloch, and Blum, but how to preserve the signs of life of these societies destroyed by the expansion of European societies and the extraction of their natural resources. This conception can be described as "cryopolitical," following the analyses of Kowal and Radin, since it is carried out in museums, laboratories, zoological parks, and nature reserves, where the living is "frozen" on the threshold between life and death. Through a modern transformation of what Chamayou and Mbembe have called "cynegetic power," Lévi-Strauss describes forms of thought in societies of hunters who live in a permanent state of war against their human and non-human enemies, and who, caught up in a permanent process of dissolution

## 118 *Planetary health*

and recomposition, are constantly reinventing the social order through the exchange and communication of signs. The problem posed by Lévi-Strauss is how the cryopolitics of museums can do for hunting societies, in a horizon marked by ecological crisis, what the anthropology of kinship had to achieve in a socialist horizon: manifest the ideal of justice through the diversity of its social forms.

This scientific and political journey through the two world wars of the twentieth century sheds light on Claude Lévi-Strauss's 1996 text on the "wisdom lesson of mad cows," which I believe should be taken as the basis for a politics of zoonoses in the era of pandemic viruses and planetary health. This text, which appeared in Italian in 1996 in the newspaper *La Repubblica*, the day after the British government revealed cases of Bovine Spongiform Encephalopathy in humans, comments on the claim that "mad cows," who had consumed animal meal and then transmitted the prion that causes nerve degeneration, were "cannibals." Such a qualification could mean that nature would take revenge for the perversion of the industrial system, which had transformed domesticated animals into monsters, and that humans could only respond to this revenge by mass slaughter of sick animals, according to the pastoral rationality of sacrifice.[76] More subtly, however, Lévi-Strauss argues that European societies should treat their cows in the same way as the so-called cannibal societies of Amazonia treat the animals of the forest: they would release them back into the wild, where they would be hunted, and they would keep some of them as domestic partners and as agents for "monitoring energy sources and machines."[77] In this technological utopia, which Lévi-Strauss takes from Auguste Comte, "cannibal cows" occupy an intermediate position between the human society and animals returned to the wild.[78] Lévi-Strauss thus replaces the modern tripartition between the civilized, the domesticated, and the savage with an Amerindian tripartition between the human, the humanized animal, and the animal reservoir.[79]

*Participation*                                    119

What first appears to be the musings of an anthropologist observing European societies through his "view from afar" is indeed a powerful proposal to reintroduce cynegetic power when sovereign power and pastoral power fail to make sense of the zoonoses caused by an increasingly meaningless industrial system. This text, inspired by Michel de Montaigne and Jean-Jacques Rousseau, goes far beyond a wisdom lesson on the compassion that the slaughter of "cannibal cows" arouses in European spectators. It also echoes Immanuel Kant's *Was ist Aufklärung?*, in which Michel Foucault saw the first philosophical reflection of the Enlightenment movement that transformed European societies at the end of the eighteenth century.[80] Kant defined the Enlightenment as the possible shift for every human being, thanks to education and discussion, from a minor use of reason in the private sphere to a major use in the public sphere. In the same way, Lévi-Strauss distinguishes between a utilitarian use of every living being for the purposes of yield and an aesthetic use for the purposes of conservation. He sees in the industrial and political revolution of the late eighteenth century an extension to all areas of life of this distinction that emerged with the Neolithic revolution. In a cynegetic reversal of Kant's analysis, Lévi-Strauss defines the Enlightenment as a passage from "wild thought" to "domesticated thought," which enables him to reformulate the critical question at the time of ecological crises.

Perhaps one day, the "mad cow crisis" will hold as important a place in the history of European emancipation as the French Revolution, in that it forced humans to extend the Enlightenment to all living beings.[81] We would thus understand why Claude Lévi-Strauss, who commented as little on current affairs as Immanuel Kant, published on this crisis two articles, which can be compared to the famous *Was ist Aufklärung?* Taking up the lessons of "cannibal societies" on the relations between humans and animals, and proposing to release animals into the wild and keep some for machine monitoring, Lévi-Strauss places the techniques of the "virus

120 *Planetary health*

hunters," which were then implemented in the U.S.A. and China, within a long history of animal domestication and of the indigenous knowledge that remains available to limit its damage. The "wild" is not what domestication has taken us away from, and which would always threaten to return through pathogenic viruses, but a reserve of signs from which all societies can draw, whatever their position on a scale of "civilization," "progress," or "development," to mitigate the consequences of unlimited productive growth. French socialism, transformed by Lévi-Strauss through social anthropology, combining Eastern European linguistics and Northern American cybernetics, then led him to integrate into the ideal of solidarity inherited from the French Revolution the diversity of signs that humans produce in their relations with animals and plants to prepare for catastrophes.[82]

Lévi-Strauss thus encourages us to think of solidarity as an ideal form to be achieved, rather than as a given thing to be studied. He breaks with a substantialist conception of solidarity, which describes the links between living beings in the face of an external evil, to build a formalist conception of solidarity, which analyzes the chains of signals at different scales of living beings to transmit ambivalent information. I will now develop this conception by using the immunological concept of the sentinel. Since it articulates pandemic preparedness and the participation of living beings in an ideal of planetary solidarity, the politics of zoonoses redefines the notions of immunity, conceived of as defending the organism against pathogenic microbes perceived as enemies in a fight for life, and sentinel, conceived of as carrying early warning signals on the boundary between the organism and what is external to it. In what way, then, can the sentinel appear as a figure of emancipation in the age of pandemic viruses?

# 6

# Sentinels:
# Building a new form of solidarity

## 6.a The frontiers of the immune system

Discussions of the notion of biopolitics after its revival by Michel Foucault have often focused on the notion of immunity.[1] This enables us to understand how power in European societies moved from sovereignty over a land to security over a territory, from the moment when sanitary techniques such as vaccination enabled it to act on its population as closely as possible to life itself, and not just to defend it against enemies on a frontier. Immunity is in fact both a military and a sanitary concept, which places it at the point of transition from sovereign power to biopolitics, where biopolitics can again and again tip over into sovereign power. I will show, however, that it also engages what I call cynegetic power and cryopolitics, and that it redefines the social body from boundaries that are not only political and territorial, but also specific and ontological.

The previous discussion of the links between preparedness and participation in social democracy shows that the register of war used by sovereign power, when it declares that the pandemic virus is an enemy from which the nation must be protected on its borders, and by pastoral power, when it asks populations for a sacrifice in the face of such a threat, is also compatible with a cynegetic power, which watches for signs of the enemy's presence at the edge of the territory by taking its perspective. "Virus hunters" use the notion of sentinel for pandemic preparedness in this sense, to describe a site for early detection of warning signals. By drawing on the register of sensitivity and feeling, the notion of sentinel inscribes pandemic preparedness into a shared experience, and allows individuals to participate in governmental forms of preparedness.

The term "immunity" first had a legal meaning in ancient Rome: it referred to citizens who were relieved of the obligations imposed on all (*municipia*) or to soldiers who stayed behind in battle.[2] As a specialist of literature, Ed Cohen goes back to this etymology, comparing the Roman conception of the body as a reserve of property to be defended against an enemy with the Native American conception of the body as a gift to be received from nature.[3] In 1852, Dr. Chrestien, a disciple of Broussais' vitalism at the Montpellier School of Medicine, defined "morbid immunity" as "the faculty of often resisting the diseases that surround us on all sides (. . .) This exemption is due to a force of resistance more or less inherent in life."[4] Claude Bernard's research on diabetes later showed that the organism, which he defined as an "interior milieu," is a dangerous environment for the individual himself. Claude Bernard considered the organism as a set of physiological functions, using an experimental method that varies its elements in order to observe its reactions and control its pathologies. Louis Pasteur, by applying this method to plant, animal, and human microbes, made it possible to extend the use of vaccination. He devised methods for attenuating virulence, thus fabricating immunity in the laboratory, but he failed to explain immunity, and he had to rely on Élie Metchnikoff to do so.[5]

Historian Anne-Marie Moulin recalls that two conceptions of immunity collided at the turn of the twentieth century: the chemical theory developed in Germany and the biological theory developed in France. Virchow described immunity as an inflammation of cells, using dyes to track the cells that come to the point of infection, notably the globules present in pus formation. This theory corresponds to the democratic orientation of Virchow, the first thinker of social medicine

## The frontiers of the immune system 123

in Germany, who wrote: "We no longer regard blood cells as gendarmes commanded by the state police to escort unwanted foreigners and those without passports back to the border."[6] Élie Metchnikoff, trained in Ukraine through a socialist reading of Darwin, challenged this democratic vision by observing a phenomenon he called "phagocytosis": the digestion by the body's own cells of a foreign body. By distinguishing between microphages (the white blood cells that "eat" the intruders) and macrophages (the cells that "eat the leftovers"), Metchnikoff proposed a first theory of the immune system, in the sense of a hierarchy between cells endowed with different functions in response to a threat. "It's not only the blood that is equipped with a kind of surveillance," he wrote. "(. . .) In the organism of man and the majority of animals, there is a whole system of such guardians, always represented by different species of phagocytes."[7] Metchnikoff conceived of generalized surveillance in the cooperation of cells with each other in the face of an enemy perceived on the other side of the organism's frontier, for, unlike the nervous system, which reports information to a center, the brain, the immune system must coordinate the vital reaction throughout the organism in a decentralized way.[8]

While Metchnikoff's pupils at the Institut Pasteur, such as Jules Bordet, were pushing his hypotheses on phagocytosis, Koch's pupils, taking up Virchow's principles, were pushing the hypothesis of cell-to-cell communication. In 1891, Paul Ehrlich coined the concept of antibodies to describe receptors that attach themselves to cells and direct them within the organism, regulating its reaction. Whereas Pasteur's line of research was based on cell observation, Virchow's line of research proposed a chemical method for classifying antibodies. The notion of the immune system really took shape in the middle of the twentieth century, integrating these two lines of research. Two English-trained biologists, the Australian Frank Macfarlane Burnet and the Lebanese Peter Medawar, were awarded the Nobel Prize in 1960 for their work in embryology

124                           *Sentinels*

and transplant pathology, which showed how cells specialize over time through a form of intolerance to other cells. Burnet formalized this observation through what he called the "theory of clonal selection," showing that the organism acquires over time the ability to distinguish between self and non-self in the set of cells it encounters.[9] Burnet applied the same reasoning to ecosystems, which he conceived of as balanced assemblages disrupted by external pathogens conceived as invasive species.[10] The making of the immune system was described by Burnet as an evolutionary progression from hunter cells developing large quantities of antibodies to catch viruses, to the domestication of viruses through antigens recognized by the immune system.

Is it possible to conceive of such a system of cell-to-cell communication other than through the virilist and militarist model of reinforcing self-defence systems? This question, posed by feminist biologists in the 1990s,[11] was answered within immunology through the distinction between innate and acquired immune systems, which earned Jules Hoffman, Bruce Beutler, and Ralph Steinmann the Nobel Prize in 2011. While the first two studied innate immunity in insects and mice, the third studied the role of "dendritic" cells in the formation of acquired immunity.[12] These cells, which sprout arms or "dendrites" analogous to synapses in the brain, and are distributed throughout the body, possess hundreds of sensors that detect specific proteins in pathogens, and receptors that can attach to other immune cells (B cells, T cells, macrophages, NK cells . . .). By attaching themselves to other cells in this way, they exchange chemical molecules called cytokines and chemokines, which trigger a signaling cascade described as "inflammation," a normal process by which the body processes and regulates abnormal information.[13] Some virologists explain the lethality of zoonotic viruses such as H5N1 or SARS-Cov by the fact that they bypass or "lure" dendritic cells, leading other immune cells to trigger an excessive signaling cascade, called a "cytokine storm."[14] In this case,

*The frontiers of the immune system* 125

inflammation, an adaptive reaction to the arrival of unfamiliar biological information through a slight rise in fever, becomes a veritable panic: it leads the organism to die not from this biological information, which seeks only to reproduce itself in the host, but from its inability to process it in a regulated manner.[15]

Anthropologist David Napier has described these recent advances in immunology with reference to his own research into the treatment of HIV/AIDS on the island of Bali in Indonesia. He underlines the analogies between the biomedical conception of this pathology, according to which immunity produces a multiplicity of antibodies that come to meet viruses to capture their information, and the conception of Javanese societies, according to which one must wear a mask in social interactions to be attentive to the ambivalence of the signs that link appearances to invisible entities.[16] Napier points out that when Descartes presented himself as a "masked philosopher" in order to found modernity on consciousness revealed to itself, he took up an animist technique of seeing himself from the perspective of the enemy – the Evil Genius who deceives the Cogito – and transformed viral appearance into a resource for the construction of his sovereignty.[17]

Through this animistic perspective, the immune system is similar to a "search engine" in the computer sense, as it searches for the right antibody for each antigen, and can go off the rails if the information doesn't suit it and multiplies virally. Cartesian consciousness is no longer a point of reference to regulate this information economy, since it is itself the product of a process of mask duplication, which Napier compares to "reverse engineering," a method by which DNA is made from available pieces of RNA sequence.[18] According to Napier, immunology, far from supporting neo-liberal visions of individuals competing in risk-taking enterprises, and of a state guaranteeing their safety through the police, shows that culture is constituted in a relationship of curiosity between living beings and the outside world, which must be protected by social institutions maintaining a reservoir of possibilities not exploited by individuals.[19] Napier recalls that Élie Metchnikoff's theory was influential when soldiers returned from the trenches in 1918. "The avant-gardes, which were military before they were artistic, were formed on the idea that when you get out of the trenches, you can find information: if you go too far, you don't come back, but if you don't go far enough, you learn nothing!"[20] Immunity, thought of from the island of Bali, where the refinement of cultural forms is inseparable from constant attention to the war between visible and invisible entities, thus links invention and protection in a permanent dynamic of exploration of the environment by the living organism.

I arrived at a similar hypothesis through my investigation of bird 'flu in southern China. The "virus hunters" I worked with apply the notion of sentinel to the immune cells who capture the information of microbes on the boundaries of the organism, but also to the territory of Hong Kong, which they consider an outpost of global health in the face of a Chinese governement they suspect of concealing its outbreaks. Hong Kong's Department of Agriculture veterinarians also use this term for poultry, which farmers leave as unvaccinated so that they show the first signs of avian influenza viruses: these are "sentinel chickens," or literally in Chinese, "whistling soldier chickens" (*shaobingji*). The sentinel is therefore not just a metaphor for thinking of human territories in terms of the body's defenses, but a real relationship between humans and animals: it's a living being exposed to a zoonosis and bearing the early warning signals before that zoonosis spreads to all living beings. By introducing virus-hunting techniques into poultry farms, the "sentinel chicken" is a relational operator situated at the crossroads of cynegetic and pastoral power, but also at the crossroads between the individual organism and the political organism.

Immunology has used the notion of sentinel over the last twenty years, while it was gaining ground in ecological knowl-

*Remembering the signs of the past*  127

edge, to think about the ways in which territories are exposed to threats: pandemics, global warming, species extinction, nuclear radiation, chemical pollution ... This notion must be distinguished from other ways of thinking about future threats, such as the Jewish prophet, the Roman oracle, the medieval herald or the statistical indicator of liberal societies, because the sentinel is anchored at the borders of a territory whose vulnerabilities it reveals through early warning signals.[21]

While this notion takes up surveillance techniques that have a long history in European societies, it is also part of a recent colonial history, during which Europe built sentinel posts across the globe to detect threats that might hinder its occupation of the globe. The challenge in a post-colonial world is to understand how these sentinel posts can be reappropriated by non-European societies to inject non-modern ways of thinking. To do this, we need to understand how the sentinel has transformed cynegetic power in modern times.[22]

## 6.b Remembering the signs of the past to prepare for future disasters

The history of immunology has enabled me to construct the notion of the sentinel through recent scientific research and its geopolitical implications in southern China for the preparation of pandemics of zoonotic origin. But I give this notion a broader meaning based on an anthropology of hunter-gatherer societies and a philosophy of life itself. I would therefore like to conclude my analysis by clarifying the concept of the sentinel in the light of two philosophers (Henri Bergson and Michel Foucault) and two anthropologists (Lucien Lévy-Bruhl and Claude Lévi-Strauss) who have been central to my reflection on this notion. If these are four French men living in the twentieth century, it doesn't mean that the male gender and the French way of life are necessary to think about sentinels. It means that France is a local space in which the experience of the modern revolution has been reflected in ways I believe

## 128 *Sentinels*

should inform our global experience of sentinels within a horizon of emancipation. I define modernity as an effort to extend to all living beings the forms of consciousness that the philosopher René Descartes defined in the sixteenth century for the scientific rationality that was emerging.[23] This effort took place in France through a political revolution, but it was an extension of the industrial revolution in England, and was oriented toward the ideal of justice by German philosophy, in a way that has been borrowed and subverted in the rest of the world over the last two centuries.

Henri Bergson used the tools of philosophy to answer the question that experimental biology and chemistry posed at the beginning of the twentieth century when they discovered the phenomenon of antibodies: how does the past exist in the body in the form of memory traces? If preserving the past in memory enables the body to act on things and open up possibilities for the future, how does the mode of existence of the past differ from that of things? In *Matière et mémoire* (*Matter and Memory*, 1896), Bergson discussed the psychology of the brain, then in full development in France and Germany, but immunology confirmed ten years later his thesis of the reality of the mind proven by its capacity for anticipation: because things are indeed movements, the mind, which is a trace of movements in the brain, can act in return on things.[24] But immunology also makes it possible to question the most fragile point of Bergson's philosophy: the privilege he gives to personal consciousness, what he calls the "deep self,"[25] and which is due to the central role of the brain in his demonstration of the reality of the mind. In *L'évolution créatrice* (*Creative Evolution*, 1907), Bergson described the way in which the "vital impulse" (*élan vital*) diffracts into a plurality of living species. He asserts that humanity stands at the tip of one of these branches, where mankind becomes aware of itself, while microbes multiply on another branch.[26] While he lucidly recognized that humanity was not the sole purpose of living things, and that microbes, with their greater capacity for adaptation, would undoubtedly outlive humanity, Bergson ignored recent discoveries in immunology, which showed that without the microbes that enable our organism to adapt to a changing environment, we would probably not have a conscious life.[27]

The essential contribution of Bergson's philosophy is placing at the center of anthropology the principle of thermodynamics, formulated a century earlier by Sadi Carnot: if the quantity of energy in a system necessarily decreases, life can be defined as the creation of new forms that reverses this tendency, so that humanity must balance these two tendencies to destruction and creation.[28] In *Les deux sources de la morale et de la religion* (*The Two Sources of Morality and Religion*, 1932), Bergson considers the conditions under which human societies can move from the "closed" to the "open," from war between groups to universal democracy; he thus echoes Kant's observations on the driving role of the French Revolution in the realization of democratic ideals.[29] He notes that the war that had just taken place was caused by population growth: this pushed peasants off their land and into industry, where they found themselves as "internal emigrants,"[30] and produced new needs for "comfort, amusement and luxury,"[31] leading to excessive consumption of fuel and raw materials.

Bergson suggested that the League of Nations, whose creation he strongly supported,[32] should take measures to limit the demographic increase. "What if our life were to become more ascetic?"[33] To answer this question, Bergson formulated two "biological laws" of history: the "law of dichotomy," according to which history splits into two "tendencies which began by being two photographic views of one and the same tendency,"[34] and the "law of double frenzy," according to which humanity goes to the end of one vital tendency before turning to the opposite tendency. After praising simplicity and vegetarianism, Bergson reminds his reader that "machinism," whose detrimental effects on workers' bodies were highlighted by many of his contemporaries, is historically linked to the spirit of democracy through the legacy of the encyclopedists of the

130 *Sentinels*

eighteenth century.[35] He concludes that we must always combine "the mechanical" and "the mystical," the construction of machines to relieve humans of hunger and the call of a great soul to carry them toward more democracy. Bergson's last book famously ends with an exhortation to convert pleasure into joy, and to "make just the extra effort required for fulfilling, even on their refractory planet, the essential function of the universe, which is a machine for the making of gods."[36]

This book played a major role in the post-war humanities in France.[37] Indeed, it confronted philosophy with the human sciences to reflect on the relations between life and power. Bergson draws on the ethnology of Lucien Lévy-Bruhl and the psychology of William James to criticize Émile Durkheim's sociology for basing morality on a sense of obligation. This notion plays a central role in Durkheimian sociology, as it designates both the inner feeling of constraint that the individual receives from an external source of rules, "society," and the desire the individual feels to relate to others through these rules. Bergson notes that obligation is both what awakens the most archaic memories in humanity, as shown by the biblical story of the "forbidden fruit,"[38] and what occupies a very restricted function in moral life, when human actions are formatted in a rule by a prohibition and a sanction. According to Bergson, the greater part of our moral life follows habits within the framework of a restricted group, and sometimes opens up to the call of a genius or a hero who carries us toward the whole of humanity. Intelligence projects these two sources of morality into an intermediate space between the "closed" and the "open," that of speculative intelligence, which is mobilized by Kantian and utilitarian morality when they aim to rationally justify the rules of social life.

The book's two central chapters examine how this moral distinction between habit and appeal, between the closed and the open, operates in the mental life of humanity. Bergson discusses Lévy-Bruhl's theory of "primitive mentality" to show that the hunter, when invoking the spirit of his prey, compen-

*Remembering the signs of the past*     131

sates for the margin of uncertainty in his action by prolonging it with an intention.[39] He then draws on James's psychology to show that mystics, when faced with a catastrophic event such as an earthquake, are able to personalize this event by seeing it as a familiar sign of a divine presence. The difference between the primitive hunter and the mystical genius, says Bergson, is that the former resorts only to fragmentary entities to personalize animals and plants, because he remains caught up in the circle of his society, whereas the latter resorts to complete entities because he (or she, as many creative mystics are women) recovers contact with the vital impulse.[40]

It could well be said, then, that Bergson combines sovereign power, pastoral power, and cynegetic power in a way that anticipates the genealogy of techniques of power proposed by Foucault. His critique of obligation is a critique of sovereignty: it targets a conception of power that is exercised over a limited territory through the application of a rule common to all men and formulated by intelligence. His description of "static religion" is an analysis of what hunters do when they attribute ghostly personalities to animals and plants. His praise of "dynamic religion" is a genealogy of pastoral power, since the great mystics express their love of God by building convents where they invent new rules for living together, through which God acts in each person in a singular way.[41] Bergson thus splits the sovereign obligation between the "fabulatory function" of hunting societies – i.e. their ability to tell stories to "insure against fear" – and the institutional creation of the great shepherds of humanity – capable of taking humanity beyond the forms of life already in use – in the same way as he splits the vital impulse between the "mechanical" and the "mystical." It could be said, then, that Bergson's entire philosophy is a reflection on "cryopolitics," showing how, by diffracting into a plurality of tendencies, life warms up what may appear to intelligence as species frozen in a conservatory, and transforms differences of degrees into differences of nature.[42]

132                           *Sentinels*

Bringing Bergson's philosophical anthropology into line with Foucault's genealogy of forms of power is more than just a formal game, since both were confronted with the problem posed by Friedrich Nietzsche at the end of the nineteenth century: if humanity is a living species endowed with consciousness, how can biological knowledge shed light on the political and moral problems it poses? Foucault borrows Nietzsche's genealogical method, which, far from projecting a biological ideology like that of Social Darwinism onto humanity, follows the proliferation of discourses and power mechanisms to identify alternatives within life itself, and thus offers affordances for critical thinking.[43] Foucault takes up Nietzsche's critique of consciousness as the basis of morality to radicalize his conception of life as a set of forms, in the moment when structuralism takes hold in mathematics, biology, and anthropology. In *Les mots et les choses* (*The Order of Things*, 1966), Foucault draws on the concept of the structural unconscious developed by Lévi-Strauss and Lacan to recount a history of sciences that narrates not the progress of a collective conscious subject, but a succession of systems of thought, which he calls *episteme*. The genealogical method enables Bergson and Foucault to place Kant's transcendental subject within the history of humanity as a living species on a finite planet. For both Bergson and Foucault, if systems of thought and forms of power are frozen views on a vital impulse, or blocks of ice in the middle of an ocean of discourse,[44] the role of philosophy is to escape from the fossilized forms of thought and power in an effort to return to "life itself" plunging back into its icy waters to warm it up.

How, then, can we explain Foucault's shift from one system of thought to another? In this book, I have shown that Foucault thinks of historical transformations through the schema of doubling. The human body is split by instances of power through tests or ordeals (*épreuves*), as when the body of the possessed woman caught up in pastoral power in the eighteenth century is split between the disciplinary subject

*Remembering the signs of the past* 133

and the biopolitics of the population in the nineteenth century. Foucault follows these diabolical splits with a malicious pleasure, reconstructing a history of the Western subject not as the progress of a consciousness, but as constituted on the thresholds between the devices of knowledge and power that have succeeded one another in the West. Indeed, life itself can be perceived as a test or an ordeal through which individuals produce knowledge about themselves as social subjects.[45] Foucault's entire work is therefore concerned with this philosophical question: how does the history of forms of subjectivity transform human relationship to truth and justice?

In his 1979–1980 lecture at the Collège de France entitled *Le gouvernement des vivants* (*The Government of the Living*), Foucault analyzed the techniques of subjectivation associated with the production of truth. He compared "ancient wisdoms," from Sophocles' *Oedipus-King* to Seneca's letters, with "Christian spirituality," based on the writings of Tertullian and Cassian. Whereas for the Greeks and Romans, the subject constructs one's self in relation to truth through a public account of one's actions, which splits him or her into a series of actors exposed before a supreme judge, for the early Christians, the subject does so through a private account of his or her faults, which splits him or her before an inner tribunal. These narratives take two forms, penitence in Tertullian and the direction of conscience in Cassian, which seem to prefigure pastoral and sovereign power in the classical age. Indeed, Tertullian was the first to see Christian baptism not as the attainment of a perfect life, but as a preparation for death through the recognition of a sinful life. He transforms "the fear of destiny, the fear of decrees and of the gods" into a "fear of oneself, the fear of what one is."[46] Origen, following Tertullian, thus distinguishes between two baptisms: that which the Christian receives during lifetime, and that which he or she receives at the moment of his or her death, the first being merely the preparation for the second, which gives access to perfect

134 *Sentinels*

life. "Mortification and the struggle against the enemy" thus become the condition of the Christian's entire life, through "constant tests of truth": "to keep watch on ourselves, to bring the truth itself into us, and to those who look on us, who keep watch on us, judge us and guide us, to the pastors therefore, we have to offer the truth of what we are."[47]

Cassian's technique of "conscience direction" differs from pastoral power in that one individual hands over his or her will to another, so as to move toward truth and perfection through obedience and contrition.[48] According to Foucault, the theme of the apocalypse at the end of the Middle Ages introduces a tension into pastoral power, since the return of Christ signifies the end of the power of the shepherd who has received the delegation.[49] We can therefore assume that sovereign power was invented at the beginning of the Classical Age in response to this apocalyptic discourse, by adopting the techniques of conscience direction to guarantee the security of citizens within a closed territory and no longer, like pastoral power, over a moving flock. Indeed, Foucault points out that when Descartes defines the modern subject as a thinking substance, paving the way for Hobbes' metaphysical definition of sovereign power, he extracts the technique of conscience direction from the pastoral power with which it was entangled, since the Cogito escapes the temptation of the Devil and the doubt of the Evil Genius, to hand it over to sovereign power.[50] Whereas monastic narratives used to model relations between humans on relations between animals – for example, when monks compare themselves to roosters watching over the henhouse to prevent the Devil from entering[51] – and while pastoral knowledge was based on an attention to the hierarchy within the flock – the shepherd used to rely on the leading sheep rather than on a dog trained to relay human authority[52] – techniques for the direction of conscience leave room only for relations between humans and God, with animals gradually becoming things under the gaze of the sovereign.[53] Preparing for death no longer implies watching over the animals, but seeing in

*Remembering the signs of the past*    135

God: sovereign power requalifies all things through the possibility of its intervention.

In his last lecture at the Collège de France, entitled *Le courage de la vérité* (*The Courage of Truth*), Foucault returned to pastoral power, analyzing for the first time its relations with a real animal, the rooster, rather than a metaphorical animal like sheep in his previous analyses. He refers to a book by Georges Dumézil,[54] which comments on Socrates' last sentence according to Plato's account in the *Phaedo*: "Crito, we owe a cock to Aesculapius." According to Foucault, Socrates is not offering a sacrifice to thank Aesculapius for having cured him of the disease of life, as interpreted by Nietzsche; he is not remembering an illness he had in his life, as interpreted by Wilamowitz; he is not asking the rooster to guide him to hell, as interpreted by Cumont: he is telling his disciples that they must continue to care for their souls even after his death. This interpretation leads Foucault to translate one of Socrates' sentences not, as is customary, "We are in prison" or "We are in a military surveillance post" but "We are on a sentinel post."[55] As the prison where Socrates and Crito converse is a place where pastoral power is exercised, Foucault concludes that the disease for which Socrates owes a rooster to Aesculapius is the disease that Socrates tried to cure in his conversation with Crito, as it liberated him from opinion and built his own relationship to truth. Sacrifice to the god establishes a continuity between the care that humans take of themselves, in their relationship to truth, and the solicitude of the gods toward humans. "It was precisely out of concern for us," says Foucault, "that they sent Socrates to teach us to take care of ourselves."[56] In this sense, pastoral power can be defined by the test that all human beings undergo following Socrates: "to make people live and accept death."

What does it mean to consider Socrates, the founder of Western philosophy, as a sentinel, rather than as a subject who sacrifices himself to trigger self-consciousness?[57] In this book, I have showed that this means adding to sovereign power and

136 *Sentinels*

pastoral power, through which Foucault analyzes the long-term transformations of the Western subject, a cynegetic power that extends Foucault's genealogy beyond Western societies. To do this, I have drawn on the two French anthropologists who took up this philosophical question: Lucien Lévy-Bruhl and Claude Lévi-Strauss. Both studied how "savage" or "primitive" societies developed ways of thinking about their environment that eluded domestication by "modern" or "civilized" societies. This method has been criticized as a "Great Divide" resulting from Europe's colonization of the rest of the world.[58] But for them, it was more a question of understanding how the threshold between the wild and the domestic was made elsewhere than in capitalist societies, where it is submitted to objectives of performance, and thus of questioning, in the wake of their socialist commitment, how it could realize the ideal of truth and justice within a horizon of emancipation. The concept of sentinel, which Lévy-Bruhl and Lévi-Strauss do not use as such, enables us to analyze this threshold between the wild and the domestic where the sentinel perceives warning signals of future events.

Lucien Lévy-Bruhl defended a thesis on responsibility at the Sorbonne in 1884, in which he analyzed non-modern forms of justice, at a time when the French Republic was sending defendants of the Commune to New Caledonia.[59] He was also cousin by marriage to Alfred Dreyfus, the French officer accused by the General Staff (*Etat-Major*) of treason because he was Jewish, and who survived the penal colony of Cayenne, in French Guiana, only to testify on his return to his innocence and to colonial violence.[60] Jean Psichari, a specialist of Greek languages and Ernest Renan's son-in-law, wrote a public letter to Alfred Dreyfus in 1898: "Every Frenchman should be grateful to you. You have been there like a soldier at his post. As an advanced sentinel, you have seen the day of justice finally dawn."[61] This letter is part of a series of interventions, notably by Lucien Herr, Émile Durkheim, and Jean Jaurès, aimed at presenting Dreyfus and his defender in the

*Remembering the signs of the past*     137

army, Colonel Picquart, as the bearers of a new military ethics formed by the republican culture of letters and sciences, and not by the hereditary virtues defended by an aristocracy perceived as decadent and degenerate.[62] Dreyfus, who came from the emancipated Jewish petty bourgeoisie,[63] thus appeared to his defenders as a sentinel of the ideal of truth and justice, able to regenerate not only the French army but also the university and public health by perceiving in advance the signs of justice to come.

We can thus understand the affinities that developed between Durkheimian sociology and Pasteurian microbiology in the wake of the Dreyfus Affair. Their aim, using ethnographic data on the most diverse societies and experimental methods applied in the laboratory, was to study the signs through which the health of the organism is regulated. This is why Lévy-Bruhl studied techniques for anticipating the future, such as divination and oneiromancy, which are not based on a mechanical conception of phenomena. Lévy-Bruhl takes up Nicolas Malebranche's conception of participation, according to which second causality is the opportunity for first causality (God, according to Malebranche, society, according to Lévy-Bruhl) to make itself visible in the accidents of sensible life.[64] To participate, in this perspective, is to see behind things an invisible force that makes them foreseeable but never makes itself visible, which we can call, to reconcile Malebranche's theology and Lévy-Bruhl's anthropology, an ideal of justice and truth whose value is universal even if its realizations are variable.

Claude Lévi-Strauss continued this movement, drawing on the structural linguistics he discovered while in exile in New York. Semiotics, defined by Saussure as a science of the life of signs, enabled him, as he put it in his "Introduction to the work of Marcel Mauss," to stop looking for the social origin of the symbolic – as Durkheim still did, by deriving social life from a founding sacrifice – and instead look for the symbolic origin of the social. Lévi-Strauss thus proposed a new alliance

138 *Sentinels*

between social anthropology and molecular biology, by analyzing the codes through which the most diverse human societies create order differently according to their environment, based on a small number of universal structures. Lévi-Strauss thus responded to the problem of war, which indirectly affected him since it forced him into exile as a result of laws targeting the Jews of France, with a conception of immunity close to that proposed by Metchnikoff: not a defense of life against an enemy, but a chain of signals designed to interpret ambivalent information.

Lévi-Strauss himself described his experience of war, in the opening of his ethnographic narrative *Tristes tropiques*, published in 1954, with a strange sentence that seems to link modern forms of power to the techniques of hunter-gatherer societies: "I already felt like game for concentration camps."[65] His entire anthropology aims to show that the thought of hunter-gatherer societies, preserved in museums and libraries in the form of signs, can re-found modern societies on a new theory of social exchange. If Lévy-Bruhl thought of sentinels as part of a cynegetic power, where signs of the future duplicate living bodies, Lévi-Strauss thinks of them as part of cryopolitics, since the signs carried by sentinels can be preserved in institutions to become legible. For these two French Jewish anthropologists, the sentinel is inseparable from an experience of the emancipation of Judaism in the Republic, formulated in an 1885 pamphlet preserved at the Universal Israelite Alliance: "When you open a cage full of birds accustomed to slavery, they don't all take flight at the same time."[66] We can thus understand why these two anthropologists were fascinated by the way of thinking of the Bororo people of Amazonia, who affirm in their rituals that they "are" Ara parrots.[67]

The sentinel is the living being who perceives warning signals on the boundary between the wild and the domestic, a boundary that varies from one society to another, but which gives rise to forms of anticipation that re-enact the ideal of

*Remembering the signs of the past* 139

living together. This is the first step in a chain of signals that is increasingly formalized through the figures of the whistle-blower and the expert.[68] It is the result of a capacity for vigilance distributed to all living beings, which does not presuppose self-consciousness. We think of sentinels today from our experience of soldiers who have been patrolling public spaces to exercise vigilance against terrorist threats for a quarter of a century, but the concept of vigilance has a longer genealogy: it comes from the experience of the Communards who, in preparation for the Prussian army's attack on Paris, elaborated the collective forms of the ideal of truth and justice.[69] All over the world, there are territories where the military logic of the sentinel is subverted by new forms of attention to living beings and vigilance against environmental threats. In France, the movement entitled "Soulèvements de la terre" (Uprising of the Earth), resonating with mobilizations in defense of the environment against extractivist projects around the world, taught us that the ideal of truth and justice does not only unfold in the sky of ideas and in the space of the courts: it is at work in territories where citizens are inventing new forms of living together. Sentinels of zoonoses are on the front lines of this struggle.[70]

# Conclusion:
# Environmental pathologies, animal studies, and the critique of capitalism

By questioning the forms of domestication that humans underwent during the Covid-19 pandemic, this book came to ask a seemingly strange question: does the integration of animals into globalized monitoring systems of zoonoses contribute to their emancipation? It has mobilized the concept of biopolitics to think about the "animal question," which at the start of this century has perhaps replaced the "social question" that was central to political thinking over the previous two centuries, in such a way that "animal studies" have emerged as a growing field added to, and sometimes competing with, social sciences. Taking as a starting point not the legal categories imposed by the state, but the surveillance practices disseminated by experts, this book has started from Michel Foucault's reappraisal of the term "biopolitics" to analyze relations between knowledge and power, and to reformulate the modern problem of emancipation. This problem, from the perspective of biopolitics, is not to determine whether living beings can become aware of their alienation and claim rights for themselves within a just society, but to study how they participate in several regimes of knowledge and power in which forms of subjectivation are possible faced with the ambivalent information carried by viruses – and their pre-modern forms: monsters, devils, ghosts.[1]

By pluralizing the forms of biopolitics, between what I have called disciplinary power, governmental power, and cryopolitics, and studying them as transformations of older forms of power (sovereign, pastoral, and cynegetic), I have sought to

## Conclusion 141

interrogate these different forms in the light of the ideal of truth and justice that has reorganized modern societies. While animal rights activists often imitate the sovereign state they challenge by making animals subjects of law in shelters, refuges, and sanctuaries,[2] I have highlighted other relationships between humans and animals in farms, markets, and laboratories, which I describe as a politics of zoonoses, in the sense that they consider some animals as sentinels for pathologies also affecting humans. I then studied a third form of power involving human–animal relations, cryopolitics, which aims to conserve some animals in nature reserves, zoos, or museums to protect them from the threat of extinction and to perceive the signs they carry in an aesthetic way. The transformation of cynegetic power into cryopolitics thus shifts the focus from the population to the collection as an object of power, from the animal reservoir of a zoonosis to a reserve for animal conservation.

I now want to recapitulate these different forms of power in a table, which summarizes the results of a survey, while concealing the trials and errors involved. I have chosen to distinguish between pre-modern and modern forms, not in order to re-establish a grand division whose evils social anthropology has shown us, but to question, following Foucault, the effects of the revolutionary break (at once economic, political, and ideological, as Marx showed) on the reorganization of relations between living beings. This is why I have described pre-modern forms more in terms of ontologies and schemes of relation, taking this term from the anthropology of nature proposed by Philippe Descola, and modern forms more in terms of ideals and grammars of justification, drawing inspiration from the sociology of critique elaborated by Luc Boltanski.[3]

I showed that the two forms of power that Foucault distinguishes in modernity under the term "biopower" (discipline and governmentality) found pre-modern equivalents in sovereign power and pastoral power. I then added two forms that seemed to better account for the phenomena I had observed

142 *Conclusion*

while following "virus hunters": cynegetic power and cryopolitics. The essential point here is not to look for effects of symmetry, but to understand, for each form of power, the constitutive test (*épreuve*) that subjects pass through rituals in the pre-modern regime and through knowledge in the modern regime. Being a good ruler, a good shepherd, or a good hunter does not imply the same tests, in the sense of techniques for perceiving invisible entities. These tests are transformed when they include the knowledge of modernity, such as psychiatry, hygiene, or ecology, thus redefining in varying ways what modernity has called health. While pre-modern societies include knowledge in their rituals, only modern societies reorganize techniques of power around forms of knowledge that extend to the whole of humanity across the planet, which explains why such a scale of knowledge forced pre-modern societies to reorganize in order to resist it (see Table 1).

By using zoonotic viruses as operators of variation to study forms of power in human–animal relations, this book also turns them into weapons for the critique of domestication and capitalism. If the forms of injustice produced on a large scale by the planetary extension of capitalism have caused "pathologies of freedom,"[4] and if public health systems have failed to remedy the inequalities it has amplified,[5] the pathologies of the environment that result from the industrialization and commodification of living beings have also given rise to criticism, of which environmental movements are the most audible spokespersons.[6] Pandemic viruses can therefore be seen by these movements as operators to criticize modern capitalism in the various contexts where they appear.

This book has shown that the ontological and political status of a pandemic virus differs depending on whether it is collected in animal reservoirs, imagined in stories of anticipation, pushed to a state border, tracked by tests and digital applications, attenuated by vaccine campaigns or stored in laboratories. The error of conspiracy theories is to think that the same virus is manipulated by globalized actors to impose

*Conclusion* 143

## Table 1

| Ontologies | Forms of pre-modern power | Forms of modern power | Ideals |
|---|---|---|---|
| **Naturalism** Scheme of relations: Punishment | **Sovereign power** Test: Make die and let live Ritual: Torture Value: Security Space: Territory | **Disciplinary powers** Test: Make people live and let them die Knowledge: Psychiatry Value: Mental health Space: Barracks, hospital, prison Nation-state | **Equality** Law (*lex*) |
| **Analogism** Scheme of relations: Protection | **Pastoral power** Test: Make people live and accept death Ritual: Sacrifice Value: Salvation Space: Herd | **Government** biopolitics Test: Make people live and let them die Knowledge: Hygiene Value: Public health Space: City Welfare state | **Liberty** Norm (*nomos*) |
| **Animism** Scheme of relations: Predation | **Cynegetic power** Test: Make the animal and delegate its death Ritual: Slavery Value: Abundance Space: Animal reservoir | **Cryopolitics** Test: Keep collections alive and differ their death Knowledge: Ecology Value: Global health Space: Museum reserve International organization and local association | **Solidarity** Morals (*ethos*) |

144        *Conclusion*

fear and sell vaccines; it is symmetrical with theories of the capillarity of power, depicting the mutations of the virus and the internalization of its fear as an interminable imposition of power on individuals. Both of these errors stem from a unilinear conception of power, from its origin to its dissemination, whereas power takes different forms, which I have described as cynegetic, pastoral, sovereign, disciplinary, biopolitical, and cryopolitical. The map of forms of power that I propose does not aim to deactivate critique but, on the contrary, to rearm it by giving it the tools it needs to understand the world of planetary health. Using the methods of Philippe Descola and Luc Boltanski, combining ontologies of relations with grammars of justification, this book provides tools to identify the hybridizations between forms of power and the points of support they offer to critique in relations between life and death.[7]

Back in 1976, Michel Foucault questioned whether biopolitics could be overturned and subverted by the fact that it concerned living and acting subjects. The zoonoses that have multiplied since this date (Ebola, "mad cow disease," avian and swine influenza, respiratory syndromes such as SARS or Covid) force us to think about the possibilities for emancipatory biopolitics including sick animals and pandemic viruses, which must be "allowed to live" by returning them to a wild space, or "made to live" by renegotiating their relations with humans.[8] Among all the critical figures in contemporary biopolitics, this book has developed the figure of the sentinel because it questions the thresholds between nature and culture, between the domestic and the wild, between the military and the sanitary that are constitutive of modernity. The sentinel is defined as a permanent state of vigilance delegated to a living being on the frontier of a collective, which leads it to recompose itself as a result of the perception of warning signals about threats coming from outside the inhabited territory. The collective's border is thus not a cut-off point that enables it to protect itself, but a space of communication that forces it to explore its outside.

*Conclusion* 145

If living beings are defined by their ability to perceive signs, from the level of relations between cells and microbes to that of geopolitical relations, via that of relations between human and animal bodies, then we can indeed speak of an extension of the ideal of truth and justice to all living beings on the occasion of a pandemic. For the warning signals must be true and accurate to trigger a response adapted to the stakes of the always potentially catastrophic encounter between living beings. Whereas sovereign power is exercised by law and discipline, and pastoral power by norms and statistics, sentinels force the authorities to keep in close touch with the diversity of customs by practicing "ethology," which defines *ethos* as the behavior of living beings in general, and not just the moral conduct of humans.[9] Zoonoses trigger mechanisms for anticipating and imagining catastrophes on a global scale, because the physiology and ethology of the animals that transmit them are comparable to those of humans, and lead them to react in a similar way to the pathogens that affect humans. This is why planetary health produces solidarity between living beings across species, not in the erasure of their differences faced with a common enemy, but in the variety of their lifestyles revealed by viruses. Communicating about the ways bats, pangolins, minks, deer, birds, rats, pigs, cattle, and non-human primates inhabit the world is a more respectful anticipation of the diseases they share with us than preemptively slaughtering them for harboring pandemic viruses.[10] We are exposed to pathogens that we share with other animals, and therefore pandemics are opportunities to display and curate our relations with these animals across a variety of species. Such would be the lesson of the Covid-19 pandemic, on which the anthropologist of the future could conclude her exhibition.

# Notes

## Opening

1 See Alejandro de la Garza, "The surprisingly long history of the ventilator, the machine you never want to need," *Time*, April 7, 2020.

2 See Bruno Strasser and Thomas Schlich, "A history of the medical mask and the rise of throwaway culture," *Lancet* 396 (10243), 2020.

3 See Anne-Marie Moulin, *L'aventure de la vaccination* (Fayard, 1993); Philippe Sansonetti, *Tempête parfaite. Chronique d'une pandémie annoncée* (Seuil, 2020); Anne-Marie Moulin and Gaëtan Thomas, "L'hésitation vaccinale, ou les impatiences de la santé mondiale," *La vie des idées*, May 4, 2021.

4 See Séverine Arsène (ed.), "Façonner l'Internet chinois: Dispositifs politiques, institutionnels et technologiques dans la gouvernance de l'Internet," *Perspectives chinoises*, 2015: 4.

5 See Linfa Wang and Christopher Cowled, *Bats and Viruses: A New Frontier of Emerging Infectious Diseases* (Wiley, 2015); Antoine Laugrand and Frédéric Laugrand, *Des voies de l'ombre: quand les chauves-souris sèment le trouble* (Muséum national d'histoire naturelle, 2023); Frédéric Keck and Arnaud Morvan, *Chauves-souris. Rencontres aux frontières entre les espèces* (CNRS Editions, 2021).

6 K. Xiao, J. Zhai, Y. Feng, N. Zhou, X. Zhang, J.J. Zou, N. Li, Y. Guo, X. Li, X. Shen, et al., "Isolation of SARS-CoV-2-related coronavirus from Malayan pangolins," *Nature* 583, 2020.

7 See Chris Coggins, *The Tiger and the Pangolin: Nature, Culture, and Conservation in China* (University of Hawai'i Press, 2003);

Kong Xiao et al., "Isolation of SARS-CoV-2-related coronavirus from Malayan pangolins," *Nature* 583, 2020; Mathieu Quet, "Le pangolin pris au piège de la commodisation de la nature," *La vie des idées*, April 28, 2020.

8 See Françoise Fenollar et al., "Mink, SARS-CoV-2, and the Human–Animal Interface," *Frontiers of Microbiology* 12, 2021; Alexander Etkind, "Barrels of fur: Natural resources and the state in the long history of Russia," *Journal of Eurasian Studies* 2 (2), 2011.

9 See Jianzhong Shi et al., "Susceptibility of ferrets, cats, dogs, and other domesticated animals to SARS-coronavirus 2," *Science* 368 (6494), 2020.

10 See Smriti Mallapaty, "How sneezing hamsters caused a Covid outbreak in Hong Kong," *Nature*, February 4, 2022; Hui-Ling Yen et al., "Transmission of SARS-CoV-2 delta variant (AY.127) from pet hamsters to humans, leading to onward human-to-human transmission: a case study," *Lancet* 12: 399 (10329), March 2022.

11 See Suresh V. Kuchipudi, "Multiple spillovers and onward transmission of SARS-Cov-2 in free-living and captive White-tailed deer," *PNAS* 119 (6), 2021.

12 See Najmul Haider et al., "COVID-19-Zoonosis or Emerging Infectious Disease?" *Frontiers of Public Health* 8, 2020.

## Introduction

1 See Paul Rabinow, Preface to Clémentine Deliss (ed.), *Object Atlas. Fieldwork in the Museum* (Kerber, 2012).

2 See Mathieu Potte-Bonneville, "Covid-19: *une crise biopolitique?*," *AOC*, June 19, 2020.

3 The most assertive use of the notion of biopolitics to fuel conspiracy theory is that of the *Manifeste conspirationniste*, published anonymously by Seuil in 2022. Through the style of denunciation, it combines the assignment of a historically coherent cause with the pinpointing of its ramifications in all areas of everyday life. "What is happening is the recomposition of a civic body, no longer on a political, but a biopolitical basis" (p. 69); "the management of the Covid-19 epidemic marks the

148 *Notes to pp. 3–6*

absolute triumph of biopolitics as a logic at the same time as its practical defeat in open country, unable as it is to cope with a virus that is not so fatal after all" (p. 210).

4　See Barbara Katz Rothman, *The Biomedical Empire. Lessons Learned from the Covid-19 Pandemic* (Stanford University Press, 2022), p. 24: "Marx was right: the state has essentially become the managing agent of bourgeois interests. Foucault was ultimately wrong: the state has not so much used biopower as biopower has used the state."

5　Michel Foucault, *History of Sexuality I*, trans. Robert Hurley (Pantheon Books, 1978), p. 143.

6　Claude Lévi-Strauss, *Wild Thought*, trans. Jeffrey Mehlman and John Leavitt (University of Chicago Press, 2021), p. 185.

7　Two interviews I gave at the beginning of the Covid-19 pandemic were given this title, even though I was questioning its relevance: "Les chauves-souris et les pangolins se révoltent." Interview with Joseph Confavreux, *Mediapart*, March 20, 2020; "La vengeance du pangolin." Interview with François Moutou and Baptiste Roger-Lacan, *Le Grand Continent*, April 1, 2020.

8　See Gil Bartholeyns, *Le hantement du monde. Zoonoses et Pathocène* (Dehors, 2021), p. 90. Covid-19 is characterized as a "broad-spectrum" zoonosis, as it is transmitted by a large number of animal species. See Gwenael Vourch, François Moutou, Serge Morand, and Elsa Jourdain, *Les zoonoses. Ces maladies qui nous lient aux animaux* (Quae, 2021), p. 18. Jacques Derrida (*Specters of Marx: The State of the Debt, the Work of Mourning and the New International*, trans. Peggy Kamuf, Routledge 1994), defines specters in terms of the frequency of the visible and the frequentation of the invisible.

9　See Philippe Descola, *La nature domestique. Symbolisme et praxis dans l'écologie des Achuar* (Maison des sciences de l'homme, 1986); Eduardo Viveiros de Castro, *From the Enemy's Point of View. Humanity and Divinity in an Amazonian Society* (University of Chicago Press, 1992).

10　See Thierry Hoquet, *Le nouvel esprit biologique* (Presses Universitaires de France, 2022).

11　See Serge Morand, *L'homme, la faune sauvage et la peste* (Fayard, 2020); Marie-Monique Robin and Serge Morand, *La fabrique*

*Notes to pp. 6–9* 149

*des pandémies. Préserver la biodiversité, un impératif pour la santé planétaire* (La Découverte, 2021).

12 See Gary Becker, *The Economic Approach to Human Behavior* (University of Chicago Press, 1976).

13 See Laurie Garrett, *The Coming Plague. Newly Emerging Diseases in a World Out of Balance* (Penguin, 1995), and David Quammen, *Spillover: Animal Infections and the Next Human Pandemic* (W.W. Norton, 2012). In 1976, historian William McNeill published *Plagues and People* (Anchor Books), a book that played an important role in popularizing the notions of zoonosis and emerging infectious disease, notably when ornithologist and geographer Jared Diamond took up his theses in *Guns, Germs and Steel* (W.W. Norton, 1997).

14 See Rachel Carson, *Silent Spring* (Houghton Mifflin Harcourt, 1962); Frank Macfarlane Burnet, *Natural History of Infectious Diseases* (Cambridge University Press, 1962). Other books that sounded the alarm on environmental degradation by pointing to a systemic cause include Vance Packard's *The Waste Makers* in 1960, Murray Bookchin's *Our Synthetic Environment* in 1962, and Ruth Harrison's *Animal Machines: The New Factory Farming Industry* in 1964.

15 See Frédéric Keck, *Signaux d'alerte. Contagion virale, justice sociale, crises environnementales* (Desclée de Brouwer, 2020).

16 Of all the Foucauldian thinkers who have written on the Covid-19 pandemic, Olivier Cheval is the only one who placed the question of domestication at the center, but he sees it as domestication of the "outside" rather than domestication of the wild. See Olivier Cheval, *La domestication du monde*, followed by *Lettres sur la peste* (La Découverte, 2022).

## 1 Biopower: Disciplining individuals, regulating populations

1 See Roberto Esposito, *Bíos. Biopolitica e filosofia* (Einaudi, 2004); Thomas Lemke, *Biopolitics: An Advanced Introduction* (New York University Press, 2011).

2 See Rudolf Kjellen, *Världspolitiken 1911–1919* (Lindblad, 1920).

150         *Notes to pp. 9–11*

3   See Kenneth Cauthen, *Christian Biopolitics. A Credo and Strategy for the Future* (Abingdon Press, 1971); Dietrich Gunst, *Politik zwischen Macht und Recht* (Hase and Koehler, 1974).

4   On Foucault's shift "from the repressive hypothesis to bio-power" in the 1970s, which played a major role on American campuses heavily influenced by the thought of Theodor Adorno, Max Horkheimer, and Herbert Marcuse, see Hubert Dreyfus and Paul Rabinow, *Michel Foucault: Beyond Structuralism and Hermeneutics* (University of Chicago Press, 1984). On the contrasts between a biopolitical history of sovereignty following Michel Foucault and a more republican history such as that of Quentin Skinner, involving different returns to the "arts of governing" since Machiavelli, see Jean Terrel, "Les figures de la souveraineté" and Michel Senellart, "La critique de la raison gouvernementale," in Guillaume Le Blanc and Jean Terrel, *Les Cours au Collège de France de Michel Foucault* (Presses Universitaires de Bordeaux, 2003), pp. 101–130 and 131–149.

5   See Michel Foucault, *The Birth of the Clinic: An Archaeology of Medical Perception*. trans. A.M. Sheridan Smith (Tavistock, 1973); Paolo Napoli, *Naissance de la police moderne. Pouvoir, normes, société* (La Découverte, 2003).

6   Here we find the influence of Georges Canguilhem: see *The Normal and the Pathological*, Introduction by Michel Foucault, trans. Carolyn R. Fawcett (Princeton University Press, 1991).

7   See Luca Paltrinieri, "L'émergence et l'événement. Population et reproduction au XVIII$^e$ siècle," in Hervé Oulc'hen (ed.), *Usages de Foucault* (Presses Universitaires de France, 2014), pp. 335–354. On the history of population sciences, see Hervé Le Bras, *The Nature of Demography* (Princeton University Press, 2008); Alison Bashford, *Global Population. History, Geopolitics, and Life on Earth* (Columbia University Press, 2016); Fabrice Cahen, *Le nombre des hommes. La mesure de la population et ses enjeux (xvi$^e$–xxi$^e$ siècle)* (Classiques Garnier, 2022).

8   See Thomas Le Roux, "L'effacement du corps de l'ouvrier. La santé au travail lors de la première industrialisation de Paris (1770–1840)," *Le Mouvement Social* 234, 2011: 103–119; Jean-Baptiste Fressoz, *L'apocalypse joyeuse. Une histoire du risque technologique* (Seuil, 2012).

*Notes to pp. 11–12* 151

9 See François Delaporte, *Disease and Civilization. The Cholera in Paris, 1832*, foreword by Paul Rabinow, trans. Arthur Goldhammer (MIT Press, 1986); Patrice Bourdelais, *Une peur bleue, Histoire du choléra en France* (Payot, 1987).

10 See Lion Murard and Patrick Zylberman, *L'hygiène dans la République. La santé publique en France, ou l'utopie contrariée, 1870–1918* (Fayard, 1996); François Ewald, *The Birth of Solidarity: The History of the French Welfare State*, ed. Melinda Cooper, trans. Timothy Scott Johnson (Duke University Press, 2020); Patrice Bourdelais (dir.), *Les hygiénistes: enjeux, modèles et pratiques (xviii–xx$^{ee}$ siècles)* (Éditions Belin, 2001); Gérard Jorland, *Une société à soigner. Hygiène et salubrité publiques en France au XIX$^e$ siècle* (Gallimard, 2010).

11 Michel Foucault, *Society Must Be Defended. Lectures at the Collège de France 1975–76*, eds. Mauro Bertani and Alessandro Fontana, trans. David Macey (Picador, 2003), pp. 243–244.

12 See Lorenzo Servitje and Kari Nixon (eds.), *Endemic. Essays in Contagion Theory* (Palgrave Macmillan, 2016).

13 Arnaud Orain has studied this local knowledge of climates through the expression "*ars mercatoria*," which in the eighteenth century referred to three types of knowledge, of which Foucault retained only the first: political economy, the science of commerce and economic physics. See *Les savoirs perdus de l'économie. Contribution à l'équilibre du vivant* (Gallimard, 2023).

14 Foucault, *Society Must Be Defended*, p. 245.

15 See Georges Canguilhem, "The living and its milieu" (lecture given at the University of Strasbourg in 1946), trans. John Savage, *Grey Room* 3, 2001: 6–31; Paul Rabinow, *French Modern. Norms and Forms of the Social Environment* (University of Chicago Press, 1992); Wolf Feuerhahn, "Les catégories de l'entendement écologique: milieu, Umwelt, environment, nature . . .," in Guillaume Blanc, Élise Demeulenaere, and Wolf Feuerhahn (eds.), *Humanités environnementales. Enquêtes et contre-enquêtes* (Éditions de la Sorbonne, 2017, pp. 19–41); Gabriel Coren and Cameron Brinitzer, "Canguilhem's Milieu Today," special issue of *History and Anthropology Review*, 2019; Ferhat Taylan, *Mésopolitique. Connaître, théoriser et gouverner*

152 *Notes to pp. 12–13*

*les milieux de vie (1750–1900)* (Éditions de la Sorbonne, 2018); Andrea Angelini, *Biopolitica ed ecologia. L'epistemologia politica del discorso biologico tra Michel Foucault e Georges Canguilhem* (Firenze University Press, 2021).

16  Michel Foucault, *Security, Territory, Population: Lectures at the Collège de France, 1977–1978*, ed. Michel Senellart, trans. Graham Burchell (Palgrave Macmillan, 2007), p. 37.

17  Michel Foucault, "La naissance de la médecine sociale" (1974), in *Dits et écrits II* (Gallimard, 2001), p. 222.

18  See Michel Foucault, *Discipline and Punish: The Birth of the Prison*, trans. Alan Sheridan (Vintage Books, 1977); Robert Castel, *The Regulation of Madness: The Origins of Incarceration in France*, trans. W.D. Hall (University of California Press, 1988); Jan Goldstein, *Console and Classify. The French Psychiatric Profession in the Nineteenth Century* (Cambridge University Press, 1982).

19  See Michel Foucault, *Abnormals. Lectures at the Collège de France, 1974–1975*, eds. Valerio Marchetti and Antonella Salomoni, trans. Graham Burchell (Verso, 2003), pp. 121–122: "Psychiatry sets itself this kind of test of recognition of its royalty, of its sovereignty, of its power and its knowledge: I can identify an illness, I can discover the signs of what has never been recognized." See Frédéric Keck and Stéphane Legrand, "Les épreuves de la psychiatrie. Situation de la psychiatrie dans *Les Anormaux* de Michel Foucault," in Guillaume le Blanc and Jean Terrel (eds.), *Les Cours au Collège de France de Michel Foucault* (Presses Universitaires de Bordeaux, 2003), pp. 59–100. In this article, we propose a reading of Foucault inspired by Pierre Bourdieu's sociological reflections on tests of strength and their role in the reproduction of domination, and Luc Boltanski's on tests of greatness and their role in changing relations of domination.

20  Foucault excludes the figure of the savage, which he had already mobilized romantically in his *History of Madness*. When he points out that the monster was described in the nineteenth century as incestuous and monstrous, he asserts that anthropology has put this figure either on the side of primitive totemism with Lévy-Bruhl, or on the side of universal exchange with Lévi-Strauss (*Abnormals*, p. 104). Whereas in *The Order of Things*,

## Notes to p. 14 153

Foucault asserted that ethnology and psychoanalysis were the only forms of knowledge that could shake the modern subject, his study of the mechanisms of power denies anthropology the ability to "find signs for that which never signals itself," and reserves it for psychiatry.

21 In his 1974 lecture in Brazil, entitled "Truth and juridical forms," in James Faubion (ed.) *Foucault, Power* (New Press, 2000, pp. 31–45), Foucault claims to be part of the sociology of law tradition, which runs from Glotz to Vernant via Gernet and Dumézil, as opposed to the structural anthropology of Lévi-Strauss. "Structuralism," he says, "consists in taking sets of discourses and treating them only as statements, looking for laws of passage, of transformation, of isomorphisms between these sets of statements. That's not what interests me."

22 See Foucault, *Society Must Be Defended*, p. 241: "One of the greatest transformations of political right underwent in the nineteenth century is precisely that, I wouldn't say exactly that sovereignty's old right – to take life or to let live (*faire mourir ou laisser vivre*) – was replaced, but it came to be complemented by a new right, which does not erase the old right, but which does penetrate it, permeate it. This is the right, or rather precisely the opposite. It is the power to make live and to let die (*pouvoir de faire vivre et de laisser mourir*)." The formula proposed in *The Will to Knowledge* is less symmetrical in terms, but the italics clearly show the underlying inverted structure: "One might say that the old right to *take life* or *let live* (*faire mourir ou laisser vivre*) was replaced by a power to *foster* life or *disallow* it to the point of death (*faire vivre ou rejeter dans la mort*)." Foucault, *The History of Sexuality I*, p. 136.

23 Ibid.

24 See Gilles Deleuze, 'What is a dispositif?' in T. J. Armstrong (ed.), *Michel Foucault Philosopher* (Harvester Wheatsheaf, 1992), pp. 159–168; Giorgio Agamben, *What is an Apparatus? And Other Essays*, trans. David Kishik and Stefan Pedatella (Stanford University Press, 2009).

25 See Foucault, *The History of Sexuality I*, p. 147. The same analysis is proposed in "*Society Must Be Defended*, pp. 254–256.

26 Foucault thus distinguishes two forms of biopower, specifying

154 *Notes to p. 15*

that they "were not antithetical, however; they constituted rather two poles of development linked together by a whole intermediary cluster of relations." The first is what he calls an "anatomo-politics of the human body": this is the disciplinary power of psychiatry, which trains bodies by adding to them a soul to be educated in prison institutions. The second is what Foucault calls a "biopolitics of population": the regulatory power of public hygiene and all the related knowledge that control births and mortality. Foucault, *The History of Sexuality I*, p. 139. The same analysis is proposed in *Society Must Be Defended*, p. 243.

27 Foucault, *Society Must Be Defended*, pp. 254–261. For a review of Foucault's hypotheses on the notion of race, see Étienne Balibar and Immanuel Wallerstein, *Race, Nation, Class. Ambiguous Identities* (Verso, 1991); Elsa Dorlin, *La matrice de la race. Généalogie sexuelle et coloniale de la nation française*, preface by Joan W. Scott (La Découverte, 2006); Claude-Olivier Doron, *L'homme altéré: races et dégénérescence (xvii<sup>e</sup>–xix<sup>e</sup> siècles)* (Champ Vallon, 2016).

28 Foucault, *Society Must Be Defended*, p. 77.

29 Ibid., pp. 128–194: Foucault shows that Boulainvilliers reverses Clausewitz's formula: "Politics is war continued by other means."

30 Foucault thus echoes Lévi-Strauss's analysis in *La pensée sauvage*, who spoke of the "Boulainvilliers transformation" to describe a counter-history that deconstructs the linear temporality of revolution and progress, starting from conflicts between "races." See Claude Lévi-Strauss, *Wild Thought*, p. 298. It is astonishing that Foucault never cites this enigmatic note by Lévi-Strauss in 1962, when he comments on Boulainvilliers in four lectures at the Collège de France in February 1976. But the reference to Lévi-Strauss is implicit in Foucault's critique of the "savage" as a "sign exchanger," to which he contrasts the "barbarian" as "the man who tramples on the frontiers of states" (Foucault, *Society Must Be Defended*, p. 195).

31 In this sense, those who criticize Foucault's analysis of biopower for not leaving space for the return of sovereignty in the 1990s through the visibility of new forms of killing and new practices for treating the dead (euthanasia, death penalty, cremation . . .)

*Notes to pp. 16–17* 155

miss the point, since it is their justification rather than their visibility that is at stake for Foucault: see Emmanuel Taïeb, "Du biopouvoir au thanatopouvoir," *Quaderni*, 62, 2006: 5–15. The concept of "necropolitics" coined by Achille Mbembe is more interesting; it is part of an economy of colonial warfare, as we shall see in the next chapter.

32 See Giorgio Agamben, *Homo Sacer: Sovereign Power and Bare Life*, trans. Daniel Heller-Roazen (Stanford University Press, 1998); *The Open. Man and Animal*, trans. Kevin Atell (Stanford University Press, 2003). Agamben takes the distinction between *bios* and *zoē* from Hannah Arendt, *The Human Condition* (University of Chicago Press, 1958).

33 Antonio Negri and Michael Hardt, *Empire* (Harvard University Press, 2001); *Multitude: War and Democracy in the Age of Empire* (Penguin, 2004); *Commonwealth* (Harvard University Press, 2011).

34 See Frédéric Keck, 2003 "La subjectivité révolutionnaire. A propos d'*Empire* de Michael Hardt et Toni Negri," *Actuel Marx*, 3: 157–166, and "Les usages du biopolitique," *L'Homme, Revue française d'anthropologie*, 187–188, 2008: 295–314.

35 See Georges Canguilhem, "Le concept et la vie," in *Études d'histoire et de philosophie des sciences concernant les vivants et la vie* (Vrin, 1994); Sarah Franklin, "Life itself: Global nature and the genetic imaginary," in Sarah Franklin, Celia Lury, and Jackie Stacey (eds.), *Global Nature, Global Culture* (Sage, 2000); Sarah Franklin and Margaret Lock (eds.), *Remaking Life and Death/ Toward an Anthropology of the Life Sciences* (Oxford University Press, 2001); Jörg Niewöhner, "Epigenetics: Embedded bodies and the molecularisation of biography and milieu," *BioSocieties* 3(6), 2011: 279–298.

36 See Paul Rabinow, *Making PCR, A Story of Biotechnology* (University of Chicago Press, 1996); *French DNA. Trouble in the Purgatory* (University of Chicago Press, 1999); Nikolas Rose, *The Politics of Life Itself. Biomedicine, Power and Subjectivity in the Twenty-First Century* (Princeton University Press, 2006).

37 See Paul Rabinow, Nikolas Rose, "Biopower today," *BioSocieties* 1, 2006: 195–217.

38 See Paul Rabinow, "Artificiality and enlightenment: from

156 *Notes to pp. 17–18*

sociobiology to biosociality," in *Essays on the Anthropology of Reason* (Princeton University Press, 1996), pp. 91–111. This article was introduced into the philosophical debate on genetics by Ian Hacking in "Genetics, biosocial groups and the future of identity," *Daedalus*, 135 (4), 2006: 81–95.

39  See Filippa Lentzos and Nikolas Rose, "Governing insecurity. Contingency planning, protection, resilience," *Economy and Society* 38 (2), 2009: 230–254; Stephen Collier, Andrew Lakoff and Paul Rabinow, "Biosecurity. Towards an anthropology of the contemporary," *Anthropology Today* 20 (5), 2004: 3–7.

40  Arthur Rimbaud, Letter to Paul Demeny, May 15, 1871, quoted in Paul Rabinow, "Artificiality and enlightenment: From sociobiology to biosociality," p. 92. The letter continues: "He will have to make his inventions felt, palpated, and listened to. If what he brings back from *over there* has shape, he gives shape; if it's formless, he gives formlessness. Find a language."

41  See Marylin Strathern, *The Gender of the Gift. Problems with Women and Problems with Society in Melanesia* (University of California Press, 1988); *After Nature. English Kinship in the late Twentieth Century* (Cambridge University Press, 1992).

42  Marylin Strathern, *Reproducing the Future. Anthropology, Kinship and the New Reproductive Technologies* (Manchester University Press, 1992), p. 56. In a lecture entitled "Refusing Information," given in 1996 at the University of Toronto for a symposium entitled "Governing medically assisted human reproduction," Strathern says: "If the very concept of 'biological kinship' becomes absorbed by the concept of technologically assisted relations, then what we mark as 'social' will also have become redistributed among diverse ways of thinking about kinspersons" (*Property, Substance and Effect. Anthropological Essays on Persons and Things* (Athlone, 1999), p. 84). The edition of this essay in this collection opens with a "paraphrase" by Paul Rabinow: "What is new in the present age is that people have produced a machine, a discourse that can absorb any part of discourse" (p. 72). We recognize here the conception of bricolage proposed by Lévi-Strauss in *La pensée sauvage*.

43  See Didier Fassin, *When Bodies Remember Experiences and Politics of AIDS in South Africa* (University of California Press,

*Notes to pp. 18–19*     157

2007); Didier Fassin and Samuel Lézé, *La question morale. Une anthologie critique* (Presses Universitaires de France, 2013). The anthropology of ethics was developed from an ethnography of millenarian groups in Greece and the United States by James Faubion (see *An Anthropology of Ethics*, Cambridge University Press, 2012) and from a study of Jain groups in India by James Laidlaw: see the "Undefined work of freedom: Foucault's genealogy and the anthropology of ethics," in James Faubion (ed.), *Foucault Now: Current Perspectives in Foucault Studies* (Polity, 2014), pp. 23–37.

44  Dominique Memmi, *Les gardiens du corps. Dix ans de magistère bio-éthique* (EHESS, 1996); *Faire vivre et laisser mourir: le gouvernement contemporain de la naissance et de la mort* (La Découverte, 2003); with Didier Fassin (ed.), *Le Gouvernement des corps* (EHESS, 2004); *La seconde vie des bébés morts* (EHESS, 2011).

45  Didier Fassin, *Humanitarian Reason: A Moral History of the Present*, trans. Rachel Gomme (University of California Press, 2011). See also Guillaume Lachenal, Céline Lefève, and Vinh-Kim Nguyen (eds.), *La médecine du tri. Histoire, éthique, anthropologie* (Presses Universitaires de France, 2014).

46  Didier Fassin, *Life: A Critical User's Manual* (Polity, 2018). Didier Fassin takes up Ferenc Fehér and Agnes Heller's criticism that the notion of biopolitics does not speak of politics but rather of governmentality, and proposes replacing it with the expression "politics of life." See Didier Fassin, "Another politics of life is possible," *Theory, Culture & Society*, 26, 2009: 44–60.

47  See Didier Fassin and Mariella Pandolfi (eds.) *Contemporary States of Emergency: The Politics of Military and Humanitarian Interventions* (Zone Books, 2013); Didier Fassin and Marion Fourcade (eds.), *Pandemic Exposures. Economy and Society in the Time of Coronavirus* (Hau Books, 2022). On the link between biopolitical government by emergency and environmental racism, see Ben Anderson et al., "Slow emergencies. Temporality and the racialized biopolitics of emergency governance," *Progress in Human Geography*, 44 (4), 2019: 621–639.

48  The question of the possibility of introducing imperceptible signs of suffering into medical power is at the heart of Luc

158                    *Notes to pp. 20–23*

Boltanski's sociology, as I showed in "Luc Boltanski et la critique du pouvoir médical," *Critique* 920–921, 2023: 45–57.

49  The first mass culling to protect a farm from a zoonosis took place in 1983 in Pennsylvania (17 million birds slaughtered to control bird 'flu), but it was presented as an industrial accident: see Peter Doherty, *Sentinel Chickens. What Birds Tell Us about Our Health and the World* (Melbourne University Press, 2012), p. 74. The mass slaughter of cattle in Europe and poultry in China in 1997, on the other hand, was presented as a moral scandal.

## 2  Pastoral power: Watching over humans like sheep

1  Michel Foucault, *Security, Territory, Population: Lectures at the Collège de France, 1977–1978*, pp. 123ff., and *"Omnes et singulatim*: Towards a critique of political reason," The Tanner Lectures on Human Values 1979, pp. 225–254.

2  Ibid., p. 228.

3  See Jérôme Baschet, *La civilisation féodale: de l'an mil à la colonisation de l'Amérique* (Flammarion, 2006). Baschet sees a contestation of the power of the Christian Church rather from the margins of the colonized world than from its center (the Zapatista communities of Chiapas), which leads him to a powerful diagnosis of the Covid-19 pandemic: *Basculements. Mondes émergents, possibles désirables* (La Découverte, 2021).

4  See Foucault, *Security, Territory, Population*, pp. 191ff. and Jean-Claude Monod, *L'art de ne pas être trop gouverné* (Seuil, 2019).

5  See Michel Foucault, "The subject and power," *Critical Inquiry* 8(4), 1982: 783.

6  See *Security, Territory, Population*, p. 175: "Sacrificial reversal involves the pastor accepting the danger of dying in order to save the souls of others. And it is precisely when he accepts dying for others that the pastor is saved." Here, Foucault comes close to the analyses of Judeo-Christian sacrifice by William Robertson Smith in his *Lectures on the Religions of Semites* in 1889, and by René Girard in *La violence et le sacré* in 1972. But

*Notes to pp. 23–25*

he never assumes that sacrifice makes the reality of the social attainable, for he is attentive to the splitting of the subject in "sacrificial inversion," so that there is always a remnant of sacrifice that enters into new techniques of power.

7  Foucault, *Security, Territory, Population*, p. 132.

8  Michel Foucault, "Crise de la médecine ou crise de l'anti-médecine," Lecture at the Institute of Social Medicine, Rio de Janeiro, October 1974, in *Dits et Ecrits III* (Gallimard, 1994), p. 54.

9  See Ronald Hubscher, *Les maîtres des bêtes. Les vétérinaires dans la société française (xviiie–xxe siècle)* (Odile Jacob, 1999); Daniel Roche, *Histoire de la culture équestre. xvie–xixe siècle* (Fayard, 3 vols. 2008, 2011, 2015); Delphine Berdah, "Entre scientifi-sation et travail de frontières: les transformations des savoirs vétérinaires en France, xviii–xix$^{ee}$ siècles," *Revue d'histoire moderne et contemporaine* 59 (4), 2012: 51–96.

10  *Encyclopédie ou Dictionnaire raisonné des sciences, des arts et des métiers, Supplément*, 1777, t. 3, p. 372–427, quoted in D. Roche, *Histoire de la culture équestre*, t. 3, op. cit., p. 110.

11  See Harriet Ritvo, *The Animal Estate. The English and Other Creatures in the Victorian Age* (Harvard University Press, 1987); Benedetta Piazzesi, *Del governo degli animali. Allevamento e biopolitica* (Quodlibet, 2023).

12  See Louise Wilkinson, *Animals & Disease. An Introduction to the History of Comparative Medicine* (Cambridge University Press, 1992), pp. 51–64; John Fisher, "Cattle plagues past and present: The mystery of mad cow disease," *Journal of Contemporary History* 33 (2), 1998: 215–228; Abigail Woods, *A Manufactured Plague: the History of Foot-and-Mouth Disease in Britain* (Routledge, 2004); John Law and Annemarie Mol, "Veterinary realities: What is foot and mouth disease?," *Sociologia Ruralis* 51 (1), 2011: 1–16.

13  See François Vallat, *Les bœufs malades de la peste. La peste bovine en France et en Europe XVIIIe-XIXe siècle* (Presses Universitaires de Rennes, 2009). In the same year, 1866, the United Kingdom passed the *Cattle Disease Act*.

14  See Michel Foucault, *Abnormal*, op. cit., p. 47: "The moment of the plague is that of the exhaustive sectioning (*quadrillage*)

160 *Notes to p. 26*

of the population by a political power, the capillary ramifications of which constantly reach the grain of individuals themselves, their time, habitat, their localization, and bodies." In his 1974 lecture, Foucault takes up analyses he had already presented in his 1961 thesis (*Histoire de la folie à l'âge classique* (Gallimard, 1972), pp. 13–16) and in *Surveiller et punir* in 1972 (op. cit., pp. 197–200). He returns to them in his 1978 lecture: see Foucault, *Security, Territory, Population*, p. 11.

15 Foucault, *Abnormal*, p. 45.

16 See Christos Lynteris, "The global war against the rat," *Visual Plague: The Emergence of Epidemic Photography* (MIT Press, 2022), pp. 121–153; Frédéric Keck, "Guerre d'occupation et morts en série dans *La Peste*," *Signaux d'alerte. Contagion virale, justice sociale, crises environnementales* (Desclée de Brouwer, 2020), pp. 214–222.

17 See Foucault, *Security, Territory, Population*, p. 57: "Variolation did not try to prevent smallpox so much as provoke it in inoculated individuals, but under conditions such that nullification of the disease could take place at the same time as this vaccination, which thus did not result in a total and complete disease. With the support of this kind of first small, artificially inoculated disease, one could prevent other possible attacks of smallpox."

18 See Jonathan B. Tucker, *Scourge: The Once and Future Threat of Smallpox* (Grove Press, 2002). The monkeypox epidemic, which began on May 7, 2022 with an English patient returning from Nigeria, infected over 80,000 people in 110 countries, including over 4,000 in France, and killed 65 people by December 13, 2022. It was declared an international public health emergency by the WHO on July 23, because humans have not been vaccinated against smallpox since the disease was eradicated in 1976 through a global vaccination campaign. It is a virus similar to that which has killed hundreds of millions of people in modern times, but it has circulated in rodents in Africa, with the first case of transmission to primates identified in a group of laboratory macaques in Copenhagen in 1958, and the first human case in a child in the Congo in 1970.

*Notes to pp. 27–29* 161

19  See Yves-Marie Bercé, *La naissance du vaccin. Entre utopie et rejets* (Cerf, 2020); Pierre Darmon, *Vaccinateurs et vaccinophobes. Histoire d'un complot* (Librinova, 2022).

20  See Anne-Marie Moulin (ed.), *L'aventure de la vaccination* (Fayard, 1996).

21  See François Vallat, *Les bœufs malades de la peste*, op. cit., ch. 8.

22  Quoted in Louis Nicol, "Pasteur et l'Académie vétérinaire," *Bulletin de l'Académie Vétérinaire de France* 125–10, 1972: 545–565. On the relationship between Pasteur and Bouley, see Michel Morange, *Pasteur* (Gallimard, 2022), pp. 258–260.

23  See Michel Morange, *Pasteur*, p. 324. Michel Morange points out that this "speed race" model was supported by Pasteur until Metchnikoff explained the attenuation of microbes by the formation of immune cells.

24  See Myron Schultz, "Rudolf Virchow," *Emerging Infectious Diseases* 14 (9), 2008: 1480; Abigail Nieves Delgado and Azita Chellappoo, "Zoonoses and medicine as social science. Implications of Rudolf Virchow's work for understanding global pandemics," in Vanessa Lemm and Miguel Vatter (eds.), *The Viral Politics of Covid-19. Nature, Home and Planetary Health* (Palgrave Macmillan, 2022) pp. 73–92. In 1855, Rudolf Virchow published a manual of pathology in which he distinguished between the contagious agents that produce the same effects in different animal species, and those that merely provide the opportunity for different diseases to be triggered in different species (*Handbuch der Speciellen Pathologie und Therapie. Intoxicationen, Zoonosen und Syphilis* (Verlag von Ferdinand Enke, 1855)). This was the first time the notion of contagion was used to differentiate between animal species. Virchow was committed to social democracy in Germany, which he promoted through his conception of the organism as a set of self-regulating cells.

25  Quoted in Alessandro Stanziani, *Histoire de la qualité alimentaire XIXe-XXe siècle* (Seuil, 2005), p. 230. See also Jérôme Bourdieu, Laetitia Piet, Alessandro Stanziani, "Crise sanitaire et stabilisation du marché de la viande en France, XVIIIe-XXe siècles," in *Revue d'histoire moderne et contemporaine* 51 (3), 2003: 121–156.

162 *Notes to pp. 30–31*

26 See David Barnes, *The Making of a Social Disease. Tuberculosis in Nineteenth-Century France* (University of California Press, 1995); Linda Brydes, *Below the Magic Mountain. A Social History of Tuberculosis in Twentieth-Century Britain* (Clarendon Press, 1988).

27 Alessandro Stanziani quotes an Alsatian veterinarian in 1882: "I fear that if Koch's new discovery of the bacterial nature of tuberculosis is brought into the public domain, it will again be the occasion for some exaggeration, the cause of some panic similar to that produced by the migration of trichinae. It is this panic I would like to try to prevent." (*Capital Terre. Une histoire longue du monde d'après (XIIe-XXIe siècle)*, Payot, 2021 p. 206.) See also Patrick Zylberman, "Making food safety an issue: Internationalized food politics and French public health from the 1870s to the present," *Medical History* 48(1), 2004: 1–28.

28 See Barbara Rosenkrantz, "The trouble with bovine tuberculosis," *Bulletin of the History of Medicine* 59, 1985: 155–175; Susan Jones, "Mapping a zoonotic disease. Anglo-American efforts to control bovine tuberculosis before World War I," *Osiris* 19, 2004: 133–148.

29 See Delphine Berdah, *Abattre ou vacciner? La France et le Royaume-Uni en lutte contre la tuberculose et la fièvre aphteuse (1900–1960)* (EHESS, 2018). Delphine Berdah speaks of a "double legitimization strategy" in response to controversies over vaccination accidents, notably the one that caused the death of 76 children in Lubeck, Germany, between 1930 and 1932. See Christian Bonah, *Histoire de l'expérimentation humaine. Discours et pratiques, 1900–1940* (Les Belles Lettres, 2007).

30 See Gareth Enticott, "Calculating nature. The case of badgers, bovine tuberculosis and cattle," *Journal of Rural Studies* 17 (2), 2001: 149–164; Angela Cassidy, *Vermin, Victims and Disease. British Debates over Bovine Tuberculosis and Badgers* (Palgrave Macmillan, 2019).

31 Foucault, *Abnormal*, p. 198: "The convulsive flesh is the body penetrated by the right of examination, and subject to the obligation of exhaustive confession and the body that bristles against this right of examination."

## Notes to pp. 31–34

32 Michel Pastoureau's work focuses on the transformations of this medieval bestiary: see *Une histoire symbolique du Moyen Âge occidental* (Seuil, 2004), and *L'Art de l'héraldique au Moyen Âge* (Seuil, 2009).

33 Foucault, *Security, Territory, Population*, p. 191.

34 Cf. Michel Foucault, *Birth of Biopolitics. Lectures at the Collège de France 1978–1979*, trans. Graham Burchell (Palgrave Macmillan, 2008), pp. 21–22: " only when we know what this governmental regime called liberalism was, will we be able to grasp what biopolitics is."

### 3 Cynegetic power: Catching the prey's perspectives

1 Grégoire Chamayou, *Manhunts: A Philosophical History*, trans. Steven Rendall (Princeton University Press, 2012), p. 32.

2 Ibid., p. 30.

3 Ibid., p. 33.

4 Ibid., p. 35. Chamayou quotes Hobbes, *Leviathan*, 3rd part, ch. XLII.

5 Ibid., p. 16.

6 Ibid., p. 36: "To protect the flock, sometimes one has to hunt down certain sheep, to sacrifice a few to save all the others. Here we are no longer in a logic of predatory appropriation, but rather in a rationality of salutary ablation or beneficent exclusion (. . .) The favorite image for pastoral hunting in order to exclude is health-related: metaphors of illness, gangrene or epidemic. It is necessary to prevent infection from spreading, to forestall general contagion."

7 See Carlo Ginzburg, *The Night Battles: Witchcraft and Agrarian Cults in the Sixteenth and Seventeenth Centuries*, trans. John and Anne Tedeschi (Johns Hopkins University Press, 1983); Silvia Federici, *Caliban and the Witch: Women, the Body and Primitive Accumulation* (Autonomedia, 2004).

8 See Chamayou, *Manhunts*. p. 52. The integration of Spanish settlers' dogs into the animist conceptions of Amerindian societies is the starting point of Eduardo Kohn's work: see "How dogs dream: Amazonian natures and the politics of trans-species engagement," *American Ethnologist* 34 (1), 2007: 3–24,

164                    *Notes to pp. 35–36*

and *How Forests Think. Toward an Anthropology Beyond the Human* (University of California Press, 2013). The vision of animals in dreams is metaphorically interpreted by the Runa of Ecuador as a sign that the hunt will be successful the next day, even if another species is caught. In contrast, the dream of dogs is interpreted literally by the Runa: the barking they do in their dreams is a sign of the barking they will do when they come across a jaguar or a monkey or a peccary. Kohn explains this difference by the fact that the dogs introduced by the Spanish colonists were used by the Runa as hunting companions with a low position in the hierarchy: the dogs are to the Runa as the Runa are to the colonists.

9  See Chamayou, *Manhunts*, p. 76: "The experience of hunting establishes for the prey a relationship to the world that is structured by a radical anxiety. Each perception, including that of its own body, becomes a foreboding of danger. Being constantly on the watch is what characterizes the animal, and it is in this sense that being hunted animalizes humans." See also p. 164: "Manhunt is a technique of government by making people feel insecure – putting people on edge, against the background of living in constant danger of being tracked down and deported."

10  Ibid., p. 86.

11  Ibid., p. 108. This is a quote from Alphonse Bertillon, *Identification anthropométrique: instructions signalétiques* (Imprimerie administrative, 1893), p. vii.

12  See Grégoire Chamayou, *A Theory of the Drone* (New Press, 2015).

13  See Grégoire Chamayou, *The Ungovernable Society: A Genealogy of Authoritarian Liberalism*, trans. Andrew Brown (Wiley, 2021).

14  See Achille Mbembe, *Critique of Black Reason*, trans. Laurent Dubois (Duke University Press, 2017). In the introduction to this book, Mbembe quotes Grégoire Chamayou's *Theory of the Drone*, but also Françoise Vergès, *L'Homme prédateur. Ce que nous enseigne l'esclavage sur notre temps* (Albin Michel, 2011).

15  See Jean and John Comaroff (eds.), *Law and Disorder in the Postcolony* (University of Chicago Press, 2006)

16  See Achille Mbembe, "Necropolitics," *Public Culture* 15 (1),

2003: 11–40. Mbembe quotes Paul Gilroy, *The Black Atlantic: Modernity and Double Consciousness* (Verso, 1993).

17  Achille Mbembe, "Necropolitics," op. cit., p. 35. On mass massacres in the German colonies, see Casper W. Erichsen, *The Kaiser's Holocaust: Germany's Forgotten Genocide and the Colonial Roots of Nazism* (Faber and Faber, 2010). On the tension between biopolitics and genocide in the Nazi regime, see Christian Ingrao, *The SS Dirlewanger Brigade: The History of the Black Hunters*, trans. Phoebe Green (Skyhorse, 2011) and *The Promise of the East: Nazi Hopes and Genocide, 1939–43* (Polity, 2019).

18  Mbembe, "Necropolitics," pp. 54–58.

19  See Mbembe, *Critique of Black Reason*, pp. 224–246.

20  Ibid., p. 260.

21  These analyses by Marx, taken up by Lenin and Luxemburg, are reflected in Claude Lévi-Strauss's famous 1953 text "Race and history," which replaces the Marxist concept of a reserve of capital in the colonies with the more structuralist concept of a reserve of structures in the human brain. It is astonishing that no discussion of this text (such as Wiktor Stockzkowski, *Anthropologies rédemptrices. Le monde selon Lévi-Strauss* (Hermann, 2008)) mentions Foucault's analyses of the use of race in biopower, and no commentator on Foucault's texts on racism mentions Lévi-Strauss. This thesis also lies at the heart of Hannah Arendt's analysis of imperialism as a matrix of totalitarianism. See Hannah Arendt, *Imperialism*, part 2 of *The Origins of Totalitarianism* (Schocken 1951); André Duarte, "Hannah Arendt, biopolitics and the problem of violence: from animal laborans to Homo sacer" in Dan Stone and Richard King, *Hannah Arendt and the Uses of History. Imperialism, Nation, Race and Genocide* (Berghahn Books, 2007), pp. 21–37.

22  See Michel Foucault, *Society Must Be Defended*, p. 61 ("what we see as a polarity, as a binary rift within society, is not a clash between two distinct races. It is the splitting of a single race into a superrace and a subrace"); Orazio Irrera, "Racisme et colonialisme chez Michel Foucault," in Jean-François Braunstein, Daniele Lorenzini, Ariane Revel, Judith Revel, Arianna Sforzini

# 166        *Notes to pp. 37–38*

(eds.), *Foucault(s)* (Sorbonne, 2017), pp. 125–139; Ann Stoler, *Carnal Knowledge and Imperial Power: Race and the Intimate in Colonial Rule* (University of California Press, 2010); Guillaume Lachenal, *The Doctor Who Would Be King*, trans. Cheryl Smeall (Duke University Press, 2022).

23  See Foucault, *Society Must Be Defended*, p. 103: "A whole series of colonial models was brought back to the West, and the result was that the West could practice something resembling colonization, or an internal colonialism, on itself."

24  See Michel Foucault, *Discipline and Punish*, p. 221: "The methods for administering the accumulation of men made possible a political takeoff in relation to the traditional, rit-ualistic, costly, violent forms of power, which soon fell into disuse and were superseded by a subtle, calculated technology of subjection." This passage is picked up and commented on by Pierre Macherey in *Le sujet des norms* (Amsterdam, 2014), pp. 211–212. On the reversible transformation of people into commodities in slavery, see Igor Kopytoff, "The Cultural Biography of Things. Commodification as a Process," in Arjun Appadurai (ed.), *The Social Life of Things: Commodities in Cultural Perspective* (Cambridge University Press, 1986), pp. 64–91.

25  See Mbembe, *Critique of Black Reason*, p. 14. This is Edward Tylor's definition of animism as the perception of a body doubled by the soul on the occasion of the death of a loved one or a premonitory dream. In *Politique de l'inimitié* (La Découverte, 2016), p. 194, Mbembe takes up Philippe Descola's definition of animism as the imputation of inten-tions analogous to those of humans to non-human natural or supernatural entities. It should be pointed out that the term "predation" is not negative in anthropological works following Descola, where it designates a modality of relationship between humans and non-humans on the occasion of the hunt, but it has become so in post-colonial literature following Mbembe, where it designates violence against living beings.

26  See Sophie Houdart and Olivier Thiery (eds.), *Humains, non-humains. Comment repeupler les sciences sociales* (La Découverte, 2011), pp. 65–74; Frédéric Keck, Ursula Regehr and Saskia

Walentowitz, "Anthropologie: le tournant ontologique en action," *Tsantsa* 20, 2015: 34–41; Martin Holbraad and Morten Pedersen, *The Ontological Turn: an Anthropological Exposition* (Cambridge University Press, 2017).

27  See Eduardo Viveiros de Castro, *From the Enemy's Point of View. Humanity and Divinity in an Amazonian Society* (University of Chicago Press, 1992); "Cosmological deixis and Amerindian perspectivism," *Journal of the Royal Anthropological Institute* 4, 1998: 469–488.

28  See André-Georges Haudricourt, "Domestication des animaux, culture des plantes et traitement d'autrui," *L'Homme*, 1962, tome 2 no.1: 40–50. On the posterity of this article, see Carole Ferret, "Vers une anthropologie de l'action. André-Georges Haudricourt et l'efficacité technique," *L'Homme* 202, 2012: 113–139. It is surprising that neither Foucault, nor Chamayou or Mbembe cite this essential article for the anthropology of hunter-gatherer societies in their analyses of pastoral and hunting power. Philippe Descola cites this 1962 text as much as Viveiros' 1998 article in *Beyond Nature and Culture*.

29  See Christophe Bonneuil, *Des savants pour l'empire. La structuration des recherches scientifiques coloniales au temps de "la mise en valeur des colonies françaises," 1917–1945* (Orstom, 1991); Grégory Quenet, *Versailles, une histoire naturelle* (La Découverte, 2015); Hélène Blais, *L'Empire de la nature. Une histoire des jardins botaniques coloniaux (Fin XVIIIe siècle – années 1930)* (Champ Vallon, 2023).

30  Pierre Vidal-Naquet, *The Black Hunter: Forms of Thought and Forms of Society in the Greek World* (Johns Hopkins University Press, 1986), p. 135.

31  Jean-Pierre Vernant and Pierre Vidal-Naquet, *Myth and Tragedy in Ancient Greece*, trans. Janet Lloyd (Princeton University Press, 1990); *Cunning Intelligence in Greek Culture and Society* (University of Chicago Press, 1991).

32  Alain Schnapp, *Le chasseur et la cité. Chasse et érotique en Grèce ancienne* (Albin Michel, 1997), p. 63. See also François Hartog, *The Mirror of Herodotus. The Representation of the Other in the Writing of History*, trans. Janet Lloyd (University of California Press, 2009).

168  *Notes to pp. 41–42*

33 See Jean-Pierre Filiu, *Le milieu des mondes. Une histoire laïque du Moyen-Orient de 395 à nos jours* (Seuil, 2021), p. 210.

34 See Anand Pandian, "Pastoral power in the postcolony. On the biopolitics of the criminal animal in south India," *Cultural Anthropology* 23(1), 2008: 85–117, and Kriti Kapila. *Nullius: The Anthropology of Ownership, Sovereignty, and the Law in India*, (Hau Books, 2022), pp. 81–93. Kriti Kapila describes how the Indian government categorized the Andaman Islands as "terra nullius," even though they are home to hunter-gatherer societies described as "sentinels."

35 See Lawrence Cohen, "The other kidney. Biopolitics beyond recognition," *Body and Society* 7 (2–3), 2001: 9–29.

36 See Krithika Srinivasan, "The biopolitics of animal being and welfare. Dog control and care in the U.K. and India," *Transactions of the Institute of British Geographers* 38, 2013: 106–119

37 See Kaushik Sunder Rajan, *Biocapital. The Constitution of Post-Genomic Life* (Duke University Press, 2006); *Pharmocracy. Trials of Global Biomedicine* (Duke University Press, 2017).

38 See Brian Lander, *The King's Harvest. A Political Ecology of China from the First Farmers to the First Empire* (Yale University Press, 2021); Roel Sterckx, *The Animal and the Daemon in Early China* (State University of New York Press, 2002).

39 See Thomas T. Allsen, *The Royal Hunt in Eurasian History* (University of Pennsylvania Press, 2011).

40 See Ruth Rogaski, *Hygienic Modernity. Meanings of Health and Disease in Treaty-port China* (University of California Press, 2004); Luca Gabbiani, *Pékin à l'ombre du landat céleste. Vie quotidienne et gouvernement urbain sous la dynastie Qing (1644–1911)* (EHESS, 2011); Pierre Singaravélou, *Tianjin Cosmopolis. Une autre histoire de la mondialisation* (Seuil, 2017).

41 See Frank Dikötter, *The Discourse of Race in Modern China* (Oxford University Press, 2015); Ari Larissa Heinrich, *Chinese Surplus. Biopolitical Aesthetics and the Medically Commodified Body* (Duke University Press, 2018).

42 See Florence Bretelle-Establet and Frédéric Keck, "Les épidémies entre Orient et Occident," *Extrême-Orient Extrême*

*Occident* 37, 2014: 5–19; Susan Greenhalgh, "The Chinese biopolitical. Facing the twenty-first century," *New Genetics and Society* 28 (3), 2009: 205–222.

43 See Christos Lynteris, "Skilled natives, inept coolies: Marmot hunting and the great Manchurian pneumonic plague (1910–1911)," *History and Anthropology*, 2012: 3. "The construction of an anthropological combination of local knowledge and hygiene, which problematized coolies as unhygienic because they lacked local knowledge, while valorizing Mongolian and Buryat marmot hunters as hygienic because they possessed local knowledge, was a vital part of the Chinese state's biopolitical reform." See also Christos Lynteris, *Ethnographic Plague: Configuring Disease on the Chinese-Russian Frontier* (Palgrave Macmillan, 2016).

44 This critical ethnographic gesture can be found in Charles Stépanoff's work on hunting societies in Tuva (Eastern Siberia) and Perche (France): *Chamanisme, rituel et cognition chez les Touvas (Sibérie du Sud)* (Editions FMSH, 2014); *Voyager dans l'invisible. Techniques chamaniques de l'imagination* (La Découverte, 2019); *L'animal et la mort. Chasses, modernité et crise du sauvage* (La Découverte, 2022). According to Stépanoff, hunter-peasants in the Perche region do not distinguish between the wild and the domestic when they explore a place they know in search of game, whereas forest managers see it as a delimited space in which they carry out acts of "taking" (*prise*). By justifying hunting with fixed-rate targets, they turn the forest into a valuable resource. "The contemporary hunter, claiming to be 'France's leading ecologist', is now a population statistician, an indispensable 'regulator' of overpopulated animals, a necessary cog in the functioning of living environments" (*L'animal et la mort*, p. 139). Stépanoff thus criticizes "cynegetic biopower" and emphasizes that population statistics, ignoring the uncertainty of interaction with the hunted animal, are "the exact opposite of the ethic of randomness and the gift of peasant hunting" (ibid., p. 143). Here, Stépanoff takes up the hypotheses of Roberte Hamayon and Caroline Humphrey on the importance of chance and gambling in Siberian hunting practices: see Roberte Hamayon,

170 *Notes to pp. 42–44*

La chasse à l'âme. Esquisse d'une théorie du chamanisme sibérien (Société d'ethnologie, 1990); Caroline Humphrey and Urgunge Onon, *Shamans and Elders. Experience, Knowledge and Power among the Daur Mongols* (Clarendon Press, 1996).

45 See Anna Tsing, *In the Realm of the Diamond Queen. Marginality in an Out-of-the-way Place* (Princeton University Press, 1993); James Scott, *Weapons of the Weak. Everyday Forms of Peasant Resistance* (Yale University Press, 1985). Focusing in particular on zoonoses as markers of the transition from nomadic to sedentary state, James Scott has pursued the hypothesis of alternative forms of life and thought to pastoral and state domestication in the nomadic societies of Southeast Asia, through a set of seminal books that are more historical frescoes than ethnographic surveys: *Seeing Like a State: How Certain Schemes to Improve the Human Condition Have Failed* (Yale University Press, 1998); *The Art of Not Being Governed: An Anarchist History of Upland Southeast Asia* (Yale University Press, 2009); *Against the Grain: A Deep History of the Earliest States* (Yale University Press, 2017).

46 See Anna Tsing, *Friction: An Ethnography of Global Connection* (Princeton University Press, 2005).

47 See Frederico Rosa, *L'Âge d'or du totémisme. Histoire d'un débat anthropologique (1887–1929)* (CNRS Éditions, 2003).

48 See Elizabeth Povinelli, *Geontologies. A Requiem to Late Liberalism* (Duke University Press, 2016), p. 9: "Foucault's concept of biopolitics has hardly been shielded from accusations of narcissistic provinciality. This provinciality becomes apparent when biopolitics is read from a different global history – when the geontology of biopower is assigned a different social geography."

49 Ibid., p. 11.

50 Taking up Achille Mbembe's proposition that European biopolitics rested on a hidden necropolitics in the colonies, Povinelli writes: "Biopower (governance by life and death) has long depended on an underlying geontopower (the difference between the living and the inert). And, just as necropolitics operated openly in colonial Africa only to reveal its form in Europe, geopower has long operated openly in late colonial

*Notes to pp. 44–45* 171

liberalism and been inserted into the ordinary operations of its governance of difference and markets" (ibid., pp. 12–13).

51 Elizabeth Povinelli points out that it doesn't matter whether what Mbembe, following Chamayou, calls "cynegetic" power is described as totemistic or animistic, as long as the anthropologist can describe how this power comes into tension with pastoral and sovereign power (*Geontologies*, pp. 39–40). Povinelli reviews a chapter in Tim Ingold's *The Perception of the Environment* (Routledge, 2000) entitled "Totemism, animism and the depiction of animals."

52 See Fabiana Jardim, Annika Skoglund, Anindya Purakayastha, and David Armstrong, "Virus as a figure of geontopower, or how to practice Foucault now? A conversation with Elizabeth A. Povinelli," *Foucault Studies* 35, 2023: 226: "I'm more into what Eduardo Viveiro de Castro calls a predator/prey mentality than a friend/enemy mentality."

53 While visiting a fossil exhibition at the Queensland Art Gallery with his Aboriginal friends, a child asked his grandmother: "Were dogs here before the dinosaurs?" (Elizabeth Povinelli, *Geontologies*, op. cit., p. 85). See also Deborah Bird Rose, *Le rêve du chien sauvage. Amour et extinction* (La Découverte, 2020).

54 See Petronella Vaarzon-Morel, "Alien relations: Ecological and ontological dilemmas posed for indigenous Australians in the management of 'feral' camels on their lands," in Françoise Dussart and Sylvie Poirier (eds.), *Entangled Territorialities. Negotiating Indigenous Lands in Australia and Canada* (University of Toronto Press, 2017), pp. 186–211.

55 See Barbara Glowczewski, *Rêves en colère. Alliances aborigènes dans le Nord-Ouest australien* (Plon, 2004), p. 223.

56 See Arnaud Morvan, "Le virus, la chauve-souris et le totem. Ethnographie des relations inter-espèces dans le contexte biosécuritaire australien," *Anthropologie & Santé* 22, 2021. http://journals.openedition.org/anthropologiesante/6942

57 See Eben Kirksey and Stefan Helmreich, "The emergence of multispecies ethnography," *Cultural Anthropology* 25 (4), 2010: 545–576.

58 See Stefan Helmreich, *Alien Ocean. Anthropological Voyages*

172                    *Notes to pp. 45–46*

in *Microbial Seas* (University of California Press, 2009); Eben Kirksey, *Freedom in Entangled Worlds. West Papua and the Architecture of Global Power* (Duke University Press, 2012).

59   See Kirksey and Helmreich, "The emergence of multispecies ethnography," p. 545.

60   See Lewis Henry Morgan, *The American Beaver and His Works* (Lippincott Co, 1868); Harold Conklin, "An ethnoecological approach to shifting agriculture," *Transactions of the New York Academy of Sciences* 17 (2): 133–142. Ethnozoology studies local conceptions of animals in indigenous societies, contrasting them with the global conceptions of Western zoology.

61   See Stefan Helmreich, "Species of biocapital," *Science as Culture* 17(4), 2008: 463–478. Helmreich also speaks of "microbiopolitics": see Heather Paxson and Stefan Helmreich, "Perils and promises of microbial abundance, novel natures and model ecosystems, from artisanal cheese to alien seas," *Social Studies of Science* 44(2), 2014: 165–93; Heather Paxson, "Post-Pasteurian cultures: The microbiopolitics of raw-milk cheese in the United States," *Cultural Anthropology* 23(1), 2008: 15–47.

62   Kirksey and Helmreich, "The emergence of multispecies ethnography," art. cit. p. 557. Stefan Helmreich notes in particular that recent research in microbiology has gone beyond the paradigm of genealogy by sexual descent to show horizontal transfers of information between microbes. See Stefan Helmreich, "Trees and seas of information: Alien kinship and the biopolitics of gene transfer in marine biology and biotechnology," *American Ethnologist* 30 (3), 2003: 340–358.

63   See Celia Lowe, "Viral clouds. Becoming H5N1 in Indonesia," *Cultural Anthropology* 4, 2010: 625–649. Celia Lowe has previously studied how biodiversity managers in Indonesia have participated in the construction of a post-colonial democratic society, and describes the biosecurity measures imposed by bird 'flu as a threat to this movement: see *Wild Profusion: Biodiversity Conservation in an Indonesian Archipelago* (Princeton University Press, 2007).

64   Celia Lowe ("Viral clouds," p. 629) quotes Gilles Deleuze and Félix Guattari: "We form a rhizome with our viruses, or rather

*Notes to pp. 47–49*  173

our viruses cause us to form a rhizome with other animals."
(*A Thousand Plateaus: Capitalism and Schizophrenia*, Athlone, 1988), p. 11.

65  Leeuwenhoek's invention of the microscope was one of a series of techniques disseminated in the Netherlands that taught children to see the world small in a box, no doubt reflecting the country's role in the globalization of trade since the sixteenth century: see Thomas Beaufils, *Histoire des Pays-Bas: de l'Antiquité à nos jours* (Tallandier, 2018).

66  Paul de Kruif, *Microbe Hunters* (Harcourt, 1926), p. 228.

67  Ibid., p. 377.

68  Ibid., p. 256.

69  Ibid., p. 321.

70  Ibid., p. 336. De Kruif took part in the controversy between Ross and Grassi over the discovery of the role of mosquitoes in malaria transmission: see Jan Peter Verhave, "Clifford Dobell and the making of Paul de Kruif's *Microbe Hunters*," *Medical History*. 54(4), 2010: 529–536.

71  De Kruif, *Microbe Hunters*, p. 266.

72  See Warwick Anderson, "Natural histories of infectious diseases: Ecological vision in twentieth-century biomedical sciences," *Osiris* 19, 2004: 39–61. Warwick Anderson, starting from a Foucauldian hypothesis on the role of the military in the use of race by colonial medicine, gradually came to focus more and more on the figure of the virus hunter: see *Colonial Pathologies. American Tropical Medicine, Race, and Hygiene in the Philippines* (Duke University Press, 2007); *The Collectors of Lost Souls. Turning Kuru Scientists into Whitemen* (Johns Hopkins University Press, 2008).

73  Edmond Sergent and Étienne Sergent, "Études épidémiologiques et prophylactiques du paludisme en Algérie, en 1904," *Annales de l'Institut Pasteur* 19 (3), 1905: 129–164.

74  Louis Tanon, "Le rat, réservoir de virus pour la peste," in *Congrès Colonial National de la Santé Publique et de la Prévoyance Sociale. Marseille, 11–17 Septembre 1922: Organisation du Congrès, Comptes Rendus des Séances* (Marseille, Commissariat général de l'exposition coloniale, 1922), pp. 249–255, quoted in Matheus Alves Duarte da Silva, Oliver French, Frédéric Keck,

174 *Notes to pp. 49–53*

and Jules Skotnes-Brown, "Introduction: Disease reservoirs: From colonial medicine to One Health," *Medical Anthropology* 42(4), 2023: 318.

75 See Christos Lynteris, *Visual Plague. The Emergence of Epidemic Photography* (MIT Press, 2022).

76 Theobald Smith, "Animal reservoirs of human disease with special reference to microbic variability," *Bulletin of the New York Academy of Medicine* 4(4), 1928: 477.

77 Ibid., p. 496.

78 Karl Friedrich Meyer, "The animal kingdom. A reservoir of disease," *Proceedings of Internal Medicine Chicago* 8 (14–15), 1931: 234–261.

79 Burnet, who was a keen collector of beetles in his youth, linked the practices of microbiologists to the British tradition of naturalists, while pointing out that "this essentially amateur type of observer has been replaced by the professional biologist, whose systematic investigations of a terrain once known as nature have given dignity to the science of ecology," *Natural History of Infectious Diseases* (Cambridge University Press, 1972), p. 5.

80 See Susan Jones, "Population cycles, disease, and networks of ecological knowledge," *Journal of the History of Biology* 50 (2), 2017: 357–391.

81 Charles Elton is also the author of *The Ecology of Invasions by Animals and Plants* (University of Chicago Press, 1958).

82 Karl Friedrich Meyer, "Infectious Disease," *Science* 94(2441), review by F.M. Burnet, *Biological History of Infectious Disease*, quoted in M. Honigsbaum, "'Tipping the balance': Karl Friedrich Meyer, latent infections, and the birth of modern ideas of disease ecology," *Journal of the History of Biology* 49 (2), 2016: 286.

83 See Susan Jones and Ana Amramina, "Entangled histories of plague ecology in Russia and the U.S.S.R.," *History and Philosophy of the Life Sciences* 40 (3), 2018: 1–21.

84 See Pierre-Olivier Méthot, "'Birth, life, and death of infectious diseases': Charles Nicolle (1866–1936) and the invention of medical ecology in France," *History and Philosophy of the Life Sciences*, 41 (2), 2019; Maurice Huet, *Le pommier et l'olivier:*

*Charles Nicolle, une biographie (1866–1936)* (Sauramps, 1995); Kim Pelis, *Charles Nicolle, Pasteur's Imperial Missionary. Typhus and Tunisia* (University of Rochester Press, 2007).

85 Kim Pelis, *Charles Nicolle*, op. cit., p. 73.

86 Charles Nicolle, *Naissance, vie et mort des maladies infectieuses* (Alcan, 1930), pp. 13–14.

87 Maximilien Sorre, "Complexes pathogènes et géographie médicale," *Annales de géographie* 42 (235), 1933: 1–18, quoted in Gil Bartholeyns, *Le hantement du monde. Zoonoses et Pathocène* (Dehors, 2021), p. 90.

88 Ibid., p. 81.

89 See Catherine and Raphaël Larrère, "L'animal, machine à produire: la rupture du contrat domestique," in Florence Burgat and Robert Dantzer (eds.), *Les animaux d'élevage ont-ils droit au bien-être?* (Éditions de l'INRA, 2001), pp. 9–24; Jocelyne Porcher, *Eleveurs et animaux, réinventer le lien* (Presses Universitaires de France, 2002).

90 See René Dubos and Barbara Ward, *Only One Earth: The Care and Maintenance of a Small Planet* (Andre Deutsch, 1972); Mark Honigsbaum, "René Dubos, tuberculosis, and the 'ecological facets of virulence'," *History and Philosophy of Life Sciences* 39 (3), 2017: 1–15.

91 See Angela Creager, *The Life of a Virus. Tobacco Mosaic Virus as an Experimental Model, 1930–1965* (University of Chicago Press, 2002).

92 See Greer Williams, *Virus Hunters. The Lives and Triumphs of Great Medical Pioneers* (Hutchinson, 1960), p. xii: "The hunt for wild viruses, as virologists call those which have not been tamed through laboratory manipulation, is quite a different story from that of the fat, easy-to-grow one-celled form of plant life known as bacteria. For one thing, viruses, traveling mainly by person-to-person contact or possibly from some distance through the air, resist treatment with the miracle drugs."

93 Ibid., p. 406.

94 See Anne-Marie Moulin, *Le dernier langage de la médecine. Histoire de l'immunologie, de Pasteur au Sida* (Presses Universitaires de France, 1991), pp. 74–77.

95 Joshua Lederberg, Robert E. Shope, and Stanley C. Oaks Jr.

176 *Notes to pp. 56–60*

(eds.), *Emerging Infections: Microbial Threats to Health in the United States* (National Academies Press, 1992).

96 Joshua Lederberg, "Infectious history," *Science* 288, 2000: 289.

97 Robert Gallo, *Virus Hunting: AIFDS, Cancer and the Human Retrovirus. A Story of Scientific Discovery* (Basic Books, 1991), p. 3.

98 Joseph McCormick and Susan Fischer Hoch, *The Virus Hunters. Dispatchers from the Frontline* (Bloomsbury, 1997), p. 1. A similar quest to that for the Ebola reservoir in primates concerns the origins of AIDS in monkeys, even though they do not constitute a reservoir for regular transmission of HIV to humans: see Alexander F. Voevodin and Preston A. Marx, *Simian Virology* (Wiley, 2009).

99 See Robert G. Webster, William Bean, Owen Gorman, Tim Chambers, and Yoshi Kawaoka, "Evolution and ecology of Influenza A viruses," *Microbiological Review* 56 (1), 1992: 152–179.

100 Robert G. Webster, *Flu Hunter. Unlocking the Secrets of a Virus* (Otago University Press, 2018), p. 45.

101 Richard Webby and Robert G. Webster, "Are we ready for pandemic influenza?" *Science* 302, no. 5650, 2003: 1519.

## 4 Cryopolitics: Conserving collections in nature reserves

1 The notion of mutation was introduced into microbiology by Charles Nicolle, who, reading the philosopher Henri Bergson, saw it as the equivalent for microbes of what invention is for humans: see Kim Pelis, *Charles Nicolle, Pasteur's Imperial Missionary*, op. cit., p. 224. On how the mutation paradigm is transforming biotechnologies with the CRISPR technique, see Eben Kirksey, *The Mutant Project. Inside the Global Race to Genetically Modify Humans* (St. Martin's Press, 2020).

2 See Hannah Landecker, *Culturing Life. How Cells Became Technologies* (Harvard University Press, 2007), pp. 68–71. Alexis Carrel is best known today as the theorist and protagonist of a eugenics policy, through his book *L'Homme, cet inconnu*, published in Paris and New York in 1935, and his directorship of the French Foundation for the study of human

*Notes to p. 61* 177

problems, entrusted to him by the Vichy regime between 1940 and 1944. Hannah Landecker points out that Carrel was first and foremost a reader of Bergson's *Creative Evolution*, whose "operationalized philosophy of biological time" he applied in the laboratory, drawing on the invention of microcinematography by his contemporary Jean Comandon: see Hannah Landecker, "Microcinematography and the history of science and film," *Isis* 97, 2006: 121–132. She thus shows that the laboratory, far from reducing life to chemical sequences, biologizes historical time by organizing an environment in which vital duration is cultivated and controlled to produce a synchronized living: see Hannah Landecker, "Food as exposure: Nutritional epigenetics and the new metabolism," *BioSocieties* 6 (2) 2011: 167–194; "Antibiotic resistance and the biology of history," *Body and Society* 22(4), 2016: 19–52.

3   Hannah Landecker quotes a text by naturalist Edmond Perrier in *Le Feuilleton du temps* in 1912 entitled "The living world": "Cell populations were just like the infusoria whose power to multiply was already well known, so great that if all their progeny live for the normal duration of their existence, only one of these tiny beings, only tenths of a millimetre long, produces in one month, according to the calculations of the eminent naturalist M. Maupas, a mass of living substance a million times more voluminous than the sun. What a hecatomb that supposes, and what fragility!" (*Culturing Life*, op. cit., p. 99).

4   Alexis Carrel, "Tissue culture in the study of viruses," in Thomas Rivers (ed.), *Filterable Viruses* (Balliere, Tindall & Cox, 1928), p. 104, quoted in Hannah Landecker, *Culturing Life*, op. cit., p. 118.

5   Hannah Landecker cites an article in *Cryobiology* in 1964: "The refrigerator may be considered a cold cornucopia that can provide the cell culturist with a virtually unlimited supply of characterized cells" (Ward Peterson and Cyril Stulberg, "Freeze preservation of cultured animal cells," *Cryobiology* 1, 1964: 85, quoted in Hannah Landecker, *Culturing Life*, op. cit., p. 157).

6   See Carlo Caduff, *The Pandemic Perhaps. Dramatic Events in a*

178 *Notes to pp. 62–63*

*Public Culture of Danger* (University of California Press, 2015), pp. 40–50.

7 See Anna Aranzazu, "Surveillance de la grippe d'origine animale à l'OMS. Transformation de l'écologie du virus grippal, de la surveillance *in extenso* à la prévention et au contrôle des pandémies," *Revue d'anthropologie des connaissances* 10 (1), 2016: 71–93; Frédéric Vagneron, "Surveiller et s'unir? Le rôle de l'OMS dans les premières mobilisations internationales autour d'un réservoir animal de la grippe," *Revue d'anthropologie des connaissances* 9 (2), 2015: 139–162.

8 See Vincent Munster et al., "Practical considerations for high-throughput influenza A virus surveillance studies of wild birds by use of molecular diagnostic tests," *Journal of Clinical Microbiology* 47 (3), 2009: 666–673; Adrian Mackenzie, "Bringing sequences to life. How bioinformatics corporealizes sequence data," *New Genetics and Society* 22 (3), 2003: 315–332.

9 Edwin Kilbourne, afterword to Stephen Morse, *Emerging Viruses* (Oxford University Press, 1993), p. 294.

10 Carlo Caduff quotes Michael Coston, author of an online *Avian Flu Diary*, as saying: "Nature's laboratory never sleeps" (*The Pandemic Perhaps*, op. cit., p. 19).

11 See David Morens, Jeffery Taubenberger, and Anthony Fauci, "The persistent legacy of the 1918 influenza virus," *New England Journal of Medicine* 361 (3), 2009: 225: "To understand what has happened since 1918, it is helpful to think of influenza viruses not as distinct entities but as 'gene teams' that work together and must sometimes trade away one or more team members to make way for new gene 'players' with unique skills. (. . .) The 1918 influenza virus and its progeny, and the human immunity developed in response to them, have for nearly a century evolved in an elaborate dance: the partners have remained linked and in rhythm, even as each strives to take the lead. This complex interplay between rapid viral evolution and virally driven changes in human population immunity has created a 'pandemic era' lasting for 91 years and counting."

12 See Madeline Drexler, *Secret Agents. The Menace of Emerging*

*Infections* (Joseph Henry Press, 2002); Michael Dillon, "Virtual security: A life science of (dis)order," *Millennium* 32 (3), 2003: 551–558; Nicholas King, "The influence of anxiety: September 11, Bioterrorism, and American public health," *Journal of the History of Medicine and Allied Sciences* 58 (4), 2003: 433–441; Jeanne Guillemin, *Biological Weapons. From the Invention of State-Sponsored Programs to Contemporary Bioterrorism* (Columbia University Press, 2005); Bruce Braun, "Biopolitics and the molecularization of life," *Cultural Geographies* 14, 1, 2007: 6–28; Melinda Cooper, "Pre-empting emergence: The biological turn in the war on terror," *Theory, Culture & Society* 23 (4), 2006: 113–135; Joseph Masco, *The Theater of Operations. National Security Affect from the Cold War to the War on Terror* (Duke University Press, 2014).

13 See Patrick Zylberman, *Tempêtes microbiennes. Essai sur la politique de sécurité microbienne dans le monde transatlantique* (Gallimard, 2013).

14 See Kirsty Duncan, *Hunting the 1918 Flu. One Scientist's Search for a Killer Virus* (University of Toronto Press, 2003).

15 See Ann Reid, Thomas Fanning, Johan Hultin, and Jeffery Taubenberger, "Origin and evolution of the 1918 "Spanish" influenza virus hemagglutinin gene," *PNAS*, 96 (4), 1999: 1651–1656.

16 Quoted in Carlo Caduff, *The Pandemic Perhaps*, op. cit., p. 109.

17 See ibid., pp. 116–118. Caduff translates Palese's position into the vocabulary of Jacques Derrida: the virus is a piece of information that circulates in the media like an indefinitely repeatable sign, but for the biologist, a sign only has meaning in a context. Caduff analyzes the precautionary principle as "a reaffirmation of agency and sovereignty in a world that is increasingly saturated with a complex array of scientific truth claims and ambiguous or unreliable test results" (p. 144). In his view, this principle operates a "leap of faith" from the set of rationally observable viruses in laboratory space to a virus declared as potentially pandemic. Caduff thus contrasts *microbe farmers*, who exercise pastoral power in the laboratory, with *virus hunters*, who exercise predatory power in a set of scarce resources subject to competition between biologists (p. 26). He

180 *Notes to pp. 64–65*

thus criticizes the "pandemic prophecies" made by 'flu specialists on the basis of observation of the ordinary techniques of virus cultivation in the laboratory: "appreciating the routine methods of microbe farming is essential if we are to understand how statements about the future galvanize the prophetic scene of science" (p. 77).

18 Michel Foucault, *Society Must Be Defended*, p. 254.

19 See Richard Neustadt and Harvey Feinberg, *The Epidemic That Never Was. Policy Making and the Swine Flu Scare* (Vintage Books, 1983).

20 See Shanta Zimmer and Donald Burke, "Historical perspective. Emergence of influenza A (H1N1) viruses," *New England Journal of Medicine* 361 (3), 2009: 279–283.

21 Caduff picks up on Foucault's conception of virologists' biopower as a pastoral power in the laboratory hijacked by sovereign power, but he misses the hunters' work of collecting influenza viruses. By referring statements about pandemics to future events concerning humans, he fails to grasp how these statements refer to past events concerning relations between humans and non-humans. This is why I compare microbiologists not to prophets making the "leap of faith" into serious statements on the public stage, but to shamans leaping between species in ritual dances. The prophet addresses the sovereign to criticize him from the standpoint of a coming apocalypse, while the shaman addresses ordinary people to tell them stories of a time when humans and non-humans were not separated. In this cross-country race between humans and the viruses that haunt the process of animal domestication, the virologist must become a ghost hunter to run as fast as the viruses in the imagination, equipped with freezers and computers as Siberian shamans equip themselves with talismans and drums. This discussion was published in the forum around Carlo Caduff, "Pandemic prophecy, or how to have faith in reason," *Current Anthropology* 55(3): 296–315.

22 See Muriel Figuié and Tristan Fournier, "Risques sanitaires globaux et politiques nationales. La gestion de la grippe aviaire au Vietnam," *Revue d'Études en Agriculture et Environnement*

*(RAEStud)* 91(3), 2010: 327–343; Frédéric Keck, "Asian tigers and the Chinese dragon. Competition and collaboration between sentinels of pandemics, from SARS to COVID-19," *Centaurus* 62 (2), 2020: 311–320.

23 See Natalie Porter, "Bird flu biopower: Strategies for multispecies coexistence in Vietnam," *American Ethnologist* 40 (1), 2013. Natalie Porter describes these campaigns as ways of producing disciplined subjects in social communities that include animals: "Becoming subjects in bird flu biopower means engaging in work on oneself in relation to poultry" (p. 144). She points out that "biopower also operates on humans and animals collectively, as one social group composed of humans living *with* animals (. . .). Zoonoses raise new questions about humans' obligations to animal health, which spur conflicts about how humans should conduct themselves in the name of an existence they share with other species" (p. 133). See also Natalie Porter, *Viral Economies. Bird Flu Experiments in Vietnam* (University of Chicago Press, 2019); Natalie Porter and Ilana Gershon, *Living with Animals. Bonds across Species* (Cornell University Press, 2018).

24 Porter, "Bird flu biopower," p. 142.

25 See ibid., p. 139: "A chicken killed at the height of health ensures taste and profit, engenders relationships between producer and consumer, and increases a farmer's social standing. In contrast, a chicken killed because of threatening disease loses its value both as a food commodity and a generator of market relationships, and thereby compromises the farmer's reputation. When the existence of more than one species is at stake, the question of how to live becomes more complicated." All these relationships between farmers and animals in Vietnam can be seen in the work of artist Lena Bui, who accompanied international virologists to villages controlled for the risk of bird 'flu: see Frédéric Keck, "Représenter des virus dans l'air, de Londres à Canton," in *Signaux d'alerte*, op. cit., pp. 165–171.

26 See Javier Lezaun and Natalie Porter, "Containment and competition. Transgenic animals in the One Health agenda," *Social Science & Medicine* 129, 2015: 96–105.

182      *Notes to pp. 68–69*

27   See Natalie Porter, "Ferreting things out. Biosecurity, pandemic flu and the transformation of experimental systems," *Biosocieties* 11, 2016: 22–45.

28   See Frédéric Keck, *Avian Reservoirs: Virus Hunters and Birdwatchers in Chinese Sentinel Posts* (Duke University Press, 2020).

29   See Kennedy Shortridge and Charles H. Stuart-Harris, "An influenza epicentre?" *Lancet* ii (1982): 812–813. Lyle Fearnley shows that this oft-quoted text by Shortridge and Stuart-Harris, which builds on Burnet, Laver, and Webster's hypotheses on the role of birds as reservoirs for influenza viruses, was preceded by research in China by Zhu Jiming. This virologist, trained at Cambridge University in the 1940s, returned to China after the advent of the People's Republic to work at the Biological Products Research Institute in Beijing and then in Changchun. To explain the 1957 'flu pandemic other than through the evolutionary mechanisms of seasonal 'flu, Zhu Jiming wrote: "It would probably be wiser to look around for some other possible explanation such as an unexpected animal reservoir as the origin of this queer variant." ("The etiology and epidemiology of influenza. An analysis of the 1957 epidemic," *Journal of Hygiene, Epidemiology, Microbiology and Immunology* 2(1), 1958: 3, quoted in Lyle Faernley, *Virulent Zones. Animal Disease and Global Health at China's Pandemic Epicenter*, Duke University Press, 2020, p. 38). After the 1968 pandemic, Charles Stuart-Harris asked the same question: "Is there an undiscovered phantom reservoir?" (*Bulletin of the World Health Organization* 41(3–4–5), 1969, p. 492, quoted in Lyle Faernley, *Virulent Zones*, op. cit., p. 40).

30   See Leslie Sims, Thomas Ellis, Kwok Liu, Ken Dyrting, Henry Wong, Malik Peiris, Yi Guan, and Kennedy Shortridge, "Avian influenza outbreaks in Hong Kong, 1997–2002," *Avian Disease* 47 (3), 2003: 832–838.

31   See Keck, *Avian Reservoirs*, pp. 79–80.

32   See Thomas Abraham, *Twenty-First Century Plague. The Story of SARS, with a new Preface on Avian Flu* (Hong Kong University Press, 2007).

33   Lyle Fearnley describes Martin and Gilbert's research as fol-

*Notes to pp. 70–72*     183

lows: "The purview of their search expanded in a centrifugal trajectory far beyond the influenza virus to encompass the bodies and behaviors of ducks, traditional techniques of duck-husbandry, the geography of rice-paddy landscapes, wild bird migration flyways, the socio-economy of live birdmarkets and many other objects inscribed within the ever-widening circles of influenza ecology" (*Virulent Zones*, p. 10).

34  Fearnley, *Virulent Zones*, p. 16. Annual duck production in China in 2017 rose from 150 million in 1970 to 2.25 billion in 2017, for around 15 billion poultry in general raised in China each year: cf. ibid., p. 66.

35  Ibid., pp. 54–62.

36  Ibid., p. 110.

37  Fearnley notes that behind a wild goose that takes flight, ecologist Scott Newman saw human practices of experimentation (ibid., p. 118). He calls him a "goose chaser," in the sense that the hunter pursues an entity between life and death for the purpose of accumulation, whereas the chaser pursues an entity between nature and artifact to sustain his desire. Fearnley also responds to the self-deprecation of the young Chinese veterinarians working with Vincent Martin by declaring themselves unfit for "field epidemiology." He recalls the Maoist figure of the "barefoot veterinarian" (*chijiao shouyi*) who goes out into the countryside to help farmers treat diseases, and the more recent figure of the "duck doctor" who can provide farmers with the appropriate medicines without going through the health administration, even though the latter criticizes him as a "cheat" (*pianzi*) (Fearnley, *Virulent Zones*, p. 188–189).

38  See ibid., p. 44 (Webster observed "how primitive Chinese laboratories had become during the dark days of the Cultural Revolution: no deep freezers, no equipment for storing viruses for long periods of time") and p. 61 (Guo, "The Institute of Virology . . . lacked a good-quality refrigerator to keep specimens and reagents.")

39  See Lyle Fearnley, "Viral sovereignty or sequence etiquette? Asian science, open data, and knowledge control in global virus surveillance," *East Asian Science, Technology and Society: An International Journal* 14 (3), 2020: 479–505.

184 *Notes to pp. 72–73*

40  The image of a Chinese tourist eating bat soup on a Micronesian island circulated on social networks around the world, even though the Chinese don't usually eat bats. See Felipe Van der Velden, "A doença comunista e a sopa de morcegos. Sobre tráfico de animais, orientalismo e pandemia," *CAMPOS* 22 (1), 2021: 214–241. Mink mortality on markets in northern China has been put forward inconclusively as a possible origin of SARS-Cov2: see Yann Faure and Yves Sciama, "Les élevages de visons en Chine à l'origine du Covid-19? Les indices s'accumulent," *Reporterre*, 2021.

41  The most comprehensive article to date in the French press on this controversy is by Stéphane Foucart and Hervé Morin, "Emergence du SARS-CoV-2: les scientifiques dans l'impasse," *Le Monde*, December 22, 2022. The most cited and controversial article, as it clearly supports the hypothesis of a zoonotic origin, is Kristian Andersen, Andrew Rambaut, Ian Lipkin, Edward Holmes, and Robert Garry, "The proximal origin of SARS-CoV-2," *Nature Medicine* 26 (4), 2020: 450–452.

42  See David Pascall et al., ""Frozen evolution" of an RNA virus suggests accidental release as a potential cause of arbovirus re-emergence," *PLoS Biology* 18(4), 2020: e3000673.

43  See Qin Li et al., "Early transmission dynamics in Wuhan, China, of novel coronavirus-infected pneumonia," *New England Journal of Medicine*, 382, 2020: 1199–1207; Xiao, Xiao et al., "Animal sales from Wuhan wet markets immediately prior to the COVID-19 pandemic." *Scientific Reports* 11, 11898, 2021.

44  *Global Study of Origins of SARS-CoV-2: China Part*, WHO report, Geneva, 2021, p. 8.

45  See Marion Koopmans, "Origins of SARS-CoV-2: Window is closing for key scientific studies," *Nature* 596 (7873), 2021: 482–485

46  Simon Leplâtre, "Contre le Covid-19, Pékin s'en attaque aux surgelés," *Le Monde*, January 31, 2021. This accusation was followed by revelations that SARS-Cov 2 had been detected in human tissues preserved in Italy and the United States before December 2019: see Frédéric Lemaître, "La polémique sur l'origine du Covid-19 s'amplifie," *Le Monde*, December 2, 2020.

*Notes to pp. 74–77* 185

47 Giuseppina La Rosa et al., "SARS-CoV-2 has been circulating in Northern Italy since December 2019: Evidence from environmental monitoring," *Science of the Total Environment* 750, 2021: 141711.

48 See Masayoshi Maruyama, Lihui Wu, and Liu Wang, "The modernization of fresh food retailing in China," *Journal of Retailing and Consumer Services* 30, 2016: 33–39; Shuru Zhong, Michael Crang, and Guo Zeng, "Constructing freshness: The vitality of wetmarkets in urban China," *Agriculture and Human Values*, 37, 2020: 175–185.

49 See Lyle Fearnley, "Fake eggs. From counter-qualification to popular certification in China's food safety crisis," *BioSocieties* 17, 2022: 253–275.

50 Simon Leplâtre, "À Shanghaï, des morts du Covid-19 stockés dans un hangar réfrigéré," *Le Monde*, January 25, 2023. On the lengthening of waiting times at the morgue during the Covid-19 pandemic and the implementation of a "delegated biopolitics" for funeral professionals to manage this period of suspension in the "work of mourning," see Gaelle Clavandier, Marc-André Berthod, Philippe Charrier, Martin Julier-Costes, and Valeria Pangnamenta, "From one body to another. The handling of the deceased during the Covid-19 pandemic, a case study in France and Switzerland," *Human Remains & Violence. An Interdisciplinary Journal* 7(2), 2022: 41–63. On the biopolitical problems posed by the management of corpses in France, see Arnaud Esquerre, *Les os, les cendres et l'État* (Fayard, 2014).

51 An international petition was launched in 2021 to stop stockpiling vaccines until people had developed immunity to Covid: https://selfhelpafrica.org/ie/vaccine-stockpiling/

52 See Judy Siu, Yuan Cao and David Shum, "Perceptions of and hesitancy toward COVID-19 vaccination in older Chinese adults in Hong Kong: A qualitative study," *BMC Geriatry* 22(1), 2022: 288.

53 William Cronon, *Nature's Metropolis. Chicago and the Great West* (Norton, 1991), p. 254.

54 Cronon shows that Native American societies (hunters in the northern part of present-day U.S. territory, farmers in the

south) saw the pastoralist settlers' conception of nature as incompatible with their own, not least because it was based on the ownership and accumulation of natural resources: see *Changes in the Land. Indians, Colonists, and the Ecology of New England* (Hill & Wang, 1983). In the epilogue to *Nature's Metropolis* (p. 384), Cronon describes himself as "a captive of the pastoral myth": this interstitial position of the historian at the crossroads of cynegetic and pastoral power enables him to criticize forms of sovereignty, in particular the accumulation made possible by property rights.

55  See Georgina André, "Wuhan, d'un centre industriel secondaire à une 'Chicago de l'Est'," *Géoconfluences*, 2020. http://geoconflu ences.ens-lyon.fr/informations-scientifiques/dossiers-regionaux/ la-chine/articles-scientifiques/wuhan

56  See Frédéric Keck, Afterword to *Les sentinelles des pandémies* (Seuil, 2021).

57  Cronon's description of the replacement of bison by cattle draws too clear a distinction between American and Native American knowledge. Recent environmental history has shown that certain Indian tribes were interested in slaughtering bison for the trade, and that "repentant" butchers became major figures in American conservationism, such as William Hornaday, taxidermist at the Smithsonian Institution. See Andrew Isenberg, *The Destruction of the Bison. An Environmental History, 1750–1920* (Cambridge University Press, 2020). Similarly, veterinarians today mix virological and ecological knowledge with farming knowledge.

58  Michael Bravo and Gareth Rees, "Cryo-politics: Environmental security and the future of Arctic navigation," *Brown Journal of World Affairs* 8(1), 2006: 205–215.

59  See Joanna Radin, "Planning for the past. Cryopreservation at the farm, zoo and museum," in Nélia Dias and Fernando Vidal (eds.), *Endangerment, Biodiversity and Culture* (Routledge, 2015), pp. 218–240; Emma Kowal and Joanna Radin, "Indigenous biospecimen collections and the cryopolitics of frozen life," *Journal of Sociology* 51, 2015: 63–80; Joanna Radin and Emma Kowal, *Cryopolitics: Frozen Life in a Melting World* (MIT Press, 2017).

Notes to pp. 78–80

60  Radin and Kowal, *Cryopolitics*, p. 3.

61  See Elisa Stella, Lorenzo Mari, Jacopo Gabrieli, et al., "Permafrost dynamics and risk of anthrax transmission: A modelling study," *Scientific Reports* 10, 16460, 2020.

62  See Johnny Bunning, "The freezer program. Value after life," in Radin and Kowal, *Cryopolitics*, pp. 215–243; Anya Bernstein, *The Future of Immortality: Remaking Life and Death in Contemporary Russia* (Princeton University Press 2019); Abou Farman, *On Not Dying: Secular Immortality in the Age of Technoscience* (University of Minnesota Press, 2020).

63  See Klaus Hoeyer, "Suspense. Reflections on the cryopolitics of the body," in Radin and Kowal, *Cryopolitics*, pp. 205–214; Thomas Lemke, "Conceptualizing suspended life: From latency to liminality," *Theory, Culture & Society*, 40 (6): 69–86.

64  See Rebecca Woods, "Nature and the refrigerating machine: The politics and production of cold in the nineteenth century," in Radin and Kowal, *Cryopolitics*, pp. 89–116. Rebecca Woods shows that freezing techniques enabled the British Empire to export meat over long distances and for periods of up to a year. "Just as it promised to equalize supply and demand between the various parts of the British Empire, the technology of artificial cold and manufactured ice offered to solve the problem of tropical climates. Standardizing the temperature of the Empire was one of the most exciting potential applications of the novel technology, even though such climatic applications were far more speculative than their use in the frozen meat trade" (p. 107).

65  Ibid., p. 6.

66  See Foucault, *Society Must Be Defended*, p. 221, quoted in Radin and Kowal, *Cryopolitics*, p. 7: "The man who died had, as you know, exercised the sovereign right of life and death with great savagery (. . .) and at the moment when he himself was dying, he entered this sort of new field of power over life which consists not only in managing life, but in keeping individuals alive after they are dead."

67  Ibid., p. 8.

68  Ibid., p. 8.

69  Ibid., p. 9. This is a reference to Lauren Berlant's book, *Cruel Optimism* (Duke University Press, 2011).

188 *Notes to pp. 80–81*

70 For an extension of Kowal and Radin's hypotheses on cry-opolitics in indigenous studies, see Kim Tall-Bear, "Beyond the life/not life binary. A feminist-indigenous reading of cryo-preservation, interspecies thinking and the new materialisms," in Radin and Kowal, *Cryopolitics*, pp. 179–202; Hi'ilei Julia Kawehipuaakahaopulani Hobart, *Cooling the Tropics* (Duke University Press, 2022).

71 See Rodney Harrison, "Freezing seeds and making futures: Endangerment, hope, security, and time in agrobiodiver-sity conservation practices," *Culture, Agriculture, Food and Environment* 39 (2), 2017: 80–89.

72 Matthew Chrulew, "Freezing the ark. The cryopolitics of endan-gered species," in Radin and Kowal, *Cryopolitics*, pp. 283–307. See also Carrie Friese, *Cloning Wild Life. Zoos, Captivity and the Future of Endangered Animals* (New York University Press, 2013).

73 See Éric Baratay and Elisabeth Hardouin-Fugier, *Zoos. Histoire des jardins zoologiques en Occident (XVIe-XXe siècle)* (La Découverte, 1998). Éric Baratay has developed a method that can be described as "cynegetic" (in the sense that Carlo Ginzburg refers to the work of the hunter in his analysis of the "indexical paradigm" in social history), enabling him to "take the animal's perspective" through the archives kept by zookeep-ers and veterinarians: see *Le Point de vue animal. Une autre version de l'histoire* (Seuil, 2012); *Animal Biographies: Toward a History of Individuals*, trans. Lindsay Turner (University of Georgia Press, 2022).

74 See Bastien Picard, 2018. "Jeux de captures. Transactions ludiques animales et humaines dans les zoos d'Europe occiden-tale," *ethnographiques.org*, 36, 2018. https://www.ethnographi ques.org/2018/Picard

75 Matthew Chrulew, "Freezing the ark," p. 298–299.

76 In 2014, a giraffe was killed at Copenhagen Zoo, then butch-ered and fed to the lions, as its genetic heritage was deemed insufficiently interesting for captive breeding programs. This spectacular form of "make die," which is often invisible, is accompanied by reintroduction programs that can be inter-preted as "letting animals live," even if they always result in

*Notes to pp. 81–82* 189

significant mortality. At the beginning of the twentieth century, for example, zoo animals were slaughtered on a massive scale to control tuberculosis: see Violette Pouillard, *Histoire des zoos par des animaux. Impérialisme, contrôle, conservation* (Ceyzérieu, Champ Vallon, 2019), p. 207. After the Second World War, they were increasingly justified in the name of selecting individuals to enhance group performance to manage reproduction through a "breed and cull" process that "aims to let animals reproduce, allowing them to express the behaviors surrounding births, and then to eliminate all or some of their offspring, preferably after birth or at a time corresponding to weaning or emigration, with the aim of maintaining the desired group size and composition" (ibid., p. 313). These animal health standards are codified by the International Union of Directors of Zoological Gardens, whose biopolitical effects Violette Pouillard analyzes as follows: "If the zoo is becoming one world, the world is also becoming one big zoo, under the action of the increasingly fine surveillance network woven by conservationists" (ibid., p. 417).

77 On the use of digital monitoring technologies to track and model the behavior of animal populations in nature reserves, see Etienne Benson, *Wired Wilderness. Technologies of Tracking and the Making of Modern Wildlife* (Johns Hopkins University Press, 2011); Irus Braverman, "Governing the wild: Databases, algorithms, and population models as biopolitics," *Surveillance & Society* 12 (1), 2014: 15–37; Antoine Doré, "L'exercice des biopolitiques: Conditions matérielles et ontologiques de la gestion gouvernementale d'une population animale," *Revue d'Anthropologie des Connaissances* 7(4), 2013: 837–855; Rafi Youatt, "Counting species. Biopower and the global biodiversity census," *Environmental Values* 17, 2008: 393–417; Jamie Lorimer, *Wildlife in the Anthropocene. Conservation after Nature* (University of Minnesota Press, 2015).

78 Matthew Chrulew, "Animals as biopolitical subjects," in Matthew Chrulew and Dinesh Wadiwel, *Foucault and Animals* (Brill, 2016), p. 228.

79 See Matthew Chrulew, "Reconstructing the worlds of wildlife: Uexküll, Hediger, and beyond," *Biosemiotics* 13 (1): 137–149.

190          *Notes to pp. 82–84*

80   Heini Hediger, *Wildtiere in Gefangenschaft* (Benno Schwabe & Co, 1942), trans. Geoffrey Sircom as *Wild Animals in Captivity. An Outline of the Biology of Zoological Gardens* (Butterworth, 1950), quoted in Matthew Chrulew, "Freezing the ark," op. cit., p. 283.

81   Heini Hediger, "Des Zoo im Kühlschrank. Fragwürdige Futurologie," *Der Zoologische Garten*, 56(2), 1986: 86, quoted in Chrulew, "Freezing the ark," p. 300.

82   Thomas Birch, "The incarceration of wildness: Wilderness areas as prisons," *Environmental Ethics* 12 (1), 1990: 3–26. Birch follows Roderick Nash's criticism in *Wilderness and the American Mind* (Yale University Press, 1982).

83   William Cronon, "The trouble with wilderness, or getting back to the wrong nature," *Environmental History* 1 (1), 1996: 7–28.

84   See Bernhard Gissibl, Sabine Höhler, Patrick Kupper, *Civilizing Nature. National Parks in Global Historical Perspective* (Berghahn, 2012).

85   See Guillaume Blanc, *Une histoire environnementale comparée de la nation* (Publications de la Sorbonne, 2015), p. 86: "those who define 'natural regions' appeal to scientific authorities endowed with the 'power to make people see and believe, to make known and recognize', and these authorities in reality and in reason found the arbitrary division they intend to impose.' Here, the division is the work of the nation, and the national park must, for those who walk through it, symbolize it." Here Guillaume Blanc quotes Pierre Bourdieu's definition of symbolic violence in "L'identité et la représentation," *Actes de la recherche en sciences sociales*, 35, 1980: 65–66.

86   Guillaume Blanc (p. 132) takes the term "frozen" from historian Bertrand Hirsch in his preface to Marie-Christine Cormier-Salem et al. (eds.), *Patrimonialiser la nature tropicale. Dynamiques locales, enjeux internationaux* (IRD Editions, 2002).

87   Blanc, *Une histoire environnementale comparée de la nation*, pp. 50, 63 and 94.

88   See ibid., p. 220, and *L'invention du colonialisme vert. Pour en finir avec le mythe de l'Éden africain*, preface by François-Xavier Fauvelle (Flammarion, 2020). These terms can be shocking

*Notes to pp. 84–86* 191

because they suggest a divide between a bad nature invented by racism and colonialism, and a good nature protected by global ecology. But these two contrasting visions of nature stem from the same projection of the national imaginary, which Guillaume Blanc proposes to deconstruct. He thus plays on the divide between nature and culture, without seeking, like Philippe Descola, to overcome it by providing agency to the human and non-human agents who suffer from this divide.

89  See Thomas Zeller, *Consuming Landscapes. What We See When We Drive and Why It Matters* (Johns Hopkins University Press, 2022).

90  See John Sandlos, "Federal spaces, local conflicts: national parks and the exclusionary politics of the conservation movement in Ontario, 1900–1935," *Journal of the Canadian Historical Association* 16 (1), 2005: 293–318. See also Stéphane Héritier, "La nature et les pratiques de la nature dans les montagnes canadiennes. Le cas des parcs nationaux des montagnes de l'Ouest (Alberta et Colombie Britannique)," *Annales de géographie* 649 (3), 2006: 270–291; Paul Kopas, *Taking the Air. Ideas and Change in Canada's National Parks* (University of British Columbia Press, 2007).

91  Jules Skotnes-Brown, "Preventing plague, bringing balance. Wildlife protection as public health in the interwar union of South Africa," *Bulletin of the History of Medicine* 95 (4), 2021: 464–496. See also Jane Carruthers, *National Park Science: A Century of Research in South Africa* (Cambridge University Press, 2017).

92  David Bruce et al., "Experiments to ascertain if the domestic fowl of Uganda may act as a reservoir of the virus of sleeping sickness (Trypanosoma Gambiense)," *Proceedings of the Royal Society of London* 83 (564), 1905: 328–334, quoted in Matheus Alves Duarte da Silva, Oliver French, Frédéric Keck, and Jules Skotnes-Brown, "Introduction: Disease reservoirs. From colonial medicine to One Health," *Medical Anthropology: Cross-Cultural Studies in Health and Illness* 42(4), 2023: 311–324.

93  See John MacKenzie. *The Empire of Nature. Hunting. Conservation and British Imperialism* (Manchester University

192 *Notes to pp. 86–89*

Press, 1988); William Beinart and Lotte Hughes (eds.), *Environment and Empire* (Oxford University Press, 2007).

94  https://www.who.int/fr/news-room/fact-sheets/detail/trypanosomiasis-human-african-(sleeping-sickness)

95  Jean Dorst, *Avant que nature meure. Pour une écologie politique* (Delachaux et Niestlé, 1965), p. 470. This book is prefaced by Roger Heim, director of the MNHN, who also prefaced the French translation of *Silent Spring* published by Plon in 1963, and who himself published a defense of nature reserves with Armand Colin in his seminal 1952 book *Destruction et protection de la nature.*

96  Daniel Lewis, *The Feathery Tribe. Robert Ridgway and the Modern Study of Birds* (Yale University Press, 2012), p. 49.

97  Mark Barrow, *Nature's Ghosts. Confronting Extinction from the Age of Jefferson to the Age of Ecology* (University of Chicago Press, 2009), pp. 152–153.

98  C. Lévi-Strauss, *Wild Thought*, op. cit., p. 247. In this passage, Lévi-Strauss rehabilitates Comte's hypothesis of fetishism as a prefiguration of his analysis of savage thought. On the meaning of this rehabilitation, see my Notice, ibid., p. 1808.

99  Claude Lévi-Strauss, *Paroles données* (Plon, 1984), p. 28, quoted in Vincent Leblan, *Aux frontières du singe. Relations entre hommes et chimpanzés au Kakandé, Guinée (XIXe-XXIe siècle)* (Éditions de l'EHESS, 2017), p. 17. Vincent Leblan follows the ape hunters both historically and ethnographically to trace the interactions between human and non-human primates in what are today constructed as nature reserves.

100  Lévi-Strauss, *Wild Thought*, p. 237.

101  See Georges Charbonnier, *Entretiens avec Claude Lévi-Strauss* (Pocket, 1963), p. 45: "We should not distinguish between societies 'without history' and societies 'with history'. In fact, all human societies have an equally long history, going back to the origins of the species. But, whereas so-called primitive societies bathe in a historical fluid to which they strive to remain impervious, our societies internalize history, so to speak, to make it the driving force behind their development." Maurice Godelier reformulates this distinction as follows: "For Lévi-Strauss, human history would only really begin with

*Notes to pp. 89–90*

the appearance of 'hot' societies, whose logic and movement are based on the existence of social contradictions between orders, castes or classes, contradictions that have nothing in common with those of the 'cold', more egalitarian societies known to mankind before they domesticated plants, animals and their own thoughts." (*L'idéel et le matériel*, Fayard, 1984), pp. 22–23.

102 Eduardo Kohn, *How Forests Think: Toward an Anthropology beyond the Human* (University of California Press, 2013), p. 182.

103 For the British Colonial Empire, see Carla Yanni, *Nature's Museums. Victorian Science and the Architecture of Display* (Athlone, 1999). For the Portuguese Colonial Empire, see Ricardo Roque, *Headhunting and Colonialism. Anthropology and the Circulation of Human Skulls in the Portuguese Empire, 1870–1930* (Palgrave Macmillan, 2010). For the German Colonial Empire, see Andrew Zimmerman, *Anthropology and Antihumanism in Imperial Germany* (University of Chicago Press, 2001). For the French Colonial Empire, see Nélia Dias, *Le Musée d'ethnographie du Trocadéro (1878–1908). Anthropologie et muséologie en France* (CNRS Editions, 1991), and Claude Blanckaert (ed.), *Le Musée de l'Homme. Histoire d'un musée laboratoire* (Muséum national d'histoire naturelle/Editions Artlys, 2015). For the Italian Colonial Empire, see Lucia Piccioni, "Empreintes de l'altérité. Moulages faciaux africains et conceptions de la "race" dans l'Italie fasciste," in Frédéric Keck (ed.), *Valeurs et matérialités* (Presses de l'ENS/musée du quai Branly), pp. 81–94. For the Russian and Soviet Empires, see Ksenia Pimenova, "Muséographie de réappropriations: la momie de la 'Princesse altaïenne' dans un musée sibérien" in Frédéric Keck (ed.), *Valeurs et matérialités*, op. cit., pp. 61–80.

104 See Joanna Radin, "Latent life: Concepts and practices of tissue preservation in the international biological program," *Social Studies of Science* 43 (4), 2013: 484–508; "Collecting human subjects: Ethics and the archive in the history of science and the historical life sciences," *Curator. The Museum Journal* 57 (2), 2014: 249–258; *Life on Ice. A History of New Uses for Cold Blood* (University of Chicago Press, 2017).

# Notes to pp. 91–92

105 See Emma Kowal, "Spencer's double: The decolonial afterlife of a postcolonial museum prop," *BJHS Themes* 4, 2019: 70; *Haunting Biology. Science and Indigeneity in Australia* (Duke University Press, 2023).

106 Michel Foucault, "Des espaces autres," in *Dits et écrits IV*, op. cit., p. 759. This text prompted the development of *heterotopy studies* as a subfield of Foucauldian studies (see Peter Johnson, "The geographies of heterotopia," *Geography Compass* 7 (11), 2013: 790–803). But the Foucauldian approach to museums has too often described the enclosure of living beings at the expense of the dialectic between the invisible reserve and the visible exhibition space: see Tony Bennett, *The Birth of the Museum. History, Theory, Politics* (Routledge, 1995). Research in maintenance studies, on the other hand, emphasizes all the work involved in keeping works in storage: see Fernando Domínguez Rubio, *Still Life. Ecologies of the Modern Imagination at the Art Museum* (University of Chicago Press, 2020); Jérôme Denis and David Pontille, *Le soin des choses. Politiques de la maintenance* (La Découverte, 2022); Tiziana N. Beltrame and Yaël Kreplak, *Les Réserves des musées. Écologies des collections* (Les presses du réel, 2024).

107 I borrow "inscription," in the sense of the production in the laboratory of written traces that circulate in scientific publications, from Bruno Latour and Steve Woolgar in *Laboratory Life. The Social Construction of Scientific Facts* (Sage, 1979).

108 I borrow the definition of the collection by Luc Boltanski and Arnaud Esquerre in *Enrichment: A Critique of Commodities*, trans. Catherine Porter (Polity, 2020). According to these sociologists, the form "collection" appears at the beginning of the nineteenth century as a systematic organization of things in series so as to reveal lacks. Because capitalism produces an ever-increasing number of commodities, and because technological revolutions are rapidly turning them into waste, things that are devalued in what Boltanski and Esquerre call the "standard" form of capitalism find themselves revalued in what they call the "collection" form. This fundamental sociological work says nothing, however, about the transi-

*Notes to pp. 93–94*    195

tion from pre-capitalist to capitalist forms of "collecting," or about the techniques used to maintain the collection over time.

109 Antoine Doré shows how the evidence of wolves (hair, droppings, urine, etc.) collected by hunter-gatherers has been transformed into an "organized collection of scriptural and biological samples" through genetic sequencing, enabling biomathematical models to simulate the dynamics of lupine populations in a territory, and to justify the killing (described as "harvesting") of some wolves by managers, or the authorization given to breeders to kill them in a logic more akin to the sovereign vengeance of pastoral power. See Antoine Doré, "L'exercice des biopolitiques. Conditions matérielles et ontologiques de la gestion gouvernementale d'une population animale," *Revue d'anthropologie des connaissances* 7 (4), 2013: 837–855. See also Ghassan Hage, *Alter-Politics: Critical Anthropology and the Radical Imagination* (Melbourne University Press, 2015); *Is Racism an Environmental Threat?* (Polity, 2017).

110 See Clémentine Deliss and Frédéric Keck, "Occupy Collections!," *South as a State of Mind*, 7, 2016: 49–58; Lotte Arndt, "Les survivances toxiques des collections coloniales," *Trouble dans les collections*, 2, 2021; Mathilde Gallay-Keller, Serge Reubi and Mélanie Roustan, "Le vivant et la collection," *Gradhiva*, 36, 2023: 10–27.

111 Foucault uses this term in his lecture of January 30, 1980, in reference to Paul Feyerabend, *Against Method: Outline of an Anarchistic Theory of Knowledge* (Verso Books, 1975). However, this book is less in the anarchist tradition than in a liberal practice close to the Dadaist movement. "The position I am proposing does not exclude anarchy, but you can see that it in no way implies it, that it does not cover it or identify with it. (. . .) I'd say that what I'm proposing to you is rather a kind of (an)archeology" (*On the Government of the Living*, op. cit., p. 153).

112 See Will Kymlicka and Sue Donaldson, *Zoopolis: A Political Theory of Animal Rights* (Oxford University Press, 2011); Joëlle Zask, *Zoocities. Des animaux sauvages dans la ville* (Premier Parallèle, 2020).

196    *Notes to pp. 94–97*

113    See Sophie Houdart and Olivier Thiery, *Humains, non-humains. Comment repeupler les sciences sociales* (La Découverte, 2011).

## 5 Planetary health: Anticipating disasters with animals

1    See Irus Braverman (ed.), *More-than-One Health. Humans, Animals, and the Environment Post-Pandemic* (Routledge, 2022), and Jérôme Michalon, "One Health au prisme des sciences sociales: quelques pistes de lecture," *Bulletin de l'Académie Vétérinaire de France* 172 (1), 2019: 118–122.

2    https://oneworldonehealth.wcs.org/About-Us/Mission/The-2019-Berlin-Principles-on-One-Health.aspx

3    See Alicia Davis and Jo Sharp, "Rethinking One Health. Emergent human, animal and environmental assemblages," *Social Science & Medicine*, 258, 2020: 113093; Nicolas Lainé and Serge Morand, "Linking humans, their animals, and the environment *again*. A decolonized and more-than-human approach to 'One Health'," *Parasite* 27 (55), 2022.

4    See Bruce Wilcox, Alonso Aguirre, and Pierre Horwitz, "Ecohealth. Connecting ecology, health and sustainability," in Alonso Aquirre, Raymond Ostfield, and Peter Daszak (eds.), *New Directions in Conservation Medicine. Applied Cases of Ecological Health* (Oxford University Press, 2012), pp. 17–32.

5    "Safeguarding human health in the Anthropocene epoch: Report of The Rockefeller Foundation-Lancet Commission on planetary health," *The Lancet*, November 14, 2015. See Warwick Anderson and James Dunk, "Planetary health histories. Toward new ecologies of epidemiology?" *Isis*, 113 (4) 2022: 767–788.

6    I use the term coined by Claude Lévi-Strauss to describe the way in which "wild thought" breaks down problems at one level of generality in order to recompose them at a higher level of generality: "The only thing that can be conceded to advocates of totemism is the privileged role falling to the notion of species as a logical operator" (*Wild Thought*, p. 184).

7    See Pieter Johnson and David Thieltges, "Diversity, decoys and the dilution effect. How ecological communities affect disease

*Notes to pp. 97–99*     197

risk," *Journal of Experimental Biology* 213 (6), 2010: 961–70. For a presentation of the dilution effect, see Marie-Monique Robin and Serge Morand, *La fabrique des pandémies*, op. cit.

8   See Anthony J. McMichael, *Climate Change and the Health of Nations* (Oxford University Press, 2017); Colin Carlson et al., "Climate change increases cross-species viral transmission risk," *Nature* 607, 2022: 555–562; Camilo Mora et al., "Over half of known human pathogenic diseases can be aggravated by climate change," *Nature Climate Change* 12, 2022: 869–875.

9   See Elisa Stella, Lorenzo Mari, Jacopo Gabrieli, et al., "Permafrost dynamics and risk of anthrax transmission: a modelling study," *Scientific Reports* 10, 2020: 16460.

10   I posed this question in the conclusion of my book *Un monde grippé* (Flammarion, 2010), in reference to the reflections of Charles Péguy and Georges Sorel.

11   See Paul Fauconnet, *La responsabilité* (PUF, 2023), introduced and edited by Sacha Lévy-Bruhl.

12   See Andreas Malm, *Fossil Capital: The Rise of Steam Power and the Roots of Global Warming* (Verso Books, 2016); *The Progress of The Storm: Nature and Society in a Warming World* (Verso Books, 2017); *How to Blow Up a Pipeline: Learning to Fight in a World on Fire* (Verso Books, 2021).

13   Andreas Malm, *Corona, Climate, Chronic Emergency: War Communism in the Twenty-First Century* (Verso Books, 2020).

14   See ibid., p. 81: "Covid-19 is one manifestation of a secular trend running parallel to the climate crises, a global sickening to match the global heating."

15   Ibid., p. 50. Robert Wallace uses Marx-inspired "evolutionary epidemiology" and "dialectical biology" to show that the concentration of animals in factory farms is a direct factor in increasing the risk of pathogen emergence. Malm cites Wallace's *Big Farms Make Big Flu. Dispatches on Infectious Disease, Agribusiness, and the Nature of Science* (Monthly Review Press, 2016). See also Robert Wallace, Deborah Wallace, and Rodrick Wallace, *Farming Human Pathogens. Ecological Resilience and Evolutionary Process* (Springer, 2009); Robert Wallace, *Dead Epidemiologists. On the Origins of COVID-19* (Monthly Review Press, 2020). Wallace often quotes Marxist geographer and

198                    *Notes to pp. 100–102*

historian Mike Davis, who proposed the first social science analyses of the bird 'flu pandemic: see *The Monster at Our Door. The Global Threat of Avian Flu* (Verso Books, 2005).

16  Malm, *Corona, Climate, Chronic Emergency*, p. 78.

17  See Nicolas Framont, *Parasites* (Les liens qui libèrent, 2023); Arnaud Esquerre, *Ainsi se meuvent les vampires* (Fayard, 2022).

18  Malm, *Corona, Climate, Chronic Emergency*, p. 119.

19  Ibid., p. 142.

20  Malm cites Lenin's words on the urgent need to create *zapovednik*, nature reserves that became hunting reserves until they were closed by Stalin in 1951, quoted in Vesely, "Vladimir Iljic Lenin and the conservation of nature," *Zoologicke Listy*, 18–19, 1970: 18–198. He also cites Douglas Weiner's *Models of Nature. Ecology, Conservation and Cultural Revolution in Soviet Russia* (Indiana University Press, 1988).

21  Malm, *Corona, Climate, Chronic Emergency*, p. 152. This is a quote from Daniel Bensaïd, "Leaps! Leaps! Leaps!" in Sebastian Budgen, Stathis Kouvelakis, and Slavoj Zizek (eds.), *Lenin Reloaded: Toward a Politics of Truth* (Duke University Press, 2007), p. 153.

22  See Judith Shapiro, *Mao's War against Nature. Politics and the Environment in Revolutionary China* (Cambridge University Press, 2001); Michael Hathaway, *Environmental Winds. Making the Global in Southwest China* (University of California Press, 2013).

23  See Robert Weller, *Discovering Nature. Globalization and Environmental Culture in China and Taiwan* (Cambridge University Press, 2006).

24  Malm, *Corona, Climate, Chronic Emergency*, p. 172: "Zoonotic spillover is, unfortunately, not a viable insurrectionary tactic from persecuted fauna, because it can easily spillback and infect wild animals."

25  Malm, *Corona, Climate, Chronic Emergency*, p. 170–174. Malm cites Theodor Adorno, *Modèles critiques. Interventions, répliques* (Payot, 2003), p. 178 and Max Horkheimer, *Eclipse de la raison* (Payot, 1974), p. 116.

26  Malm, *Corona, Climate, Chronic Emergency*, p. 173.

27  See Bruno Latour, "Biopouvoir et vie publique," *Multitudes*

1 (1), 2000: 94: "If the word 'biopower' is used to designate the authority by which some biologists avoid discussion, [. . .] I have no problem with it [. . .]. If, on the other hand, 'biopower' designates a radical break in the history of politics, as is claimed following Michel Foucault, I am much more skeptical."

28  See Bruno Latour, *The Pasteurization of France*, trans. Alan Sheridan and John Law (Harvard University Press, 1988), p. 104: "By using the microbe, whose virulence can be varied, as a veritable 'clutch', [the Pasteurians] can pass from one discipline to another and move in a single movement from contagions to phagocytes, from these to cheeses, and on to diastases and drains (. . .): they were able to renew medicine without ever taking disease as the object of study, and to renew politics and hygiene without ever taking the poor or social outcast as a unit of analysis."

29  See Bruno Latour, *We Have Never Been Modern*, trans. Catherine Porter (Harvard University Press, 1993); *Politics of Nature: How to Bring the Sciences into Democracy*, trans. Catherine Porter (Harvard University Press, 2004).

30  See Frédérique Aït-Touati and Emanuele Coccia (eds.), *Le cri de Gaïa. Penser la Terre avec Bruno Latour* (La Découverte, 2021).

31  See Bruno Latour, *Facing Gaia: Eight Lectures on the New Climatic Regime*, trans. Catherine Porter (Polity, 2017), pp. 86–88: "Lovelock's problem is new: how to speak about the Earth *without taking it to be an already-composed whole*, without adding to it a coherence it doesn't have, and yet without de-animating it by representing the organisms that keep the thin film of critical zones alive into mere inert, passive passengers on a physico-chemical system? His problem is to understand in what respect the Earth is active, but without endowing it with a soul; and to understand, too, what is the immediate consequence of the Earth's activity: in what respect can one say that it *retroacts to the collective actions of humans*. (. . .) Pasteur, after describing how his microbes worked, immediately tried to convince surgeons that with their infected scalpels they were unwittingly killing their patients. Similarly, Lovelock, as soon as he had drawn Gaia's face, tried to persuade humans that

200 · *Notes to pp. 103–104*

they had a strange fate: they had inadvertently become Gaia's *malady*."

32 See ibid., pp. 245–246: "Instead of imagining that you have no enemies because you live under the protection of (allegedly depoliticized) Nature, can you designate your enemies and delineate the territory you are prepared to defend? (. . .) The front line not only divides each of our souls, it also divides all the collectives on the topic of all the cosmopolitical problems we have confronted."

33 See ibid., p. 251.

34 See ibid., p. 257: Latour takes the notion of simulation to mean both a scientific model and a theatrical performance.

35 See also Bruno Latour, *After Lockdown: A Metamorphosis*, trans. Julie Rose (Polity, 2021), p. 161: "Earth is not an all-encompassing form. We're confined to it, but it's not a prison, it's just that we're rolled up in it. Emancipation doesn't mean leaving it, but exploring its implications, folds, superimpositions and interweavings."

36 Bruno Latour and Nikolaj Schultz, *Mémo sur la nouvelle classe écologique* (La Découverte, 2021), p. 72.

37 See Bruno Latour, "Quel État peut imposer des 'gestes barrières' aux catastrophes écologiques?," *Esprit*, July–August 2020.

38 See Michel Callon, Pierre Lascoumes, and Yannick Barthe, *Acting in an Uncertain World: An Essay on Technical Democracy*, trans. Graham Burchell (MIT Press, 2011); Noortje Marres, *Material Participation. Technology, the Environment and Everyday Publics* (Palgrave Macmillan, 2012).

39 Latour refers to Marx's materialism when he writes with Schultz: "To be a materialist today is to take into account, in addition to the reproduction of material conditions favorable to humans, the conditions of habitability of planet Earth" (*Mémo sur la nouvelle classe écologique*, p. 23). But the call for a change of cosmology can appear as a new idealism based on the ideal of habitability, which would be the ecological version of the ideal of justice. See Sacha Lévy-Bruhl, "Changer de cosmologie ou refaire du socialisme?," *AOC*, July 13, 2022, and Ulysse Lévy-Bruhl, "Politique et cosmologie chez Bruno Latour. Vers un éco-socialisme latourien?," Master 2 thesis,

UFR de Philosophie, Université Paris 1–Panthéon Sorbonne, 2022.

40 See Patrice Maniglier, *Le philosophe, la terre et le virus* (Les Liens Qui Libèrent, 2021), pp. 106–107: "The pandemic has synchronized us as never before. It is a rather Durkheimian experience, as if human sociality in general, in its greatest extension, found for the first time in this virus a concrete symbolization. Durkheim insisted on the need for symbols to underpin social experience, insofar as this presupposed the passage from the diversity of particularities to the unity of a collective consciousness. The notion of a 'global world' has therefore undoubtedly found its first symbol in the pandemic, and thus perhaps the beginning of a moral reality that it had previously lacked."

41 See Bruno Latour, "Imaginer les gestes-barrières contre le retour à la production d'avant-crise," *AOC*, March 29, 2020.

42 Ibid.: "there was indeed a bright red alarm signal in the global economic system, hidden from everyone, with a good big handful of hardened steel that the heads of state, each in turn, could pull at once to stop 'the train of progress' with a great screech of brakes."

43 Ibid. Latour refers here to Pierre Charbonnier, *Abondance et liberté. Une histoire environnementale des idées politiques* (La Découverte, 2020).

44 Burke described the French people under the Revolution as a "*swinish multitude*," and Rivarol wrote: "the populace is always and in every country the same, always cannibalistic, always anthropophagous" (quoted in Frédéric Brahami *La raison du peuple. Un héritage de la Révolution française (1789–1848)* (Les Belles Lettres, 2016), p. 85. According to Brahami, the work of socialists like Proudhon and Leroux consisted in thinking of a rationality of the people at a level prior to the untraceable sovereignty, in the plurality of "mores" that became the subject of "social science." The reactionary thinker Bonald was the first to use this expression, later borrowed by the French socialists. Besides these debates on the social, the French Revolution redefined the status of animals by demonstrating the violence of which they were both the source and the object, and by reducing

them to signs on display in the public arena, in the context of the civilization of the savage. See Pierre Serna, *Comme des bêtes. Histoire politique de l'animal en Révolution (1750–1840)* (Fayard, 2017), p. 219: "For a section of society appalled by the disorder of the Revolution, the latter did not invent a new humanity through the birth of the citizen, it made possible a kind of revolution against the human race, irreparably split in two between the good people, the 'honest people,' as they called themselves after Thermidor, and the herd of semi-beasts to be watched, tamed, domesticated, caged if need be."

45  See Pierre Charbonnier, "La naissance de l'écologie de guerre," *Le Grand Continent*, March 18, 2022.

46  See Stephen Collier, Andrew Lakoff, and Paul Rabinow, "Biosecurity: Towards an anthropology of the contemporary," *Anthropology Today*, 20(5), 2004: 3–7.

47  See Luigi Pellizoni, "The time of emergency. On the governmental logic of preparedness," *Sociologia Italiana*, 16, 2020: 39–54.

48  See Brian Massumi, *Ontopower. War, Powers, and the State of Perception* (Duke University Press, 2015). Whereas deterrence, according to Massumi, produced fear around an objective cause whose realization it prevents (the nuclear threat), preemption produces fear from a virtual cause whose potentialities it never ceases to deploy (terrorism). We are here in the context of what Massumi calls an "onto-power" that produces the reality it needs to legitimize itself, thus destroying any possibility of contesting it, as it becomes coextensive with life defined as a proliferating potentiality of emergence.

49  Stephen Collier and Andrew Lakoff, *The Government of Emergency. Vital Systems, Expertise, and the Politics of Security* (Princeton University Press, 2021), p. 97.

50  Ibid., p. 278.

51  See Herman Kahn, *Thinking about the Unthinkable* (Horizons, 1962); Sharon Ghamari-Tabrizi, *The Worlds of Herman Kahn: The Intuitive Arts of Thermonuclear War* (Harvard University Press, 2005); Tracy Davis, *Stages of Emergency. Cold War Nuclear Civil Defense* (Duke University Press, 2007), pp. 51–53.

*Notes to pp. 110–112* 203

52 See Sandrine Revet, "'A small world'. Ethnography of a natural disaster simulation in Lima, Peru," *Social Anthropology/ Anthropologie Sociale* 21, no. 1, 2013: 1–16.

53 See Andrew Lakoff, *Unprepared. Global Health in a Time of Emergency* (University of California Press, 2017).

54 Hurricane Katrina, which devastated Louisiana in 2005, demonstrated the incompatibility between prevention and preparedness. The Bush administration was accused of letting the protections of New Orleans collapse under the cyclone's impact, instead of supporting the underprivileged populations in the neighborhoods exposed to flooding and inhabited mainly by African-Americans, because it had invested massively in the preparedness techniques of the Homeland Security Department in the wake of September 11, 2001. See Romain Huret, *Katrina, 2005. L'ouragan, l'État et les pauvres aux États-Unis* (EHESS, 2010).

55 Stephen Collier and Andrew Lakoff, *The Government of Emergency*, op. cit., p. 10. The notion of reflexivity is taken here from sociologist Ulrich Beck.

56 Ibid., p. 335.

57 On this notion, see Stephen Collier and Andrew Lakoff, "The vulnerability of vital systems: How 'critical infrastructure' became a security problem" in Michael Dunnet and Kristen Kristensen (eds.) *The Politics of Securing the Homeland. Critical Infrastructure, Risk and Securitisation* (Routledge, 2008).

58 Just before the First World War, Jean Jaurès published a book entitled *L'armée nouvelle (The New Army)*, in which he criticized the military authorities for their lack of preparation. Taking up the revolutionary concept of the people in arms, Jaurès prescribed the creation of a national reserve army to complement the active army. His aim was to use the army not only to strengthen the education of the people in fighting with the enemy, but also to guarantee social rights and the equality of citizens by insuring them against accidents. "If France wants to live truly and be assured of life, if it wants to put at the service of its ideal a national force that will forever discourage all aggression, it must demand a military institution where all able citizens are supervised, educated and prepared

204  *Notes to pp. 112–114*

for war" Jean Jaurès, *L'armée nouvelle* (L'Humanité, 1915), p. 140.

59  Letter from M. to Y. Halbwachs, November 5, 1914, IMEC, quoted in A. Becker, *Maurice Halbwachs, un intellectuel en guerres mondiales 1914–1945* (Agnès Viénot, 2003), p. 79. On the involvement of Durkheimian sociologists in the first socialist ministry of the Third Republic, see Christophe Prochasson, *Les intellectuels, le socialisme et la guerre 1900–1938* (Seuil, 1993), pp. 122–129; Christophe Prochasson and Anne Rasmussen, *Au nom de la patrie. Les intellectuels et la Première Guerre mondiale (1910–1919)* (La Découverte, 1996).

60  Lucien Lévy-Bruhl, "Réflexions sur les leçons de la guerre. Force et finesse," Archives Lucien Lévy-Bruhl / IMEC. See also Lucien Lévy-Bruhl, "L'effort industriel" in *L'effort de la France* (Librairie militaire Berger-Levrault,1915), pp. 58–70.

61  See Frédéric Keck, *Lucien Lévy-Bruhl, entre philosophie et anthropologie. Contradiction et participation* (Editions du CNRS, 2008), and *How French Modern Think. The Lévy-Bruhl Family, From Primitive Mentality to Contemporary Pandemics* (Hau Books, 2023).

62  Lucien Lévy-Bruhl was reintroduced to the *science studies* debate on participation by Christopher Kelty in *The Participant. A Century of Participation in Four Stories* (University of Chicago Press, 2019). See also the forum on the reedition of Lévy-Bruhl's article, "Primitive mentality and gambling," in *HAU: Journal of Ethnographic Theory* 10 (2), 2020.

63  See Marie-Claude Blais, *La solidarité. Histoire d'une idée* (Gallimard, 2007).

64  Lucien Lévy-Bruhl, *La mentalité primitive* (1922), ed. Frédéric Keck (Flammarion, 2010), p. 35.

65  The parallel between Marc Bloch's diagnosis in 1940 and the French government's lack of preparedness in 2020 for the Covid pandemic is made by Marie-Angèle Hermitte and Hélène De Pooter in an interview coordinated by Aliénor Bertrand, Patrick Giraudoux, and Arnaud Macé for the collective volume entitled *Le temps des pandémies* (Belin, 2023).

66  Marc Bloch, *Strange Defeat* (Oxford University Press, 1949), p. 188.

# Notes to pp. 114–117

67  See Marc Bloch, *Les rois thaumaturges* (Gallimard, 1983); *Feudal Society* (University of Chicago Press, 1964).

68  Bloch, *Strange Defeat*, p. 149.

69  Julia Bracher, *Léon Blum face à Vichy* (Bibliomnibus, 2014), p. 179–180, quoted by Milo Lévy-Bruhl in his preface to Léon Blum, *À l'échelle humaine* (Le Bord de l'Eau, 2021), p. 54.

70  See Milo Lévy-Bruhl, "Signification immédiate du Front Populaire et incompréhension ultérieure. Léon Blum et les jalons d'une doctrine socialiste oubliée," *Germinal* 7, 2023: 132–150. Léon Blum is perhaps not the most relevant thinker to consider the ecological crisis, because unlike Bloch, who develops a still very topical way of thinking about false news linked to an atmosphere that has become toxic, Blum thinks of viruses as foreign agents, against whom he reasserts the vitality of the people. Blum explains that the changes of government in France over the past two centuries "do not mark the effects of an unhealthy virus, introduced by the Democratic Revolution into the body of the nation, but on the contrary the growth troubles that this revitalized body would have to overcome before reaching its full and stable virility" (*À l'échelle humaine*, pp. 125–126). In thus contrasting "democratic virility" and "foreign viruses," Blum takes up the philosophy of progress inherited from Auguste Comte, who explains the "jolts" of history as temporary illnesses in a transition from "primitive" to "civilized" states of social thinking. Achille Mbembe quotes Léon Blum's speech to the Chamber of Deputies on July 9, 1925: "We recognize the right and even the duty of the superior races to attract to themselves those who have not reached the same degree of culture, and to call them to the progress achieved through the efforts of science and industry" (*Critique de la raison nègre*, pp. 101–102).

71  See Emmanuelle Loyer, *Lévi-Strauss: A Biography*, trans. Ninon Vinsonneau and Jonathan Magidoff (Polity, 2018), ch. 3.

72  See Jean-Pierre Dupuy, *On the Origins of Cognitive Sciences: The Mechanization of the Mind*, trans. M. B. DeBevoise (MIT Press, 2009).

73  See Collier and Lakoff, *The Government of Emergency*, p. 332: "Its procedure for simulating future attacks created a different

206 *Notes to pp. 117–118*

kind of 'archive' – an archive of *possible future events* – that would guide preparedness planning by transforming the radical uncertainty of a nuclear attack into a foreseeable contingency for which preparations could be made."

74 This is the Human Relations Area Files, which Lévi-Strauss had transferred from Yale University to the Laboratoire d'anthropologie sociale in Paris: see Rebecca Lemov, *Database of Dreams. The Lost Quest to Catalog Humanity* (Yale University Press, 2015).

75 See Lucie Fabry, "Quelles mathématiques pour l'anthropologie de la parenté et de l'alliance?," *Terrain* 2023. http://journals.openedition.org/terrain/25479

76 See Mondher Kilani, "Crise de la 'vache folle' et déclin de la raison sacrificielle," *Terrain*, 38, 2002, pp. 113–126; Florence Burgat, *L'humanité carnivore* (Seuil, 2017).

77 Claude Lévi-Strauss, *We Are All Cannibals: And Other Essays*, trans. Marie Todd (Columbia University Press, 2016), p. 115.

78 Lévi-Strauss takes up Auguste Comte's "utopian" project of opening the positivist city to workers, women, and animals, after having initially opened it to scientists and industrialists: see Vincent Descombes, "L'utopie positive," in *Régénération et reconstruction sociale entre 1780 et 1848* (Vrin, 1978).

79 Lévi-Strauss points out that, unlike European societies, which set up dualities and then resolve them by means of a conquering dialectic, Amazonian societies are based on dualities that leave open a third place to welcome the new and the foreign, which is indeed the position of the sentinel. See *The Story of Lynx*, trans. Catherine Tihanyi (University of Chicago Press, 1995). Lévi-Strauss's diagnosis of "mad cow disease" through the knowledge of "cannibalistic societies" from Amazonia and Melanesia finds a confirmation with the ongoing "chronic waste disease" that affects reindeers in Scandinavia. The health authorities rely on the knowledge of the Sami people to trace the movements of reindeers that may be affected by a prion, and to draw the distinction between wild and domestic reindeers in ways that challenge the boundaries of "domesticated thought." See Simon Maraud and Samuel Roturier, "Chronic wasting disease (CWD) in Sami reindeer herding: The socio-political dimension of

*Notes to pp. 119–122* 207

an epizootic in an indigenous context," *Animals* 11(2), 2021: 297.

80 See Michel Foucault, "What is Enlightenment?," in Paul Rabinow (ed.), *The Foucault Reader* (Pantheon Books, 1984), pp. 32–50. This famous text by Kant opposes the counter-revolutionary interpretation of the French Revolution as a generalization of terror, emphasizing the interest that all European peoples took in the spectacle of the Revolution.

81 See Corinne Pelluchon, *Les Lumières à l'âge du vivant* (Seuil, 2021).

82 See Jean-Claude Milner, *Le Périple structural, figures et paradigmes* (Seuil, 2002); Gildas Salmon, *Les structures de l'esprit. Lévi-Strauss et les mythes* (Presses Universitaires de France, 2013).

## 6 Sentinels: Building a new form of solidarity

1 See Emily Martin, *Flexible Bodies. Tracking Immunity in American Culture from the Days of Polio to the Age of AIDS* (Beacon Press, 1995); Alain Brossat, *La démocratie immunitaire* (La Dispute, 2003). These works highlight the tension between the discourse of liberal democratic societies and biopolitical measures aimed at strengthening immunity. For a more ecological proposal on immunity, inspired by Peter Sloterdijk's work on spheres, see Frédéric Neyrat, "The biopolitics of catastrophe, or how to avert the past and regulate the future," *South Atlantic Quarterly* 115 (2), 2016: 247–265.

2 See Ed Cohen, *A Body Worth Defending. Immunity, Biopolitics, and the Apotheosis of the Modern Body* (Duke University Press, 2009).

3 Roberto Esposito summarizes Ed Cohen's historical genealogy based on a philosophical distinction between *immunitas* and *communitas*. Whereas in Rome, *immunitas* was separated from *communitas*, since those who protected themselves withdrew from their civil duties, in biopolitical modernity, immunity becomes the factory of citizens. "The community today appears entirely immune, attracted and opposed in the form that is its opposite. Immunity, in short, is the internal boundary that

208 *Notes to pp. 122–124*

cuts the community off, folding it in on itself" (*Immunitas. The Protection and Negation of Life* (Polity, 2018,) p. 31). Esposito refers to the work of Niklas Luhman to think of modern immunity through the law, which reflects society's internal tensions and transforms them into alarm signals for the recognition of other tensions at more abstract levels of social activity (ibid., p. 72).

4  Augustin Chrestien, *De L'immunité et de la susceptibilité morbides, au point de vue de la clinique médicale, thèse d'agrégation* (Montpellier, 1852), p. 2, quoted in Anne-Marie Moulin, *Le dernier langage de la médecine. Histoire de l'immunologie, de Pasteur au Sida* (Presses Universitaires de France, 1991), p. 23.

5  See Michel Morange, *Pasteur*, p. 286.

6  Rudolf Virchow, *Die Cellular Pathologie* (Berlin, 1871), quoted in Moulin, *Le dernier langage de la médecine*, p. 57.

7  Élie Metchnikoff, "La lutte pour l'existence entre les différentes parties de l'organisme," *Revue scientifique*, 1892, 11: 324, quoted in Moulin, *Le dernier langage de la médecine*, p. 58.

8  See Marc Daëron, *L' Immunité, la vie. Pour une autre immunologie*, with a preface by Anne-Marie Moulin (Odile Jacob, 2021).

9  See Henry Park, "Germs, hosts, and the origin of Frank Macfarlane Burnet's concept of 'self' and 'tolerance', 1936–1949," *Journal of the History of Medicine and Allied Sciences* 61, 2006: 492–534; Thomas Pradeu, *The Limits of the Self: Immunology and Biological Identity*, trans. Elizabeth Vitanza (Oxford University Press, 2012).

10  See Warwick Anderson, "Natural histories of infectious disease. Ecological vision in twentieth-century biomedical science," *Osiris* 19, 2004: 51.

11  See Polly Matzinger, "Tolerance, danger, and the extended family," *Annual Review of Immunology* 12, 1994: 991–1045; Donna Haraway, "The biopolitics of postmodern bodies. Determinations of self in immune system discourse," *Simians, Cyborgs, and Women. The Reinvention of Nature* (Routledge, 1991), pp. 203–230.

12  The term "dendritic cell" was coined by Ralph Steinman in 1973, but synapse-shaped cells had first been observed in the

*Notes to pp. 124–125* 209

skin in 1868 by Paul Langerhans, who thought they belonged to the nervous system. See Ralph Steinman and Zanvil Cohn, "Identification of a novel cell type in peripheral lymphoid organs of mice," *Journal of Experimental Medicine* 137, 1973: 1142–1162; Jacques Banchereau and Ralph Steinman, "Dendritic cells and the control of immunity," *Nature*, 392, 1998: 242–252; Warwick Anderson and Ian Mackay, *Intolerant Bodies. A Short History of Autoimmunity* (Johns Hopkins University Press, 2014), p. 125.

13  See Philippe Kourilsky, *Le jeu du hasard et de la complexité. The new science of immunology* (Odile Jacob, 2014), p. 68 and pp. 106–109.

14  See Connie Cheung et al., "Induction of proinflammatory cytokines in human macrophages by influenza A (H5N1) viruses. A mechanism for the unusual severity of human disease?," *Lancet* 360, 9348, 2002: 1831–1837; Malik Peiris, "Innate immune responses to influenza A H5N1: friend or foe?," *Trends in Immunology* 12, 2009: 574–84.

15  Citing the work of immunologist Alberto Mantovani (*Il fuoco interiore*, Milan, 2020), Roberto Esposito writes: "It seems in fact that pulmonary inflammation may result precisely from excessive, or misdirected, intervention on the part of the immune system, provoked by the encounter with the virus." Mantovani has in fact studied the decoy mechanisms by which viruses bypass the inflammatory response, and proposes that the pharmaceutical industry *scavenge* these "molecular traps" to regulate the immune response (*Immunitas*, op. cit.).

16  See David Napier, *Masks, Transformation, and Paradox* (Oxford University Press, 1986), p. 223: "Polytheism's great attention to the notion of appearance – to masks that may or may not be embodiments, to humans who may or may not be masked in their natural physical state, able or unable to shed a role – is both polytheism's great intellectual invention and its enormous emotional charge." Napier, using Lévi-Strauss's method, shows that while Barong and Rangda masks also have wide-open eyes, in Barong masks they signify protection and in Rangda masks they signify fear. Hindu tradition has introduced a third eye between these two opposing masks, to signal danger in advance,

so that the person can prepare to avoid it through sacrificial techniques. The Javanese tradition, a mixture of animism and analogism, thus solves a problem that the Christian tradition addressed by condemning the mask as a diabolical creation because it splits the person in two. See also David Napier, *Foreign Bodies. Performance, Art, and Symbolic Anthropology* (University of California Press, 1992).

17 See David Napier, *The Age of Immunology. Conceiving a Future in an Alienating World* (University of Chicago Press, 2003), p. 5: "On the microbiological level, Descartes' mask has its analogue in the virus, that only comes alive when it is 'worn' by a cell – becoming a cell that looks like its prey. The viral cell is, as it were, the 'product' of self-consciousness: it perpetuates its own stasis by donning your appearance. It looks like you. It deceives you in order to 'reverse-engineer' you. In this way, viruses are no different from Descartes' mask, since his self-conscious motives are structurally identical to the pathogenic behavior of viruses. Descartes' act of 'possessing' the other is the same act that accounts for our fear of being virally possessed."

18 See ibid., p. 2: "What Descartes did, put simply, was engage in a trial of what patent attorneys today call 'reverse engineering' – a process by which one controls another's creation by breaking it down and reassembling it. And the outcome? The Age of Enlightenment, the Age of Discovery, the homogenization and elimination of difference that has brought us from this hoary past into our 'immunological' world."

19 See David Napier, "Nonself help: How immunology might reframe the Enlightenment," *Cultural Anthropology* 27(1), 2012: 122–137.

20 See David Napier, "Nos conceptions des maladies sont culturellement construites," *AOC*, June 6, 2020.

21 See Frédéric Keck and Andrew Lakoff, "Sentinel devices" and "Figures of warning," *Limn*, 3, 2013.

22 See Davi Kopenawa and Bruce Albert, *The Falling Sky: Words of a Yanomami Shaman*, trans. Alison Dundy and Nicholas Elliott (Harvard University Press, 2023). Davi Kopenawa can be described as a sentinel when he perceives emerging diseases and global warming as the effects of "the falling sky" after the

*Notes to pp. 128–130*

arrival of Europeans among the Yanomami, and transforms this perception into action through international forums where he is the Yanomami spokesman.

23  I borrow this definition from Lucien Lévy-Bruhl in *History of Modern Philosophy in France* (Open Court-Kegan Paul, 1899).

24  See Henri Bergson, *Matter and Memory*, trans. N. M. Paul and W. S. Palmer (Zone Books, 1990).

25  See Henri Bergson, *Time and Free Will: An Essay on the Immediate Data of Consciousness* (Dover Publications, 2001).

26  See Henri Bergson, *Creative Evolution* (Dover Publications, 1998).

27  See Brett Finlay, *Let Them Eat Dirt: How Microbes Can Make Your Child Healthier* (Windmill, 2017); Martin Blaser, *Missing Microbes. How the Overuse of Antibiotics is Fueling our Modern Plagues* (HarperCollins, 2014).

28  Bergson was undoubtedly familiar with this principle through its revival in Cournot's philosophy: see François Vatin, *Economie politique et économie naturelle chez Antoine Augustin Cournot* (Presses Universitaires de France, 1998).

29  These ideas influenced Karl Popper in *The Open Society and its Enemies* (Routledge, 1945).

30  Henri Bergson, *The Two Sources of Morality and Religion*, trans. R. Ashley Audra and Cloudesley Brereton (University of Notre Dame Press, 1977), p. 289.

31  Ibid., p. 298.

32  See Philippe Soulez, *Bergson politique* (Presses Universitaires de France, 1989); Alexandre Lefebvre and Melanie White (eds.), *Bergson, Politics, and Religion* (Duke University Press, 2012).

33  Bergson, *Two Sources of Morality and Religion*, p. 291.

34  Ibid., p. 296.

35  Ibid., pp. 299–304. Bergson refers to Gina Lombroso's *Le tragedie del progresso meccanico* (Bocca, Torino, 1930).

36  Ibid., p. 317. This link between mechanics and mysticism was missed by the founder of ecological thought in France, Serge Moscovici, when he used Bergson's expression in the title of one of his books: *La machine à faire des dieux*. Moscovici takes Durkheim's theoretical tools for thinking about the creativity of the social from the effervescence of groups, which he considers

212 *Notes to pp. 130–131*

as the basis of a psychology of "active minorities" capable of challenging the dominant norms of the majority through their internal normativity. He writes: "To give a canary a more beautiful voice, all you have to do is burn its eyes with a red-hot iron. A similar operation has been performed on Durkheim's thought. By cauterizing his psychological vision of social facts, we believe we are giving his sociology a more harmonious song" (*La machine à faire des dieux*, Fayard, 1988, p. 58). For Moscovici, returning to Durkheimian sociology its eyes mean adding a social psychology that shows, for example, how one group can convince another that what it sees as blue is green. If Moscovici had started from microbiology rather than psychology, he would have given his canary not eyes to see, but a microbiota to adapt to its environment, like the canaries that miners placed in mines in the nineteenth century to alert them to firedamp explosions by fainting, and which the miners raised in such a way that they survived the shock.

37 See Georges Friedmann, *Problèmes humains du machinisme industriel* (Gallimard, 1946); Roger Bastide, *Éléments de sociologie religieuse* (Alcan, 1935); Jean Baruzi, *Problèmes d'histoire des religions* (Alcan, 1935).

38 Bergson, *Two Sources of Morality and Religion*, p. 1.

39 Ibid., p. 139: "The savage, when shooting his arrow, does not know whether it will strike the object at which he aimed; we have not here, as in the case of the animal with its prey, continuity between the gesture and the result; a gap appears, exposed to accident, attracting the unexpected." This analysis foreshadows that of eagle hunting among the Hidatsa by Claude Lévi-Strauss in *La pensée sauvage*. In *Le totémisme aujourd'hui*, Lévi-Strauss points out that Bergson was the first to formulate the idea that qualitative distinctions between animals and plants are used by human groups to distinguish between themselves, and that this is the origin of the notions of race and caste. According to Lévi-Strauss, this intuition shared by Rousseau and Bergson stems from the affinities between Bergson's metaphysics of *élan vital* and the cosmology of the North American Indians.

40 Bergson, *Two Sources of Morality and Religion*, p. 125.

41 Ibid., p. 227. For Bergson, as for Foucault, Socrates is the

*Notes to pp. 131–133* 213

first shepherd of whom the philosophical tradition has kept a trace.

42 Gilles Deleuze has pointed out that Bergson's main philosophical invention was to consider differences of degree as differences of nature, in order to solve metaphysical problems by bringing them down to the concrete living conditions of mankind on earth. See Gilles Deleuze, *Bergsonism*, trans. Hugh Tomlinson and Barbara Habberjam (Zones Books, 1988).

43 See Michel Foucault, "Nietzsche, Genealogy, History," in D. F. Bouchard (ed.) *Language, Counter-Memory, Practice: Selected Essays and Interviews* (Cornell University Press, 1977); Hubert Dreyfus and Paul Rabinow, *Michel Foucault*, pp. 155–173; Quentin Landenne and Emmanuel Salanskis (eds.), *Les métamorphoses de la "généalogie" après Nietzsche* (Presses de l'Université Saint-Louis, 2022).

44 In his Lectures at the Collège de France, Michel Foucault compares himself to a sperm whale "which breaks the surface of the water, makes a little splash, and lets believe, makes you believe or want to believe that down there where it can't be seen, down there where it is neither seen nor monitored by anyone, it is following a deep, coherent and premeditated trajectory" *(Society Must Be Defended*, p. 6) and a crayfish that "moves laterally" (*Birth of Biopolitics*, p. 80). See M. Senellart, "Le cachalot et l'écrevisse: réflexion sur la rédaction des cours au Collège de France," *Cahiers de L'Herne* 95, 2011: 153. These remarks can be compared with an enigmatic formula from *Les Mots et les choses* (Gallimard, 1966 p. 224): "cette ombre d'en-dessous, c'est la mer à boire" ("this shadow below is the sea to drink").

45 The 1982 course entitled *The Hermeneutics of the Subject* concludes with a discussion of the notion of test in Stoic asceticism through an examination of ethical exercises. Foucault characterizes the test as distinct from abstinence, according to three criteria: "First, the test always includes a certain questioning of the self by the self. Unlike abstinence, a test basically involves knowing what you are capable of, whether you can do a particular kind of things and see it through. You may succeed or fail, win or lose in a test, and through this kind of open game of the

214                    *Notes to pp. 133–134*

test, it is a matter of locating yourself, of measuring how far you have advanced, and of knowing where you are and basically what you are. (. . .) Second, the test should always be accompanied by a certain work of thought on itself. Unlike abstinence, which is a voluntary deprivation, the test is only really a test if the subject adopts a certain enlightened and conscious attitude towards what he is doing and towards himself doing it. Finally, the third difference is that (. . .) the test must become a general attitude towards reality. Ultimately, and this is the meaning of the test for the Stoics, the whole of life must become a test." Michel Foucault, *The Hermeneutics of the Subject. Lectures at the Collège de France, 1981–1982*, eds. Frédéric Gros, François Ewald, and Alessandro Fontana, introduction Arnold Davidson, trans. Graham Burchell (Palgrave Macmillan 2005), pp. 430–431. This tension within the notion of test between experience and exercise thus contains Foucault's entire philosophical itinerary, from Georges Bataille to Pierre Hadot.

46   Michel Foucault, *On the Government of the Living. Lectures at the Collège de France, 1979–1980*, eds. Frédéric Gros, François Ewald, and Alessandro Fontana, introduction Arnold Davidson, trans. Graham Burchell (Palgrave Macmillan, 2014), p. 127. On the use of early Christian texts by Foucault, and its contrast with the classical history of Christianity, see Philippe Chevallier, *Michel Foucault et le christianisme* (ENS Éditions, 2011).

47   Foucault, *On the Government of the Living*, p. 159.

48   See ibid., p. 255: "The theme of pastoral power, that is to say the fact that at the head of the flock there must be a guide who leads it to salvation (. . .) does not coincide with the idea or technique of direction (. . .), of a permanent intervention by one individual over another, with the aim of observing, getting to know, guiding and leading it point by point all the way to salvation), of a permanent intervention by one individual over another, with the goal of observing him, knowing him, guiding him, conducting him in every detail throughout his existence within a relationship of uninterrupted obedience, (. . .) even if later, when this technique of is developed within Christianity, it is situated within the realm of the pastorate."

49   Foucault, *Security, Territory, Population*, op. cit., p. 220.

*Notes to pp. 134–137* 215

50 Foucault, *On the Government of the Living*, p. 303.

51 I thank Sylvain Piron for this reference to the *Rule of the Master*, an anonymous Latin monastic document dating from the early sixth century. See Sylvain Piron, *Dialectique du monstre. Enquête sur Opicino de Canistris* (Zones sensibles, 2015); *L'Occupation du monde* (Zones sensibles, 2018).

52 I thank Charles Stépanoff for this reflection based on his forthcoming book on the history of domestication.

53 See Peter Sahlins, *1668. The Year of the Animal in France* (Zone Books, 2017).

54 See Georges Dumézil, *La courtisane et le seigneur coloré* (Gallimard, 1984).

55 See Michel Foucault, *The Courage of the Truth. Lectures at the Collège de France, 1983–1984*, eds. Frédéric Gros, François Ewald, and Alessandro Fontana, trans. Graham Burchell (Palgrave Macmillan, 2011), p. 100: "*Epimeleia* is not the warder's supervision of his slaves; it is not the prison guard's supervision of his prisoners. It is the positive concern of a father for his children, of a shepherd for his flock, of a good sovereign for the citizens of his country. It is the concern of the gods for men." Graham Burchell translates "we are on a sentinel post" by "we are on a sentry duty" (p. 99).

56 Ibid., p. 113.

57 On the different representations of Socrates in the history of philosophy, see Francis Wolff, *Socrate* (Presses Universitaires de France, 1987); Paulin Ismard, *L'événement Socrate* (Flammarion, 2017).

58 See Jack Goody, *The Domestication of the Savage Mind* (Cambridge University Press, 1977).

59 See Lucien Lévy-Bruhl, *La responsabilité* (Hachette, 1884).

60 See Peter Redfield, *Space in the Tropics. From Convicts to Rockets in French Guiana* (University of California Press, 2000), pp. 51ff.

61 Quoted in Vincent Duclert, *Alfred Dreyfus. L'honneur d'un patriote* (Fayard, 2006), p. 571. This book is a turning point in the historiography of the Dreyfus Affair, in that it describes Dreyfus as an active hero and not just a passive victim of the social process of accusation he was involved in.

62 See Ruth Harris, *Dreyfus: Politics, Emotion, and the Scandal of*

216 *Notes to pp. 137–139*

the Century (Picador, 2010). Ruth Harris shows that the Dreyfus Affair, presented in Dreyfusard historiography as the triumph of the Enlightenment over obscurantism, used occult means on both sides: clairvoyance, misappropriation of evidence, exaltation of sacrifice.

63 See Paula Hyman, *The Emancipation of the Jews of Alsace: Acculturation and Tradition in the Nineteenth Century* (Yale University Press, 1991).

64 Lévy-Bruhl takes up Durkheim's hypothesis that "society is God," but does not repeat his thesis that society is a collective Cogito that imposes itself on individuals through the categories of sacrifice. According to the philosophy of action developed by Malebranche from Descartes onwards, it is enough to start from the occasions when individuals are led to "see in God," i.e. to move from second (or mechanical) causality to first (or mystical) causality.

65 Claude Lévi-Strauss, *Œuvres*, op. cit., p. 10. Monique Lévi-Strauss also told me that her husband used to say about his fieldwork in Amazonia: "I felt like Dreyfus in Cayenne."

66 See Pierre Vidal-Naquet, *Les Juifs, la mémoire et le présent* (Maspéro, 1981), p. 79, trans. David Curtis, *The Jews: History, Memory, and the Present* (Columbia University Press, 1996).

67 I have analyzed the status of sentinels based on the observations of Israeli ornithologists Amotz and Avishag Zahavi on babblers. These small birds living in the Negev desert display sentinel behaviors that do not consist in sacrificing themselves for the collective in the face of a predator, but rather in singing and dancing to signal their singular value to the predator and the rest of the group. See Amotz and Avishag Zahavi, *The Handicap Principle: A Missing Piece of Darwin's Puzzle* (Oxford University Press, 1997); Frédéric Keck, *Avian Reservoirs*, ch. 4.

68 See Francis Chateauraynaud and Didier Torny, *Les sombres précurseurs. Une sociologie pragmatique de l'alerte et du risque* (EHESS, 1999); Francis Chateauraynaud, *Alertes et lanceurs d'alerte* (Presses Universitaires de France, 2020). In my afterword to *Sentinelles des pandémies* (Seuil, 2021), I distinguished the horizontal work of connecting living beings made by sen-

*Notes to pp. 139–141*  217

tinels with the more vertical work of whistle-blowers trying to reach a public space by the work of proof; but these are two stages in a chain of signalling aimed at an ideal of truth and justice.

69 See Louise Michel, *La Commune* (Stock, 1898).

70 See Léna Balaud and Antoine Chopot, *Nous ne sommes pas seuls. Politique des soulèvements terrestres* (Seuil, 2021), p. 232; Léna Balaud, Antoine Chopot, and Allan Wei, "La part sauvage des communs? Une enquête écologique au Marais Wiels," in Philippe Boursier (ed.), *Écologies. Le vivant et le social* (La Découverte, 2023), pp. 597–606.

## Conclusion

1 Dominique Guillo traces the contemporary program to study coevolution and interaction between humans and animals based on their shared cognition, defined as viruses or memes by Richard Dawkins. He thus takes up Alfred Espinas' and Émile Durkheim's definition of collective consciousness as parasite relations between living beings. See Dominique Guillo, *Les fondements oubliés de la culture. Une approche écologique* (Seuil, 2019) and my discussion of this book in "Les animaux contre l'État. Tournant ontologique et transformations politiques en sciences sociales," *L'Homme* 236, 2020: 177–190.

2 See Fabien Carrié, Antoine Doré, and Jérôme Michalon, *Sociologie de la cause animale* (La Découverte, 2023). This book shows how animal rights activists have moved from the street, as a space where cruelty is visible, to animal farms for industrial production or scientific research. This has led them to make closed spaces (slaughterhouses or laboratories) visible, but also to intervene in them through the alternative between sabotage and consultancy, "abolitionism or reformism," "systemic or sectoral struggle." Animal activists can be described by themselves or their opponents as whistle-blowers, terrorists, or infiltrated experts, but they could also conceive of themselves as sentinels.

3 See Luc Boltanski and Laurent Thévenot, *On Justification: Economies of Worth*, trans. Catherine Porter (Princeton

218 *Notes to pp. 142–144*

University Press, 2006) and Philippe Descola, *Beyond Nature and Culture*, trans. Janet Lloyd (University of Chicago Press, 2013). By "sociology of critique," I mean the body of work carried out by the Groupe de sociologie politique et morale in the 1980s and 1990s, following Pierre Bourdieu's "sociology of practice," to pluralize forms of action and justification, based on the refusal of opposition between theory and practice. By "anthropology of nature," I mean all the work carried out at the Laboratoire d'anthropologie sociale in the same period, starting with Claude Lévi-Strauss's work on "wild thought," to pluralize relations between humans and non-humans, based on the refusal of the opposition between nature and culture. The work of Bruno Latour, on which I opened the fifth chapter of this book, lies at the crossroads of these two lines.

4 See Axel Honneth, *The Pathologies of Individual Freedom: Hegel's Social Theory*, trans. Ladislaus Löb (Princeton University Press, 2010).

5 See Didier Fassin, *De l'inégalité des vies* (Fayard, 2020).

6 See Marie Gaille (ed.), *Pathologies environnementales. Identifier, comprendre, agir* (CNRS, 2018).

7 See Luc Boltanski, *On Critique. A Sociology of Emancipation* (Polity, 2011). Luc Boltanski shows how conspiracy theory emerged in the spy novel, taking over from the police enigma as the centralizing state was replaced by globalized networks in the twentieth century. See Luc Boltanski, *Mysteries and Conspiracies: Detective Stories, Spy Novels and the Making of Modern Societies* (Polity, 2014). On the inclusion of this sociology in a social philosophy of possibilities open to a horizon of emancipation, see Haud Gueguen and Laurent Jeanpierre, *La perspective du possible. Comment penser ce qui peut nous arriver, et ce que nous pouvons faire* (La Découverte, 2022); Bruno Frère and Jean-Louis Laville, *La Fabrique de l'émancipation. Repenser la critique du capitalisme à partir des expériences démocratiques, écologiques et solidaires* (Seuil, 2022).

8 Baptiste Morizot emphasizes that social emancipation should not be conceived in opposition to the reductionism of the life sciences, because "it is precisely these sciences (the reanimating sciences of the living) that have generated this emancipatory

*Notes to p. 145*   219

knowledge with regard to the living" (*Manières d'être vivant* (Arles, Actes Sud, 2020), p. 146, trans. Andrew Brown, *Ways of Being Alive* (Polity, 2022)). Through his writing about nature in communication with wolves, he encourages us to "make a distinction in our historical legacies between emancipations to be cherished and protected, and toxic wanderings" (p. 36). Thinking of emancipation in terms of the life sciences is the right way to go, but to do so, we need to include viruses among the signs that humans receive from other animals. The same criticism can be levelled at James Bridle's stimulating book, *Ways of Being. Animals, Plants, Machines. The Search for a Planetary Intelligence* (Penguin, 2023). In proposing to think about solidarity with the living through the sensors of artificial intelligence, Bridle says nothing about computer viruses or industrial pathologies. Bridle and Morizot's critiques can be described as aesthetic, in the sense that they magnify the capacities of life itself, but they do not provide a clinical diagnosis of the pathologies of modernity that would offer a political way out of the ecological crisis.

9   The term "ethology" was coined in 1843 by John Stuart Mill in his *System of Logic* to designate the science of human character formation, and then taken up again in 1854 by Isidore Geoffroy Saint-Hilaire to extend it to the study of animal behavior. See Stéphane Madelrieux, *La philosophie comme attitude* (Presses Universitaires de France, 2023), p. 56.

10   Since all animals have a perception of diseases transmitted from one body to another, a definition of the human exception could be: it is the only species capable of massively slaughtering another species to protect itself from a zoonosis and of imagining its own disappearance in the event of a pandemic. The history of domestication would have to be read in the light of this definition.

# Index of Names

Abraham 33
Aeschylus 40
Agamben, Giorgio 15–16, 38
Arendt, Hannah 16
Aristotle 15
Arloing, Saturnin 30
Armour, Philippe 77
Artemis 40
Augustine, Saint 16

Barré-Sinoussi, Françoise 56
Bartholeyns, Gil 54
Bataille, Georges 16
Becker, Gary 6
Benjamin, Walter 16
Bensaïd, Daniel 100
Bergson, Henri 112, 127–132
Bernard, Claude 122
Bertillon, Alphonse 35
Beutler, Bruce 124
Birch, Thomas 83
Blanc, Guillaume 83–84
Bloch, Marc 114–117
Blum, Léon 114–117
Boltanski, Luc 141
Bordet, Jules 123
Boulainvilliers, Henri de 15
Bouley, Henri 25
Bourdieu, Pierre 19

Bourgelat, Claude 24
Bourgeois, Léon 113
Bravo, Michael 78
Broussais, François 122
Bruce, David 86
Burnet, Frank Macfarlane 6,
    50–53, 57–59, 123–124
Bush, George Walker 63, 109

Calmette, Albert 30
Cassian 133
Canguilhem, Georges 12
Carnot, Sadi 129
Carrel, Alexis 60–61
Carson, Rachel 6
Cauthen, Kenneth 9
Césaire, Aimé 36
Chamayou, Grégoire 33–39, 43,
    46, 91, 113, 117
Chan, Margaret 69
Chapman, Frank 87
Chatton, Edouard 54
Chrestien, Louis 122
Chrulew, Matthew 80–82
Cohen, Ed 122
Colbert, Jean-Baptiste 24
Collier, Stephen 109–111
Conklin, Harold 45
Conseil, Ernest 53

## Index of Names

Crick, Francis 17
Cronon, William 75–77, 83
Cumont, Franz 135

d'Alembert, Jean 26
Darwin, Charles 87, 89, 123
Daszak, Peter 72
de Certeau, Michel 31
de Kruif, Paul 46–48, 55–57
de Montaigne, Michel 119
Deleuze, Gilles 46
Descartes, René 125, 128, 134
Descola, Philippe 39, 141
Diderot, Denis 24
Dorst, Jean 86
Dreyfus, Alfred 112, 116,
   136–137
Dubos, René 54
Dumézil, Georges 135
Duncan, Kirsty 63
Durkheim, Émile 105, 113,
   136–137

Ehrlich, Paul 47, 56, 123
Eisenhower, Dwight 109–110
Elton, Charles 51
Euripides 40
Evans, Alice Catherine 48

Fanon, Frantz 37
Fassin, Didier 18–19
Fischer, Hoch Susan 56
FitzSimons, Frederick 85
Foucault, Michel 2–33, 37–40,
   46, 64–65, 72, 79, 81–82,
   91, 93, 102, 119, 122, 127,
   131–136, 141, 144
Fouchier, Ron 67–68
Fukuda, Keiji 69

Gallo, Robert 56
Gambetta, Léon 115
Garvey, Marcus 36
Gates, Bill and Melinda 110
Guo, Yuanji 71
Gilbert, Marius 69
Gillen, Francis 90
Grassi, Battista 48
Guattari, Félix 46
Guérin, Camille 30
Gunst, Dietrich 9

Halbwachs, Maurice 112
Harant, Hervé 54
Hardt, Michael 16
Harrison, Ross 60
Haudricourt, André-Georges
   39–40
Hediger, Heini 82
Hegel, George Friedrich 35
Helmreich, Stefan 45
Hercules 40
Herr, Lucien 137
Herodotus 40
Hirst, George 59, 61
Hitler, Adolf 115
Hobbes, Thomas 134
Hoffman, Jules 124
Hultin, Johan 64
Hussein, Saddam 109

James, William 130–131
Jaurès, Jean 112, 114–116, 136
Jenner, Edward xi, 26

Kahn, Herman 110
Kant, Immanuel 119, 129, 132
Kawaoka, Yoshi 67–68
Kilbourne, Edwin 62

## Index of Names

Kirksey, Eben 45
Kjellen, Rudolf 9
Koch, Robert 30, 47, 67
Kohn, Eduardo 89
Kowal, Emma 78–80, 89–91, 117

Lacan, Jacques 132
Lacks, Henrietta 61
Lafosse, Philippe-Etienne 24
Lakoff, Andrew 109–111
Las Casas, Bartolomé de 34
Latour, Bruno 101–108
Laver, Graeme 57
Lederberg, Joshua 56
Lenin, Vladimir 100, 108
Lévi-Strauss, Claude 4–7, 14, 17, 46, 87–88, 116–120, 127, 132, 136–138
Lévy-Bruhl, Lucien 112–114, 127, 130, 136–138
Lewis, Sinclair 47
Liang, Qichao 41
Lincoln, Abraham 110
Lovelock, James 102, 108
Lowe, Celia 45

Malebranche, Nicolas 137
Malm, Andreas 98–101, 105–108
Mandela, Nelson 37
Manson, Patrick 48
Marcuse, Herbert 9
Margulis, Lynn 102
Marx, Karl 103, 107, 141
Martin, Vincent 69
Mauss, Marcel 112, 137
Mbembe, Achille 36–38, 41, 91, 114, 116

McCormick, Joseph 56
Medawar, Peter 123
Meister, Joseph 28
Memmi, Dominique 18–19
Metchnikoff, Elie 122–123, 126, 138
Meyer, Karl Friedrich 50–52
Montagnier, Jean-Luc 56
Montagu, Mary Wortley (Lady) 26
Morgan, Lewis Henry 45
Morton, John 90
Moulin, Anne-Marie 122

Napier, David 125–126
Negri, Antonio 16, 38
Nicolle, Charles 52–53
Nietzsche, Friedrich 132, 135
Nimrod 33–34

Origen 133
Owen, Richard 28

Palese, Peter 64
Pasteur, Louis 28, 47, 67, 104, 122
Pavlovsky, Evgeny 52
Pétain, Philippe 115
Picquart, Marie-Georges 137
Pfeiffer, Richard 61
Plato 135
Polge, Christopher 61
Povinelli, Elizabeth 43–45
Psichari, Jean 136

Rabinow, Paul 17, 109
Radin, Joanna 78–80, 89, 91, 117
Rees, Gareth 78

## Index of Names

Renan, Ernest 137
Renouvier, Charles 113
Ridgway, Robert 87
Rivet, Paul 112
Roberts, Austin 85
Roosevelt, Franklin Delano 109–110
Ross, Ronald 48
Rousseau, Jean-Jacques 119
Roze, Nikolas 17

Salk, Jonas 61
Schnapp, Alain 40
Seneca 133
Sepulveda, Juan 34
Sergent, Edmond and Etienne 49
Shi, Zhengli 72
Shortridge, Kennedy 68–69
Sims, Leslie 69
Skinner, Quentin 9
Smith, Theobald 48–50
Socrates 135
Sophocles 133
Sorre, Maximilien 54
Spencer, Walter Baldwin 90–91
Spinoza, Baruch 16
Steinmann, Ralph 124
Strathern, Marylin 18
Stuart-Harris, Charles 68

Tanon, Louis 49
Tavistock (Marquise of) 87
Taubenberger, Jeffery 64
Tertullian 133
Thomas, Albert 112
Trump, Donald 72
Tsing, Anna 43, 45
Tung, Chee-Wah 69

Ulysses 40

van Leeuwenhoek, Antoni 47
Vicq d'Azyr, Félix 25
Vidal-Naquet, Pierre 40
Villermé, Louis 11
Virchow, Rudolf 28–29, 122–123
Viveiros de Castro, Eduardo 38–39, 41
von Behring, Emil 31
von Wilamowitz, Ulrich 135
von Zenker, Friedrich Albert 29

Wallace, Robert 99
Wang, Yi 75
Watson, James 17
Webster, Robert 57, 71
Williams, Greer 55–56
Wu, Liande 42

Zedong, Mao 42